The Hero's Journey

The World of Joseph Campbell

Edited and with an Introduction by Phil Cousineau

Foreword by Stuart L. Brown, Executive Editor

The Hero's Journey

Joseph Campbell on his Life and Work

HarperSanFrancisco

A Division of HarperCollins*Publishers*

FIRST HARPERCOLLINS PAPERBACK EDITION PUBLISHED IN 1991.

Library of Congress Cataloging-in-Publication Data

Campbell, Joseph, 1904–1987
    The hero's journey: Joseph Campbell on his life and work / edited and with an introduction by Phil Cousineau; foreword by Stuart L. Brown, executive editor.
        p.   cm.
    Includes bibliographical references.
    ISBN 0-06-250171-2 (pbk.)
    1. Campbell, Joseph, 1904–1987—Interviews.   2. Mythologists—United States—Interviews.   3. Mythology.   4. Heroes.   5. Myth.
I. Cousineau, Phil.   II. Title.
BL303.6.C35A3   1991
291.1'3'092—dc20
[B]
                                                                    90-55772
                                                                    CIP

91 92 93 94 95 RRD 10 9 8 7 6 5 4 3 2 1

This edition is printed on acid-free paper which meets the American National Standards Institute Z39.48 Standard.
Designed by Detta Penna
Grateful acknowledgment is made for permission to reprint excerpts from the following works: *Bollingen: An Adventure in Discovering the Past,* by William McGuire. Copyright © 1982 by William McGuire. *The Hero with a Thousand Faces,* by Joseph Campbell. Copyright © 1949 by Joseph Campbell. *The Mythic Image,* by Joseph Campbell and M. J. Abadie. Copyright © 1981 by Joseph Campbell and M. J. Abadie. Reprinted with permission of Princeton University Press.

Illustration and photo credits begin on page 241.

Contents

They thought that it would be a disgrace to go forth as a group. Each entered the forest at a point that he himself had chosen, where it was darkest and there was no path. If there is a path it is someone else's path and you are not on the adventure.

Joseph Campbell

Foreword

Passion makes most psychiatrists nervous. "Joseph Campbell sounds like a displacement of your need for a messiah," a prominent analyst friend said to me early in my quest to assure that the best of Campbell would be memorialized on film and television. That dream materialized in the 1987 production of *The Hero's Journey,* the one-hour film from which the book you hold in your hands emerged.

Zeal for something other than sports and church makes most midwestern Presbyterians tense, and both of my aging parents clearly would have been more comfortable if this "Campbell interest" had been supplanted by my energetic support of a local congregation, or by more attention to my medical activities and financial future.

Since it is poor judgment and bad manners not to listen to mentors and parents, I have, since the inception of my long and intricate involvement with Joseph Campbell, tried not to embrace him as a cult figure, and have good and irreverent friends who assure me that I keep thinking and feeling for myself.

But as I try to place those years in perspective, the experience of it all feels more like love. Not specifically love of Campbell, but love for what happens to *others* when they see and hear him. Their pleasure—and their growth—were what kept me working on this project for more than a decade. Of course, the awareness of what would happen to others as they encountered Campbell started with my own experiences.

At age thirty-nine, in 1972, I took a sabbatical to complete a research project on homicide. While closeted in the library, I discovered that the earliest known written references to violence were mythological, and to my surprise the dynamics of domestic violence described in the ancient myths and the patterns of domestic violence in contemporary American life showed striking parallels. So I set about to read Joseph Campbell's four-volume *Masks of God*. As I finished, I realized that Campbell was remarkably connecting the symbolic, psychological, spiritual, and artistic heritages of humanity in ways that an army of scientists since Darwin had been doing in order to understand biological patterns. Along the way something in me more than intellect had been fed by these books. As I completed them, I felt differently about myself and the world. I felt at home. I wanted to learn more about what Campbell had to say and, like many others, I was curious about the man himself. The more I read, the more I was moved by an incessant urge to see that Campbell's sweeping scholarship and capacity for tolerantly blending the world's mythologies were made available to audiences outside the scholarly community.

Since I was not a television professional myself, I formed a partnership with the late Greg Sparlin, who was. Campbell, however, initially rejected our proposal to transfer his work into the television medium with the remark that *his* proper medium was print. It took many meetings to persuade him otherwise, but when we finally got his commitment, I was certain that we could get others properly exposed to Campbell's scholarship and vitality, and they would experience their own deepening of soul. It didn't matter to me at the time that few agreed with this conviction.

As with many creative projects, there were many false starts. By late 1981, I was becoming increasingly concerned about Joe's health, since he had experienced two severe bouts of pneumonia within six months. While he looked fine and sounded as eloquent as ever, the physician in me was worried. Joe was approaching eighty, and there still was no adequate filmed record of him and his work. Yes, he had published many superb books, but I felt strongly, as George Lucas was later to say, that there was a "life force" that poured out of him causing his audiences to actively initiate their own spiritual adventure. With an increased sense of urgency, I redoubled my efforts.

The formal filming of *The Hero's Journey* began in January of 1982 at Esalen, in Big Sur, California. With producer Bill Free's help, I corralled a diverse group that ranged from Joe's close poet friend, Robert Bly, to Nobel laureate Roger Guillemin, to a young woman who had never heard of Campbell before. My hope was that the mix of people, the skills of the director, David Kennard, the beauty and heritage of the setting, and the phenomenal life and energies of Joseph Campbell would provide a rich foundation for our film. Much of what you will discover in this book comes from the conversations filmed at Esalen.

Some four or five months later, as we were editing the film and poring over transcripts, I began to find myself besieged by a relentless inner voice. Inner voices, even if they were telling me to "follow my bliss," were not something I was used to. But this one kept saying, "Get Joe's next nationwide lecture series on videotape, because it will be his last." Sadly, it was.

Some people are at their best in a relaxed, informal setting. The first cut of our film used a great deal of such footage. However, the more we worked on it, the clearer it became that Campbell was at his best when *he* chose the subject matter; when he was able to use the material that he had perfected over many decades of lectures.

Betwen 1982 and early 1985, a production crew followed Campbell around the country, videotaping his last major lecture tour. We recorded "Psyche and Symbol" in Taos, New Mexico; "Transformations of Myth Through Time" in Santa Fe; "The Perennial Philosophy: Hinduism and Buddhism" at his wife Jean Erdman's Open Eye Theater in New York; "The Western Way: the Arthurian Legends" and "The Quest for the Grail" at the Palace of Fine Arts Theater in San Francisco; and "Contemporary Mythologies: James Joyce and Thomas Mann" at the California Historical Society in San Francisco. We now had a mother lode of fifty hours of Campbell's most powerful lectures, which will be available forever. I have since stopped hearing voices.

As the production crew and I followed Campbell around this country, people kept coming up to me after his lectures and seminars asking, "Who is this man Campbell? How did he get to be the person he is?" An enduring curiosity about who he was and an enchantment with him and his ideas pervaded his audiences. It was these questions that provided the stimulus that led to the final form of the first film and, ultimately, to this book.

Our final strategy for the film was to allow the viewer to process unconsciously his or her own life while watching the story of Joe's. Their own personal rites of passage, their recognition of the importance of union with nature, their need to take their own path—in short, the trajectory that Joe Campbell lived out and so magnetically demonstrated in the breadth of his scholarship—would be discovered in the vignettes and stories, monologues and inter-actions, that we had filmed. For me, the highlight of the film is the awards dinner at the New York Art's Club in 1985, where Joseph Campbell was honored for his contributions to literature. Our film had time only for excerpts from the testimonials of George Lucas, Richard Adams, James Hillman, and others, and, as much as it pained us, we were forced to cut Joe's soaring acceptance speech. Fortunately, this book has allowed us to incorporate more complete coverage of that remarkable evening, as well as to include marvelous original material that time constraints excluded from the film.

Joe always felt his ideas were more significant than his person. In the film and in the construction of this book, we have tried to make sure that it would be as he wished it—that the *ideas* speak with all of the remarkable clarity that the man was capable of generating.

The film version of *The Hero's Journey: The World of Joseph Campbell* premiered on the East Coast at the Museum of Modern Art and on the West Coast at the Directors Guild Theater in the spring of 1987. Included in this book are excerpts from his last public appearance at the West Coast premier program where, even as he approached what he himself called "The Death," he continued to provide new information and syntheses to his audiences. It was with great poignancy that I watched Joe receive his last standing ovations. He died four months later.

After much review of our transcripts and outtakes, I asked Phil Cousineau, the associate producer of the film, who, along with coproducer Janelle Balnicke, wrote its narration, to construct this book. I had been consistently impressed with his important creative contributions to all aspects of the film and to his growing devotion to Joe and Jean Campbell, and I knew that they recognized and appreciated not only the breadth of his knowledge of myth and life, but the depth of his talent.

In 1988, the national airing on PBS of *The Hero's Journey: The World of Joseph Campbell,* and Bill Moyers's six-part series, "Joseph Campbell and the Power of Myth," led to an explosive and broad response. This outpouring of interest, it seems to me, has confirmed that Joseph Campbell speaks to *all* of us.

Stuart L. Brown

Introduction

Joseph Campbell's long odyssey through the seas of ancient mythology was as much a spiritual quest as it was a scholarly one. Through his prodigious readings, writings, and travels, as well as his crossroad meetings with many of the century's most influential men and women, he discovered remarkable parallels in our world's mythological heritage and reinforcement for the deep conviction he had held since he was a young student: that there is a fundamental unity at the heart of nature.

"Truth is one, the sages speak of it by many names," he often quoted the Vedas. To synthesize the constant truths of history became the burning point of his life; to bridge the abyss between science and religion, mind and body, East and West, with the timeless linkage of myths became his task of tasks.

"My hope," he wrote in his preface to *The Hero with a Thousand Faces,* "is that a comparative elucidation may contribute to the perhaps not-quite-desperate cause of those forces that are working in the present world for unification, not in the name of some ecclesiastical or political empire, but in the name of human mutual understanding."

Campbell's comparative historical approach to mythology, religion, and literature, in contrast to the conventional scholar's emphasis on cultural differences, concentrated on similarities. He was convinced that the common themes or archetypes in our sacred stories and images transcended the variations or cultural manifestations. Moreover he believed that a re-viewing of such primordial images in mythology as the hero, death and resurrection, the virgin birth, and the promised land—the universal aspects of the soul, the blood memories—could reveal our common psychological roots. They could even show us, as seen from below, how the soul views itself.

"Myths are the 'masks of God,' " he wrote, "through which men everywhere have sought to relate themselves to the wonders of existence." The shock of recognition we receive from the timelessness of these images, from primal cultures to the most contemporary, he believed, was an illumination not only of our inward life but of the same deep spiritual ground from which all human life springs.

So as Albert Einstein pursued a unified field theory for the energies of the outer realms, Joseph Campbell dedicated himself to forging a kind of unified field theory of the equally prodigious energies of the inner realms, the personifications of which we call "the gods." And what physicists call the "fabric of reality" Campbell called "the net of gems," a sparkling metaphor from Hindu cosmology that is also a keen image for his own unique weaving together of myth, religion, science, and art. His teachers in those disciplines, he concluded, were all saying essentially the same thing: that there is a system of archetypal impulses that have stirred the human spirit throughout history. It is, as he synthesized it, "one grandiose song."

The iconoclastic road he took as scholar, teacher, and writer was not unlike the "left-hand paths" he discovered in myriad myths: what the Kena Upanishads call the crossing of "a bridge as sharp as the edge of a razor"; the taking of the "middle way" of the Buddhists; or the entering of the dark forest of the Grail Quest "where there is no way or path." Intuitively he followed his Tao of Scholarship beyond the hallowed halls of traditional academia and into a spiritual and psychological view of mythology, which embraces the transcendent Reality referred to by saints and shamans that can be directly *experienced*. This form of direct perception of what the mystics called cosmic consciousness is nothing less than a personal encounter with the gods. It is the healing vision of order underlying apparent chaos, the seizure of life-affirming Beauty in the heart of darkness. If "snatching the eternal out of the everfleeting is one of the great tricks of human existence," as Tennessee

Williams said, then those who can experience eternity *now,* from Campbell's challenging perspective, become our tricksters, our spiritual guides.

Campbell's decidedly unconventional career deprived him, he used to joke, of some prestige from his fellow scholars. But it was obvious to those of us who knew him that he took great pride in being the maverick and the "dilettante," "the one who takes delight in," as he once described his own mentor, the Indologist Heinrich Zimmer. He could afford to. His enthusiasm—literally his being full of the gods—had won him the hearts and minds of students early on in his career at Sarah Lawrence, and later, scores of artists. His own fascination with the "great stuff of myth" turned thinking into an adventure, translated knowledge into wisdom, and revealed the personal relevance of mythology for those who heard or read him. To them he was far more than the popularizer who trivializes his subject; he was what the French elegantly call the *"animateur,"* the charismatic teacher who not only animates complex material for the average audience, but evokes what Vladimir Nabakov called the *frisson,* the telling shiver of truth about your own life. For that gift alone he became one of the most beloved teachers of our time.

Yet after more than fifty years of teaching and more than twenty books, Campbell felt that his contribution was simply that he gave people "the key to the realm of the muses," that marvelous realm beyond the visible one from which imagination and inspiration could guide us in shaping our lives. In that role he was a modern *mystagogue,* a guide through the often inscrutable mysteries of the ancient texts of Beowulf, Gilgamesh, the Tibetan Book of the Dead, the Egyptian mysteries, the *Iliad* and the *Odyssey,* the Arthurian romances, the American Indian myths, Hinduism, Buddhism, and Christianity, as well as such modern myth-makers as James Joyce, Thomas Mann, and Pablo Picasso. In his rendering of these majestic narratives and images, he taught us the poet's way of "How to Read a Myth" (the original title for *The Hero with a Thousand Faces*): symbolically, metaphorically, soulfully.

But beyond his talent for "metaphorphosis," that is, his ability to read into these transformative riddles of life and death, Campbell personalized the classics like few scholars before him. To complement the rigorous methods of scholarship, he revived the art of hermeneutics—inventive interpretations in the spirit of the Hermes, the soul-guide—and fused them with the glint-in-the-eye-regaling of a wise Irish storyteller. In so doing he breathed new life into the old myths, as Albert Camus said each generation must do. As he did with one of his favorite tales, the Parsifal legend, when he threw down the gauntlet at the end of his Arthurian romance seminars. So is it going to be the Grail Quest or is it going to be the Wasteland? he would ask. Are you going to go on the creative soul's quest or are you going to pursue the life that only gives you security? Are you going to follow the star of the zeal of your own enthusiasm? Are you going to live the myth or is the myth going to live you?

And so reemerged the ecstatic scholar, a breed of thinker thought long extinct since the age of scientific rationalism. "It's not the *agony* of the quest," he often reminded his audiences, "but the *rapture* of the revelation," giving new meaning to the old saw about "rapture of the deep." Furthermore, he would add gnomishly, "Life is not a problem to be solved but a *mystery* to be lived."

But how is this possible? Can we do more than wait for the serendipitous encounter? How do we turn around the flight from mystery in this demythologized era with its overarching question: Is nothing sacred anymore? How do we separate the sham from the sublime?

Joseph Campbell's patented response to the dis-enchantment of modern life was: find your life's true passion and follow it, follow the path that is no path: "Follow your bliss." When you have the unmistakable experience of the *Aha!* then you'll know you're riding on the mystery.

Campbell's irrepressible urge to pursue his own bliss into the essential knowledge, the hidden harmonies within the dream world of myths, legends, fairy tales, folklore, poetry, literature, and art, is reminiscent of what John Keats described in Shakespeare as the "circumnavigation of the soul." While Sigmund Freud and Carl Jung rescued the soul from the oblivion of the spiritual materialism of the nineteenth century with the study of depth psychology, Campbell's cross-cultural explorations, and those of a host of other modern religious historians and anthropologists like Mircea Eliade and Claude Levi-Strauss, revived our moribund myths in their ancestral home of the stories and images of the soul. Together and alone, they were "dreaming the myth onward," as Jung advised, reweaving the ancient story-web.

Campbell's sojourn inevitably took him to the Perennial Philosophy. The sublime theme he found in the ancient Hindu and Chinese pundits, Sufi and Christian mystics, poets and philosophers from Walt Whitman to Aldous Huxley, was that deep within the human soul is a mirror of divine Reality. As above, so below. *Tat tvam asi:* Thou art That: The Kingdom of God is within us, here and now. Awakening to that mystical dimension where the very essence of the self is suddenly perceived to be one with the ultimate forces of nature, is at once the secret and the transforming journey of human life. "You are that mystery which you are seeking to know," Campbell concluded.

This spiritual perspective, Campbell believed, is not only timeless but universal. He had as great a respect for the wisdom lore of the shamans and sages of antiquity as he did for the creative visions of contemporary artists and scientists. Accordingly, like many other perennial philosophers, Campbell had very little patience, if not disdain, for any individual or chosen people mythologies that excluded others from divine revelation or claimed to possess exclusive knowledge of what he vigorously thought to be the fundamental truths, the sacred constants, of all people. *"Every people is a chosen people,"* he insisted. Every deity is a metaphor, a mask, for the ultimate mystery ground, the transcendent energy source of the universe, that is also the mysterious source of your own life—and everyone else's.

In light of this Campbell realized after years of being asked earnest questions about ultimate answers that, "When people say they're looking for the meaning of life, what they're really looking for is a deep experience of it."

As a mythologist with a metaphysical slant on life, a doctor of things-beyond-appearances, he dedicated his life to mapping out the experience of plumbing those depths, which is the journey of the soul itself. The cartography, as he drew it, was the geography of the inner or underworld, showing perilous territory to be traversed not by the faint, but by the stout of heart. If myths emerge, like dreams out of the psyche, he reasoned, they can also lead us back in. The way out is the way in. It is a movement beyond the known boundaries of faith and convention, the search for what matters, the path of destiny, the route of individuality, the road of original experience, a paradigm for the forging of consciousness itself: in short the hero's journey:

> A hero ventures forth from the world of common day into a region of supernatural wonder: fabulous forces are there encountered and a decisive victory is won: the hero comes back from this mysterious adventure with the power to bestow boons on his fellow man.

This "monomyth" lies at the core of Joseph Campbell's steadfast belief in one universal mythology. Like the legendary gryphon, the winged lion of the medieval bestiary, it was a composite, taking shape gradually, piece by piece, an innovative assemblage of key ideas from Campbell's own masters: Joyce, Mann, Jung, Zimmer, Underhill, Coomaraswamy, and Ortega y Gasset, who wrote in an influential passage that the "will to be oneself is heroism."

The monomyth is in effect a *metamyth,* a philosophical reading of the unity of humankind's *spiritual* history, the Story beyond the story. To paraphrase the ancient Japanese koan, it is the sound of one myth clapping: the universal quest for self-transformation. The journey of the hero is about the courage to seek the depths; the image of creative rebirth; the eternal cycle of change within us; the uncanny discovery that the seeker is the mystery which the seeker seeks to know. The hero journey is a symbol that binds, in the original sense of the word, two distant ideas, the spiritual quest of the ancients with the modern search for identity, "always the one, shape-shifting yet marvelously constant story that we find."

Joseph Campbell's life spanned the years from Buffalo Bill to *Star Wars;* his work from Apollo the Greek god to *Apollo* the spacecraft. His was truly a story with a thousand faces. And Stuart

Brown's dream of documenting that protean story was a vision journey in its own right.

For years Campbell had shied away from film crews, deflecting the cult of celebrity by reminding people that, "It's not me, it's the myths," and the prying eyes of biography from audiences by insisting, "I've spent all my life trying to stay out of the way of this stuff." No doubt his colorful telling of Odysseus describing himself as "No Man" to the Cyclops in Homer's great epic was as much an element of his self-image as the Grail Quest or the dream sequences from *Finnegans Wake*. Outside of a few in-depth interviews he instinctively lived out what the German poet Rainer Maria Rilke referred to when he wrote about the creative life: "True art comes from the anonymous self."

Nevertheless, there were choice passages here and there in our own filming of him over the three-year period, in the scattered interviews found in library stacks, and during our casual conversations with him about how he had recognized, in meandering through the maze of his own life, the various stages of the hero journey: the calls to adventure, the mentors and allies, the threshold guardians, the dark forest, the bringing back of the boon to the community.

Once the group decision was made to approach Joe about supplementing the original Esalen material with personal interviews at his home in Honolulu, I was elected to reassure him that now that we had the *ideas* on film, we were simply looking for the links between them. For the sake of the dramatic structure of the documentary, I told him, we thought our story would be even more compelling if we could chronicle the nature of his learning process. How did he discover the themes that became the crossbeams of his work? Why did he connect the Navaho material to the Hindu? When did he first align in his mind the twilight myths of the Celts with Joyce's nightworld novels?

Only after all the filming was completed, and we hunkered down in the editing room, did the theme of the hero journey become the Ariadne's Thread that led us through the labyrinth of film footage. Convoluted as the conversations and interviews sometimes were—ranging from the Upanishads to Kant, the Gnostic Gospels to Black Elk—there was now the *clew,** the winding thread

---

*The skein of Ariadne's thread that Theseus used to lead himself out of the labyrinth; the origin of our word *clue*.

of Campbell's path through his own labyrinth, the relevance of the work to his own life, which made sense of his sometimes arcane connections. The moments of synchronicity ("And then the whole world opened up!") that highlighted his life confirmed his deep belief that devotion to one's own inner work is the beam that keeps you on the path. Over and over again, we discovered, he looked back through the years in the manner of Schopenhauer, who wrote about the well-lived life appearing in retrospect like a well-written novel. The first encounters with friends like Jiddu Krishnamurti, John Steinbeck, Ed Ricketts, Alan Watts, and above all his wife, Jean Erdman, he would describe more like epiphanies or powerful chapters than anecdotes. And of the enormous influence he had on creative artists, he appeared profoundly grateful that such an epilogue could have been written to the story of his life's work.

Stuart Brown's eight-year labor of love, *The Hero's Journey: The World of Joseph Campbell,* premiered at the Museum of Modern Art in New York in February 1987. Seven months later Joseph Campbell died quietly in his home in Honolulu at the age of eighty-three. During the approximately ten years between Brown's vision of popularizing Campbell at a time when few people wanted to hear about mythology, and the time our film was finally released, an astonishing turnaround had taken place. Campbell's fame had spread from a devoted audience of ex-students and avid readers to popular culture. Filmmakers like George Lucas and George Miller, sculptor Isamu Noguchi, rock stars David Byrne and the Grateful Dead, priests, poets, psychologists, and even comedians, were all publicly expressing their debt and admiration of him.

The following summer, *The Hero's Journey* and Bill Moyers's interviews with Joseph Campbell, *The Power of Myth,* were shown on PBS. The ensuing "Campbell phenomenon" took everyone by surprise. Who would have believed that the American public would ever be interested in listening to a scholar and a journalist discuss religion for six hours? Nevertheless Campbell cassette and book sales soared, discussion groups formed in school rooms, ther-

therapist's offices, church basements, Zen centers, and story conference rooms in Hollywood.

The appeal went far beyond elitist debates about diffusion versus parallelism theories of anthropology, beyond the romanticizing of mythical Camelots and Troys. Instead the country was mesmerized by a passionate storyteller; a robust athlete and musician turned dignified philosopher and writer; the exciting blend of Campbell's universal humanism and secular spirituality. Here was the background music of the spheres, a skeleton key to open the door to the worlds of art, literature, and religion. Most important, he was saying that "myths have to do with how you live your life."

In an era undermined by a pervasive feeling of deep skepticism and anxiety appeared someone who insisted that we find "what electrifies and enlivens our hearts and wakes us." In fact the public found in Joseph Campbell what the poet W. B. Yeats called "the old eagle's mind," the wise old man, the rarest of archetypes in a land of eternal youth.

Campbell's message that *myths matter* galvanized the long dormant cultural discussion about the spiritual and aesthetic life. In the winter of 1986, at a memorable conference in San Francisco entitled "From Ritual to Rapture," starring Joseph Campbell, psychiatrist John Perry, and the Grateful Dead, Jerry Garcia brought the house down by confessing on stage to the old mythologist his feelings about the similarities between the ancient mystery festivals and rock concerts. "They didn't know what they were saying, and we don't know what we're saying either, but we think we're saying the same thing."

Not everyone understood myths overnight, but suddenly the old "dream of a common language" had been revived.

After its debut on public television, I took *The Hero's Journey* around the country and to Europe to show in movie theaters, university auditoriums, and at film festivals. Audiences everywhere stayed after the screenings for unusually long, probing question-and-answer sessions. When I began showing specially selected "outtakes" (passages from the hours and hours of film footage that never made the final cut of the film) to my own "Myth and Movies" seminars and continued to get delightful feedback, it became exhilaratingly clear that we had a treasure trove of material left over. I approached Dr. Brown about rescuing the hours of outtakes from the obscurity of film vaults and organizing them into a book to meet the groundswell of interest. He generously gave me access not only to the film footage but to hours of videotaped lectures and encouraged me to create a companion book to the film. For that I am deeply grateful.

My interest in working with the original transcripts was also inspired by a driving curiosity to seek out in the hieroglyphics of nearly fifteen hundred pages of disjointed conversations, interviews, and speeches, the intriguing relationship between Campbell's personal journey and the evolution of his work. How did he reconcile his accumulation of such a staggering amount of knowledge, which included an unflinching look into the dark shadows of the human condition, with a life-affirming philosophy? A seeming paradox in the heart of the labyrinth reared its minotaur head: If the old gods are dead, and the traditional myths out of date, as Campbell insisted, why even study them, let alone rhapsodize about them?

It can only be hoped that the following confluence of conversations, interviews, speeches, and book quotes evokes Campbell's moving response: that we are in what the Greeks called the time of the "metamorphoses of the gods." The images of the new gods, the new creative myths, the global vision, are being born not anew "out there" but in the mythogenic zone of the awakened human heart. There, re-formed for our different times, are the different metaphors to express the constant truths; and therein the courage can be found to join "with joyful participation in the sorrows of the world." This immortal teaching of affirmation and compassion, which Campbell found in the teachings of the Buddha, gave him the courage of his own convictions. This, I am convinced, is his greatest legacy.

The actual transformation of the transcripts into book form follows my exploration through the records of the original filming at Esalen Institute, the National Arts Club, and finally at the Campbell home in Honolulu. I also had the great fortune of being able to select passages from the videotaped lectures on "The Perennial Philosophy," "James Joyce and Thomas Mann," and "Psyche and Symbol" from Joe Campbell's last official lecture tour (which Dr. Brown, with tremendous foresight and courage, videotaped between 1982 and 1983) as well as the audiotaped panel discussion after the West Coast premiere of *The Hero's Journey* at the Director's Guild in Los Angeles in May 1987.

Considerable editing was necessary to reconstruct the parallel journey of the work and the man. Where reconstructions were needed—as when there were the inevitable but exasperating gaps in the filming because the sound dropped away or conversations overlapped—I was able to resort to my own notes taken from Campbell seminars, workshops, and personal conversations. Trusting the lead of Joe's personal asides that highlighted the entire round of filming, the story slowly unfolded chapter by chapter, as it had for him. Other stories, other renditions, will follow this one, perhaps more comprehensive and less schematic; but these interviews stand alone as the telling of the tale by the light of the fire by the teller himself. Perhaps the self-synthesis that emerges was his last brilliant metaphor, a flickering image of the task that is before all of us today.

One of the last times I saw Joe Campbell, in late spring of 1987, was in the Redwood Room of the Clift Hotel in San Francisco. That night, as we had so often before in what we called our version of the philosopher's "long conversation"—the one between minds long gone, still here, and yet to come—we spoke with great joy about two of our favorite topics: Joyce and Paris, and the bittersweet relationship between the artist and the city.

Over a final glass of Glenlivet I confided to him a favorite story of my own. A few years before I was drifting across the country on a motorcycle trip when, like a wayward traveler in an Arabian Nights tale tripping over a gold nugget hidden under a tree root in the dark forest, I discovered an uncanny scene that struck me as being at the heart of the hero's journey.

It was that of a crumbling tombstone in Boothill Cemetery in Tombstone, Arizona, the gravemarker of an old gunslinger. The epitaph read: "Be what you is, cuz if you be what you ain't, then you ain't what you is."

I can hear Joe's hearty bodhisattva laugh now and the clink of our glasses over the soothing sounds of the late-night jazz piano in the old redwood-paneled bar.

"That's it!" he cried out with that eternal look of wonder in his eyes. "That's what it's all about: the mystery of the journey. That's just marvelous!

"Now, how did that go again? 'Be what you is . . .' "

Phil Cousineau

Editor's Acknowledgments

I would like to express my deepest gratitude to all those who helped me with the development of this book. I owe a special thanks to Robert Cockrell, who first introduced me to Joseph Campbell, and eternal thanks to Stuart Brown for his unstinting support for my work on his documentary, *The Hero's Journey,* and his encouraging me to fulfill his vision of a companion book to the film.

My heart-felt thanks to Jean Erdman Campbell for her graceful comments on the first draft of the manuscript, her hospitality in Honolulu when she gave me kind access to the Campbell family photographs, and for her faith in me, all of which strengthened the courage of my convictions.

I wish to thank my editor Tom Grady, who was unwavering in his enthusiasm about this project, despite its many permutations, and a sage with his advice. Many thanks to Kevin Bentley, Arla Ertz, and all those involved at Harper & Row, San Francisco, whose patience and guidance saw this book through to its publication. I also want to thank Detta Penna for her elegant design. Vigorous thanks also to my art researcher, Lynne dal Poggetto. Her devotion will be remembered and appreciated by all those who wish to follow the footsteps of scholarship in this book. I am very grateful to the other voices in the book, those whose questions and insights brought a fresh perspective to this rich material, and to the various photographers, artists, and writers whose contributions enriched this book immeasurably.

My thanks also to my friend Tom Schlesinger with whom I first ventured onto the road of teaching and writing about the Hero's Journey, and to another close friend, Keith Thompson, whose robust conversations with me about mythology and whose key suggestions for the manuscript have made this a better book. To Robin Eschner I want to convey my everlasting thanks for her gifts of love, wit, and inspiration that helped me complete the journey.

I would also like to gratefully acknowledge the contributions of Mythology Ltd., a California Ltd. partnership, whose foresight in raising funds made possible the acquisition of this material.

Finally, I would like to dedicate this entire endeavor to Joseph Campbell, whose work changed so many of our lives by simply giving us the key to the realm of the muses.

Phil Cousineau

Chronology of Joseph Campbell's Life

1904	Born in New York City on March 26, the son of Charles W. Campbell, a merchant from Waltham, Massachusetts, and Josephine E. Lynch of New York.
1910	His father takes young Joe and his brother, Charlie, to see Buffalo Bill's Wild West Show at Madison Square Garden, and to the Museum of Natural History. His lifelong interest in Indians begins.
1913–17	Family moves to New Rochelle, New York, and his fascination with Indians and myths intensifies. At age eleven he is admitted to the adult stacks in the New Rochelle Public Library to continue his studies.
1917	Family builds bungalow in the Pocono mountains of Pennsylvania. There he meets his first mentor: Elmer Gregor, noted author of boys' books on American Indians.
1919	Tragic fire destroys the family home in New Rochelle, killing his grandmother and destroying his collection of Indian books and relics.
1919–21	Enrolls at Canterbury prep school, New Milford, Connecticut. Headmaster Dr. Nelson Hume introduces him to literature and the art of writing. His favorite subject is biology. Editor of school literary magazine, writer and business manager for school's weekly paper, plays football and field hockey. Graduates with "Head Boy" award.

1921	Enters Dartmouth College to study biology and mathematics and play freshman football.
1922	Discovers the humanities after reading Merejkowski's *The Romance of Leonardo da Vinci*. Transfers to Columbia University.
1922–27	Studies under his third mentor, Raymond Weaver. Member of track team, 1924–26, sets Columbia half-mile record. Runs in Penn Relay championships and for New York Athletic Club track teams. Also plays saxophone in jazz bands for college and fraternity dances.
1924	Meets Jiddu Krishnamurti on boat trip to Europe and becomes interested "in a vague way" in Hinduism and Buddhism.
1925	Earns BA degree from Columbia University. Runs with New York Athletic Club track team in the AAU championships in San Francisco. On a trip to Hawaii he befriends the "father of surfing," Duke Kahanamoku. Upon return he attends the Indian Rodeo in Yakima, Washington.
1926	Returns to Columbia in order to run with the track team; studies medieval literature. Completes thesis on "The Dolorous Stroke" from the Arthurian legends.
1927–28	Receives Proudfit Traveling Fellowship for two years of study in Europe. Earns MA from Columbia University. Studies Romance philology, Old French, and Provençal at the University of Paris under Joseph Bédier, noted translator of "Tristan and Iseult." Discovers modern art and modern literature, notably Joyce's *Ulysses*. Acquaintanceship with sculptor Antoine Bourdelle and owner of Shakespeare and Company, Sylvia Beach.
1928–29	Transfers to University of Munich to study Sanskrit and Indo-European philology; discovers the works of Freud and Jung, Thomas Mann, and Goethe. He returns to the United States two weeks before the Crash. Drops work on his PhD to retire to the woods of Woodstock with his sister, Alice, a student of sculptor Archipenko, renting a cabin for $20 a year. There he pursues the line of study he began in Paris.
1929–31	After futile attempts to write short stories—"Absolutely nothing that I wrote would sell"—turns to voluminous readings in modern American literature and philosophy: Hemingway, Lewis, Dewey, and Russell.
1931–32	Drives alone across the country in his mother's Model T Ford to think out his future. Stops in San Jose, California, to see old friend nutritionist Adelle Davis. She introduces him to John and Carol Steinbeck, and their neighbor, intertidal biologist Ed Ricketts. Campbell stays on in a $15-a-month cottage. Discovers Spengler in the Carmel library: "the major crisis of my intellectual life." Writes 85 colleges and universities for a job. Travels up coast of British Columbia to Alaska with Ricketts, collecting intertidal fauna, and reconfirms his belief of the relationship

	between mythology and biology. Accepts a job offer from old head-master at Canterbury.
1933	Teaches history, English, French, German, while studying Spengler, Mann, Jung, Joyce. Resigns at end of year and goes back "on the Depression." Sells first story, "Strictly Platonic," for $300, and on that plus some savings from his jazz playing days returns to Woodstock to read and write.
1933–34	Reads through the winter: Joyce, Spengler, Frobenius, Mann, Freud, Jung. Starts a novel that doesn't work. Invited to teach at Sarah Lawrence College on the recommendation of his old master, Professor W. W. Lawrence. He immediately accepts.
1938	Marries Jean Erdman, his former student from Sarah Lawrence and a member of the Martha Graham Dance Company.
1940	Meets Indologist Heinrich Zimmer, who introduces him to the founders of the Bollingen Series.
1941	Works with Swami Nikhilananda on the translation and editing of *The Gospel of Sri Ramakrishna* and the *Upanishads* for the next three years.
1942	Recommended by his mentor, Zimmer, to the Bollingen Foundation to produce premier volume in their series. The next year, Zimmer dies of pneumonia. Zimmer's widow asks Campbell to edit Zimmer's posthumous writings, to which he devotes twelve years.
1943	Campbell's first publication: Commentary to *Where the Two Came to Their Father: A Navaho War Ceremonial,* with Jeff King and Maud Oakes.
1944	Publishes *A Skeleton Key to Finnegans Wake* with Henry Morton Robinson. Writes commentary to *The Complete Grimm's Fairy Tales.* Joins editorial staff of *The Dance Observer.* Begins work on *The Hero with a Thousand Faces.*
1946	Publishes Zimmer's *Myths and Symbols in Indian Art and Civilization.*
1948	Publishes Zimmer's *The King and the Corpse.* Article on "Finnegan the Wake" appears in *James Joyce: Two Decades of Criticism.*
1949	After two other publishers reject the manuscript, Bollingen accepts *The Hero with a Thousand Faces.* Award from American Academy of Arts and Letters for *The Hero with a Thousand Faces.*
1951	Publishes Zimmer's *Philosophies of India* "Bios and Mythos: Prologemena to a Science of Mythology," an article in *Psychoanalysis and Culture: Essays in Honor of Gaza Roheim.* General editor of the series *Myth and Man,* and the volume by Carl Kerenyi, *The Gods of the Greeks.*
1952	Publishes *The Portable Arabian Nights.*
1953	Appointed president of the Creative Film Foundation, and editor of the

Papers from the Eranos Yearbooks. Publishes *Spirit and Nature*. General editor of Maya Deren's *Divine Horsemen: The Living Gods of Haiti*, the *Myth and Man* series.

1954   General editor of Alan Watts's *Myth and Ritual in Christianity*, the *Myth and Man* series. On sabbatical leave he travels in India, Ceylon, Thailand, Burma, Taiwan, Hong Kong, and Japan. Begins study of Japanese.

1955   Publishes Zimmer's *The Art of Indian Asia*. Publishes (as editor) *The Mysteries*.

1956   Lecturer at Foreign Service Institute, Department of State, Washington, D.C.

1957   Publishes (as editor) *Man and Time*. Reads first paper at the Eranos Conference in Ascona, Switzerland, "The Symbol without Meaning."

1958   Reads paper "Oriental Philosophy and Occidental Psychoanalysis," at IXth International Congress for the History of Religions, Tokyo, and Kyoto; Maruzen, Tokyo.

1959   Reads first paper at Eranos Foundation: "Renewal Myths and Rites of the Primitive Hunters and Planters." Publishes *The Masks of God: Vol. I, Primitive Mythology*.

1960   Publishes (as editor) *Spiritual Disciplines*.

1961   Publishes *The Masks of God: Vol. II, Oriental Mythology*. Appointed to Trusteeship in the Bollingen Foundation. Listed in *Who's Who in America*.

1964   Publishes (as editor) *Man and Transformation* and *The Masks of God: Vol. III, Occidental Mythology*.

1967   Named to the Board of Directors of the Society for the Arts, Religion, and Contemporary Culture.

1968   Publishes (as editor) *The Mystic Vision* and *The Masks of God: Vol. IV, Creative Mythology*. Begins long association with Michael Murphy and Esalen Institute.

1969   Publishes *The Flight of the Wild Gander: Explorations in the Mythological Dimension*.

1970   Publishes (as editor) *Myths, Dreams, and Religion*.

1972   Publishes *Myths to Live By* and edits *The Portable Jung*. Retires from Sarah Lawrence College after 38 years. Named President of the Society for the Study of Religion. Travels to Iceland and Turkey. Interview with Sam Keen in *Psychology Today*. With his wife, Jean Erdman, founds the Theater of the Open Eye in New York City.

1973	Receives the Hofstra Distinguished Scholar Award. Publishes "Erotic Irony and Mythic Forms in the Art of Thomas Mann," a broadside by Sarah Lawrence College.
1974	Publishes *The Mythic Image*.
1976	Receives the Melcher Award for Contributions to Religious Liberalism. Travels to Egypt and Greece.
1977	Edits *My Life and Lives: The Story of a Tibetan Incarnation*, by Rato Khyongla Nawang Lozang. Interview with Donald Newlove in *Esquire*.
1978	Receives Honorary PhD from Pratt Institute in Brooklyn, New York.
1983	Publishes *The Historical Atlas of Mythology: Vol. I, The Way of the Animal Powers*. Befriended by filmmaker George Lucas, who invites him and Jean to Skywalker Ranch in Northern California to see the *Star Wars* trilogy, which was greatly influenced by his work.
1984	80th birthday celebration at the Palace of Fine Arts, San Francisco, attended by 1000 people, with Sam Keen, Chungliang Al Huang, Stanley Keleman, Barbara Myerhoff, Marija Gimbutas, and Robert Bly, entitled "A Symposium on the Hero's Journey."
1985	Awarded the Medal of Honor for Literature by the National Arts Club of New York for *The Way of the Animal Powers*.
1986	Publishes *The Inner Reaches of Outer Space: Myth as Metaphor and Religion*. Participates in seminar for UC Berkeley Extension entitled: "From Ritual to Rapture," with psychiatrist John Perry and the legendary rock band, the Grateful Dead.
1987	Premier of *The Hero's Journey: The World of Joseph Campbell*, at the New Director's/New Films Festival at the Museum of Modern Art, New York. The PBS series "The Power of Myth" with journalist Bill Moyers airs. Dies in Honolulu, Hawaii, October 30.
1988	Posthumous publication of *The Power of Myth* and *The Historical Atlas of World Mythology: Vol. II, The Way of the Seeded Earth*. Joseph Campbell Chair of Comparative Mythology established at Sarah Lawrence College.

The Hero's Journey

The call to adventure signifies that destiny has summoned the hero and transferred his spiritual center of gravity from within the pale of his society to a zone unknown. This fateful region of both treasure and danger may be variously represented: as a distant land, a forest, a kingdom underground, beneath the waves or above the sky, a secret island, lofty mountaintop, or profound dream state; but it is always a place of strangely fluid and polymorphous beings, unimaginable torments, superhuman deeds, and impossible delights.

Joseph Campbell,
The Hero with a Thousand Faces

1

The Call to Adventure

Joseph Campbell was born in New York City on March 26, 1904, the son of Charles and Josephine Campbell. His passion for mythology began when he was a young boy and his father took him and his younger brother, Charlie, to Buffalo Bill's Wild West Show at Madison Square Garden, and to the Museum of Natural History, where he became fascinated with Indian totem poles. By the time he was twelve he was voraciously reading books about American Indians. He soon recognized the parallels between these stories and those of his own Roman Catholic tradition, a discovery that would fire a cross-cultural study in the arcane discipline of mythology for the rest of his life.

As a student at prep school in New Milford, Connecticut, his favorite studies were biology and math. He went on to attend Dartmouth in 1921 for one year, but felt a "complete disorientation" there and even considered dropping out of college to enter business.

In the summer of 1922 a family friend gave him a biography of Leonardo da Vinci that so inspired him he transferred to Columbia University to "shift my interest from science to cultural history" and the humanities.

Campbell poses with a young Yakima woman at the Yakima Rodeo in Yakima, Washington, 1925.

1

STUART BROWN: Can you tell us about your grandparents and your Irish background?

JOSEPH CAMPBELL: I didn't really know my grandparents well. My father's father came over at the end of the potato famine in Ireland. He was a peasant and he became a gardener on an estate in Waltham, Massachusetts. My father grew up there. And his mother, also, was from Ireland. As a boy Dad got a job in a department store and became one of their major salesmen, and then they sent him to New York to open the New York office. So I was born in New York.

I remember when I was a little boy visiting my grandfather. He had a great white beard as a grandfather ought to. That's about all I remember. That was a long, long, long way back. And my mother's father I met only once. Mother was a New York girl but

Joseph Campbell, age thirteen weeks, with his parents, Charles W. and Josephine Campbell, 1904.

her mother was from Scotland and was a pretty, lovely, wonderful woman, and she took very good care of us. My mother had a beautiful brother who was a glorious swimmer. He died of diabetes when he was around twenty-two. I can remember swimming with him when I was a kid; he was the only other person in the family that played a role at all in the building of my ideals and idealism.

I never thought very much about being thoroughly Celtic-Irish until well on in my college years, when I began to get a real sense of what the Celtic consciousness was and what a good fortune it was to come out of that realm of wonderful, rich verbal fantasy. The whole fairyland world of Europe is out of Ireland, really.

And then in my graduate years I became interested in the Arthurian material, which is thoroughly Celtic, and gradually I got a sense of my relationship to their mentality.

BROWN: What were your boyhood years like? Were you an avid student?

CAMPBELL: From very early—around four or five years old—I was fascinated by American Indians, and that became my real studying. I went to school and had no problems with my studies, but my own enthusiasm was in this maverick realm of the American Indian mythologies. We lived in New Rochelle [New York] in those years, right next door to the public library. When I

Campbell (right) at around age four with his younger brother Charlie, about 1908. In later years Campbell reveled in the family lore. He and his brother were once strolling with their grandmother and baby sister down Riverside Drive in New York City when a woman stopped them. "You seem like two nice little boys," the woman said. Joe boldly responded, "I have Indian blood in me." Then his brother piped in, "And I have dog blood."

was about eleven I had read all the books about Indians in the children's library and was actually admitted to the stacks. I remember coming home from the library with stacks of books. And I think that's where my life as a scholar began. I *know* it did.

There they all were: all the reports of the Bureau of Ethnology, [Frank H.] Cushing and [Franz] Boas, and the lot of them. By the time I was thirteen I knew about as much about the American Indian as a good many anthropologists that I have met since. They know the sociological interpretations of why the Indians are the way they are or were, but they don't know much about Indians. And *I* did know.

BROWN: Did you have any heroes in your youth? Any lionized characters who became an early mentor for you?

CAMPBELL: Well, my parents found a lovely place in the Pocono Mountains of Pennsylvania along about 1917, and right nearby was a man whose books about Indians I had been reading. And so he became my first guru, or teacher. His name was Elmer Gregor and he wrote books about American Indians. He had been out in the Indian country. In those days—this is 1912, '13, '14, '15—the Indian wars were still going on, and "the only good Indian

The Campbell family bungalow in Pike County, Pennsylvania, about 1917.

was a dead Indian" and all of that. So there were Indians in the wind, even though we were in the East.

And so this beautiful place became my real discovery of nature. My emphasis on biology and nature and the body in my writing about myth comes out of those years. It is really a combination that comes from this man, who was a naturalist as well as an Indian scholar. He put me right on the road. Elmer Gregor. I remember him as a great. We used to communicate across the dining room with Indian sign language, and all that kind of thing.

Buffalo Bill's Wild West Show (above), about 1910. This photo was taken by Campbell's father on one of the family excursions to see Buffalo Bill Cody and his spectacular troupe of cavalrymen, sharpshooters, and Indian warriors. The show ignited the young Campbell's lifelong fascination with American Indians.

Buffalo Bill Cody (right), frontier scout, hero of dime novels, and a major force in the mythologizing of the American West, enjoys a cigar and newspaper in his tent after a performance. (Courtesy of the Buffalo Bill Historical Society, Cody, Wyoming.)

My career as a mythologist began almost immediately with Buffalo Bill's Wild West Show at Madison Square Garden [1910]. He came for two or three years, then he died and the group that replaced him was called the 101 Ranch. One of the Indians in the sideshow was Irontail, whose head had just appeared on the Indian-head nickel. He'd sit in profile to the people who filed by as they took their nickels out of their pockets, looked, bowed their heads, and went on.

Joseph Campbell,
Esquire (September 1977)

BROWN: It sounds as if your interest in Indians really was rising as much out of yourself as from any direct encouragement from your family.

CAMPBELL: My parents were very, very cooperative, but I found it myself. They helped me go on with it but they were business people; they had no scholarship. But they met people who could help them find the books that I could use, and so, really, I had wonderful help there.

Meanwhile in school I was doing the things one has to do, studying what was given me to study, and I enjoyed it all. But the real stuff was off on this side.

Indeed, the first and most essential service of a mythology is this one of opening the mind and heart to the utter wonder of all being.

Joseph Campbell,
The Inner Reaches of Outer Space

BROWN: I've never heard you speak much about your own background in Roman Catholicism, the church and its rituals.

CAMPBELL: I was in a day school convent in New York with the nuns until, oh, my Lord, I was about fifteen. And when you're born in an Irish Catholic family and environment and spend your boyhood with nuns, and you're serving Mass (I was a little altar boy), you're studying the Catholic doctrine all the time with deep belief. And I think anyone who has not been a Catholic in that sort of substantial way has no realization of the ambience of religion within which you live. It's powerful; it's potent; it's life-supporting. And it's beautiful. The Catholic religion is a *poetic religion*. Every month has its poetic and spiritual value. Boy, that got into me. I'm sure that my interest in mythology comes out of that.

I notice when I read the work of scholars or artists or novelists who are really interested in myth as a life-structuring thing—not something that's just fantasy, but deeper, *significant* fantasy—nine times out of ten they were Catholics. I've been interested in what happens to people when they leave their religions. Protestants and Jews become psychologists and sociologists, and Catholics become . . . poets.

You know, it's really true!

BROWN: Did you go to parochial school or a public grade school?

CAMPBELL: I went to Canterbury School, a fine Catholic prep school, in Connecticut [1919–1921]. That's where another beginning took place. There were two particular teachers there. One was the headmaster who had founded the school, Nelson Hume, and it was from him that I learned to write. He was a marvelous, marvelous teacher. I was in a class—oh, this was real elegant—the school was newly founded so there were only about fifty boys in the school. There were six of us in my class, and we had a kind of precise attention. Every day we had to write a daily scene. Hume would come in and read out scenes and criticize and adjust them for us right there. It was every day: writing, writing, writing. And I was studying biology at that time and mathematics. Those were my principal school interests.

Of course we had to take languages, and back in those years after World War I we still weren't allowed to study German, we had to study Spanish and French. (I couldn't even have German measles—I had Liberty measles!) But the man who was our teacher in the languages was a magnificent scholar, and it was through him that I first learned that there was such a thing as Sanskrit. He was a linguist. Between him and the headmaster I discovered the world of, what can we say, academic scholarship, although I had discovered my subject myself with the Indians.

BROWN: Is there any truth to the story that you actually taught your own high school class in biology?

CAMPBELL: Yes. The headmaster, Hume, was hoping that I would become a master in his school. He gave me two opportunities to give lectures to the boys. No one else had ever had this given him. But I had that privilege. I gave a lecture once on the history of the American Indians, and another on biology and the circulation system of the blood. Those are the great, great achievements—my first lectures.

Campbell (right) and friend, John McPhee, at Canterbury School, 1920.

CAMPBELL: One of the big problems in mythology is this one of putting the individual in accord with nature. The world in which the primitive people are living becomes mythologized. One of the problems in our tradition is that the land—the Holy Land—

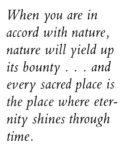

When you are in accord with nature, nature will yield up its bounty . . . and every sacred place is the place where eternity shines through time.

Joseph Campbell

7

Black Elk, only a "preacher" to the white men near the Pine Ridge Reservation where he spent his last years, but a wichasha wakon, a holy man or shaman, to his own people, the Oglala Sioux. Campbell strongly felt that his story, as told to John Neihardt in Black Elk Speaks, *is part of our "spiritual history."*

is somewhere else. So we've lost the whole sense of accord with nature. And if it's not here, it's nowhere.

ANGELES ARRIEN: American Indian mythology really brings out that reverence for nature.

CAMPBELL: I like that passage very much in the Black Elk speech in John Neihardt's book [*Black Elk Speaks*], where he's telling about his vision. He says, that he found himself on the central mountain of the world. And the central mountain of the world was Harney Peak in South Dakota. "But anywhere" he says, "is the center of the world."

And this is the basic mythological problem: Move into a landscape. Find the sanctity of that land. And then there can be the matching of your own nature with this gorgeous nature of the land. It is the first essential adaptation. Now if—as in our tradition—you think of nature as corrupt, that there are certain things in nature that should not be, then you *can't* put yourself in accord with nature. Instead you're always thinking of right and wrong, evil and good, the Devil and God. And so you're in an ethical position and it makes yielding to nature so difficult.

ARRIEN: And yet we have the four seasons, which are a constant mirror of our own process. Each one of us has a spring, we have a summer, we have a wintertime.

CAMPBELL: The poets and the artists have recognized this, in general. They have put themselves in accord with it in order to find their own inner base.

EDWARD DREESSEN: You're saying then that myth is a constant regeneration, an identification with the life process?

CAMPBELL: That's what it is; that's what it is. The amazing thing is that when you go to a sacred place you feel its sanctity. There's a little bit of it down here in this little stream [at Esalen in Big Sur, California] which the Essalen Indians regarded as sacred. The landscape here was involved in their mythologies and rituals.

I remember when I was in Iceland there was an Icelandic mythographer who took my wife and me around and showed us all the sacred places. There was one place, Thingvellir, which was where they had their annual great ceremony. You felt that this is a magical place, this is a magical place! And I had the same thing happen when I was in the great caves of Lascaux in France. Those places you don't want to leave. They grab something inside you that's very deep. Very deep and very important.

I'll never forget the experience of going to Delphi in Greece.

Campbell with Icelandic mythographer Einar Pálsson on the sacred grounds of Thingvellir, Iceland, 1972.

The temples have all been deliberately smashed by the vandalism of the Christians, but they are still there and you can see what the Greek idea of corporal beauty was. That is where the oracle, the prophetess, received inspiration in the fumes, the smoke coming up from the abyss, and she prophesied and gave statements of destiny.

And then you have on another level this beautiful theater with the wonderful valley and landscape as its backdrop and that accord with nature, that accord with nature, the bringing of nature to its high fulfillment in human nature. This is Greek. One height more as you climb and you come to the stadium, the athletic field. This is the only culture I know where this whole range of the spiritual, the religious, the aesthetic, and the physical is all put together into one picture. Any young man in Greece could participate in those games. This is the idea of the individual and the individual's quest.

Any beautiful lands like these are power spots because they help you put your own nature in accord. And art is supposed to do this also. Cézanne says somewhere, "Art is a harmony parallel to nature."

ARRIEN: That's beautiful.

CAMPBELL: Well, the basic idea in the old Bronze Age mythologies was of the cycle of the ages, the cycle of the year, and the cycle of a lifetime, all as equivalent cycles. Just think of it: cycles, cycles, cycles; nothing occurs that has not already occurred. There's nothing to it but to yield to it.

ARRIEN: Like the *Tao Te Ching* is a whole mythic motif honoring nature, a mirror of oneself.

CAMPBELL: Yes, yes. And this comes out very radically in the line between Persia and India. Zoroaster, the Persian prophet, actually attacks the Indian idea of yoga, which involves putting yourself in accord with the universe. You see?

This is two totally different mythologies, and it makes a big difference. The scientist can't tell us, and doesn't even try to tell us, whether it's a good world or a bad world; that's not his job. But the attitude of their mythology does establish Europe's relationship to nature.

Now this thing is coming in—with people in this country at any rate—of the rediscovery of nature. And through it they are rediscovering the American Indian stuff. I knew about it when I was a kid; I used to read the stuff when nobody else ever thought about it. Now it's all over the place with wonderful characters such as the medicine man Black Elk, as in *Black Elk Speaks,* which is a work that was given to us by a writer, John Neihardt, and not by an anthropologist, though he got the inner message. It's something that's making history in this country right now, spiritual history. *Black Elk Speaks:* It's *marvelous.*

When you look at that nature world it becomes an icon, it becomes a holy picture that speaks of the origins of the world. Almost every mythology that knows anything about water sees the origins of life coming out of water. And curiously, that's true. It's amusing that the origin of life out of water is in myths and then again, finally, in science, we find the same thing. It's exactly so.

I can remember when I spent a long time with an intertidal biologist, Ed Ricketts, in that area between lowtide and hightide [1931–1932]. All those strange forms, cormorants and little worms of different kinds and all. You'd hear, my gosh, this generation of life was a great battle going on, life consuming life, everything learning how to eat the other one, the whole mystery, and then from there they crawl up on the land. And also in the mythic themes generally out of the ocean, or what in India is called the milky ocean out of which the whole universe comes.

DREESSEN: The milky elixir of life.

CAMPBELL: Yes, the milky elixir of life.

ARRIEN: There's the water and here's this great rock, so here are mythic motifs.

CAMPBELL: Well, yes, and the tree and the rock are also motifs: These rocks are the enduring, and the tree the living symbol. James Joyce plays with it in *Finnegans Wake,* where he speaks about the "tree stone"—Tristan—the one who is wealthy, the eternal rock, ever-growing life.

DREESSEN: When you pick up rocks off a beach that seem to have something to do with you, you feel a connection.

CAMPBELL: Any child walking along the beach naturally picks up buried treasures, stones and shells, and things like that. And the use of the shell, the conch, as a trumpet has to do with the voice of the ocean and the summons to the people.

ARRIEN: Like the sirens.

CAMPBELL: And actually, psychologically, the ocean is the counterpart of the unconscious into which the sun of consciousness sets and out of which it comes.

Minaret of the Mosque at Samarra in Iraq. "Ascending mountains is a common metaphor for a spiritual quest and ascent."

ARRIEN: When looking at the mountains here I was thinking about René Daumal's book *Mount Analogue,* and about the mountain being a symbol of the inner quest.

CAMPBELL: When the clouds come down it's as though the heavenly powers were descending on the realm of the earth. And in the early mythologies—for instance, of ancient Sumer—the earliest emergence out of the sea of life is in the form of a mountain. The mountain is a male and female. The upper half is male and the lower half female. Then it separates and the upper half becomes the sky and the goddess is the mountain. And then the descent of the clouds is the joining of heaven and earth, which is to say the joining of the phenomenological side of life, the living in the world with its spiritual import and the juncture of the two.

This is why ascending the mountains is a standard theme for a spiritual quest and ascent. Moses goes to the top of the mountain and the God delivers the law to him. There are just no end of mountain themes.

Although Jesus' cross is not on a mountain, there was a little rise of hill there, and the mountain theme is insisted upon in the art representations of the cross.

DREESSEN: Odysseus came out of the water and came onto the land, came to the mountain. How can you describe that in mythological terms?

CAMPBELL: In the Greek world the emergence of a being out of the water is a constant theme, the boy riding the dolphin who establishes Delphi, for example. It's the emergence of life out of the sea into the world of solid circumstances. Then the end of the world, the end of a cycle of time, ends in water. That's the flood motif, which appears in all mythologies—all the cyclic mythologies—of the end of time.

Now you have that theme of being born in perfection, then gradually a sort of entropy increases, losing tension. Life depends on tension; and as soon as the polarities begin to dissolve we move into an androgynous situation of male-female barber shops! Then everything is gone back into the anthropological soup, and it's time for the world to come again. So the cycle comes out of the sea, which is a mixture of everything, and becomes defined in the forms of the landscape and life and gradually returns to the sea. This is the cycle of it all: the ages of Gold, Silver, Bronze, Iron, the Abyss, then start again.

ARRIEN: So the hero's journey is very much equated with the mountain quest?

CAMPBELL: Yes indeed. And one part of the mythological motif of the hero's journey is acquiescence. For instance, I am moving toward death, as we all are. That's also yielding. And the hero is the one who knows *when* to surrender and what to surren-der *to*. The main theme is to yield your position to the dynamic. And the dynamic of life is now this form eats that form. Yield.

That's what goes on in the world of fish. It's what the Hindus call *matsya nyaya,* the "Law of the Fish," which is that the big ones eat the little ones, and the little ones have to be smart so they can grow up.

ARRIEN: The alchemists said that we're really the weavers of all the elements—earth, fire, water, and air. And when we say somebody's in their element or out of their element, what is it really that they are saying?

CAMPBELL: Yes, well, the element of where you are is always involved in the ritual of orientation of the four quarters, as with the Indians in the ceremony of the calumet, the sacred pipe.

The pipe is a kind of portable altar, and when it's lighted it's not being smoked for fun, typically, but as a sacred act. When it is lighted the incense is, as it were, going to heaven. The pipe stem is lifted so that the sun smokes first, then it's addressed to the four quarters so you know where you are: the central mountain is right here, which is everywhere. And the celebrant smokes and then the pipe is passed around. This orientation of the quarters, I guess one could say, is the basic high cultural myth form: the centre, the quarters. And then wherever you go: Find the center. That establishes the sacred point, where the high point is, and then you have the four quarters.

We live by killing, which is what you do even when you are eating grapes. You are still killing something. Life just lives on life. And it's the one life in all of these different heads of mouths eating itself. It's a fantastic mystery. That's what's symbolized in the snake biting its own tail, the snake of life consuming itself. That's what it means.

The essence of life is that it lives by killing and eating. And that's the great mystery that myths have to deal with. The primitive★ people that live by killing have to reconcile the psyche to this thing because for them the animals are manifestations of divine powers. Not only that: They are wearing the skins of the animals, their tents are made out of the animal skins, and so they are living on death all the time in a sea of blood. And a typical myth is a kind of covenant between the animal and the human world, where it is understood that this is the way of nature and that the animals become their willing victims. They give themselves willingly with the understanding that the ritual of gratitude will be enacted to return their life to the source of life, so that another group of animals of the same kind can come to be consumed next year. For them the animals are manifestations of divine powers.

Would you like to hear a little bit of a myth on this theme?

This story is of a time when a certain tribe was facing a desperate winter. The Indians had a way to kill a whole herd of

And the whole secret of relating mythology and the spiritual life to your environment is involved in what's called landnama *by the people in Iceland: naming and claiming the land through naming the landscape, land-taking. You read the land you are living in as the holy land.*

Joseph Campbell

★[Ed. note. In his later career Campbell vigorously took on a more contemporary phrasing. Throughout his *Historical Atlas of Mythology,* and in his last lectures, Campbell referred to Jamake Highwater's use of the term "primal" cultures.]

buffalo, which gave the tribe its meat for the winter, by stampeding them over a great precipice. So the animals go over and are knocked to pieces at the bottom and then they can be killed. But this particular year when they had stampeded the buffalo and the buffalo would get to the edge, they would swerve aside—nobody was going over. So it looked bad for the tribe.

One morning a young woman gets up to get the water for her family. From the tepee she sees the buffalo just up there, right on the edge, and she says, "Oh, if you'd only come over and give food to my people for the winter, I would marry one of you." And immediately they began coming over.

Well, that was a surprise. A still larger surprise was that one of them comes up and says, "All right, girlie, we're off."

"Oh, no," she says.

"Oh, yes," he says. "Look, it's happened, and you've given your promise and we've done the work."

So he takes her by the arm (it's hard to know how a buffalo can take you by the arm but he does), and he leads her off over the hill and out onto the plains.

When her family wakes up the next morning they look around and ask, "Where's Minnehaha, anyhow?"

Then Daddy goes out, and being an Indian he knows how to read in footprints what's going on. He looks and says, "She's run off with a buffalo." He puts on his walking moccasins and he takes his bow and arrow and goes off to find his daughter among the buffalo.

After he's followed these footsteps and gone a considerable way, he comes to a wallow where the buffalo like to roll around to get the lice off. He sits down and thinks, What am I going to do?

Then he sees a beautiful magpie. Now in the hunting mythologies there are certain animals that are very clever: magpies and foxes and blue jays and ravens. These are sort of shaman animals. So the magpie comes down and begins picking around, and the father says, "Beautiful bird, my daughter has run off with a buffalo. Have you seen a young woman with the buffalo people?"

The magpie says, "Yes, there's a young woman with the buffalo over there right now."

So the father says, "Oh, will you go tell her that her father is here?"

The magpie flies over and there she is. I don't know what

she's doing—knitting or something like that—and behind her all the buffalo are having a nap. Right behind her is the great big fellow. The bird comes pecking over and says, "Your father's at the wallow."

"Oh, dear," she says. "This is dangerous. This is terrible. Tell him to wait. I'll see about this."

Presently the buffalo wakes up, the big fellow behind her, and takes off one of his horns and says, "Go get me some water."

She takes the horn and goes to the wallow and there's Daddy. Daddy grabs her and he says, "You come."

"No, no, no, this is very dangerous. Let me fix this thing up." So she gets the water and goes back to the buffalo. He takes it and sniffs and says, "Fee, fi, fo, fum, I smell the blood of an Indian."

And she says, "Oh, no."

And he says, "Yes," and he roars, and all the buffalo get up and they lift their tails and start to dance and roar and go to the wallow and trample Daddy into invisibility. He's just not there anymore; she has just wiped him out.

The girl begins to cry and the old buffalo says, "So you're crying, what's the matter?"

"It's my Daddy."

He says, "Yeah, you've lost your daddy, but we lose our wives and our uncles, our children, and everything, to feed your people."

"Well," she says, "but—*Daddy!*"

There's a kind of sympathy in the buffalo for her and he says, "Well, if you can bring your daddy back to life, I'll let you go."

So she calls the magpie and says, "Will you peck around a little and see if you can find a piece of Daddy?" And he does. He pecks around and finds a little vertebrae, a bit of backbone.

"I've got something here," he says.

"Well," she says, "that'll do." So she puts it down on the ground and takes her robe and puts it over the piece of bone and starts to chant. She chants a magical power song. And presently you can see there's a man under the buffalo robe. She looks under, and yes, it's Daddy all right. But he needs a little more singing.

And she goes on with her chant and presently he stands up. The buffalo are tremendously excited about this. And they say, "Well, now, why don't you do this for us? Why don't you bring us back to life after you've killed us all? Now we'll give you our buffalo dance, we'll tell you how to do it. And when you've slaughtered a lot of our people, you dance this dance and sing your song and we'll come every year to feed your people."

This is the origin legend of the Blackfoot buffalo society. It was published in a book I read when I was a kid by George Bird Grinnell, a really marvelous writer and collector of Indian material; it's called *Blackfoot Lodge Tales*.

Now you turn from one people to another and you get one story after another like this, of a covenant between the people and the animals, all understood to be part of the nature of the world, this life eating life. And of course, when they eat, they don't thank their idea of God for having given them the animal. They thank the animal, which is a rather appropriate act. The great ceremonies of the Northwest cult people, for instance, are ceremonies thanking the salmon of the first salmon catch for having come again this year.

It's a beautiful idea, that life is on the surface unendurable. It's a fierce, ferocious thing. Schopenhauer said in one of his best moments, "Life is something that should not have been." If it's not something that should not have been, but something that should have been, then you've got to say yea to it, that's all, the way it is.

And when Nietzsche comes along and reads Schopenhauer, he takes the other attitude toward this idea of life eating life, and he says, yes, this is not only as it is, but as it should be. It can't be otherwise. Now this brings in a terrific emphasis on what the tender-minded call violence. But that's what nature is. And every now and then you see something that opens your mind to this. Last year in *National Geographic* there was a picture that just lifted the hair on my head. It was of a gazelle being eaten by three cheetahs. And you had this animal lying on the ground with three cheetahs eating its belly while the animal was still alive and its head was lifted in a kind of plea for compassion or mercy.

Now can you say yea to that? You've got to. You must have *amor fati,* the love of fate. And it takes an awful lot of guts to *really* say yes all the way.

Life lives on life. That's what it is. And there are some traditions where eating human beings is part of the sacrament, you might say. But you have a different meditation when you have personified the food creature that way.

You must realize that in the hunting and gathering tribal

world all eating is like eating human beings, because the animals are themselves life masters. They're teaching the people the way of life. And the principal rituals have to do with gratitude and thanks to the animal that is being eaten. And these people comfort themselves in the notion that they are participating in the way of nature, in killing, in eating, in enjoying.

BROWN: And they're guilt free?

CAMPBELL: There's no guilt; there's nothing to be guilty about. Because when you are in accord with nature, nature will yield its bounty. This is something that is coming up in our own consciousness now, with the ecology movement, recognizing that by violating the environment in which we are living, we are really cutting off the energy and the source of our own living. And it's this sense of accord, so that living properly in relation to what has to be done in this world, one fosters the vitality of the environment.

CAMPBELL: One of the big disasters for the American Indian tribes on the plains was this: Their whole religious centering was in the buffalo as the prime food, and then the buffaloes are wiped out and life loses its magic. During the 1870s and 1880s one of the great projects in the conquest of the West was to annihilate the buffalo herds. When one sees the pictures of the buffalo plains that were done by George Catlin, for example, it's incredible the multitudes of animals that were there. Well, you couldn't put railroads across that land, and you couldn't plant wheat in that land. And so—not only to clear the land, but also to relieve the Indians of their food supplies so that they'd have to go onto reservations and receive handouts from the governments—the buffalo killers were sent out and the buffaloes were simply massacred.

This is entirely contrary in mode and feeling to the manner in which the Indians killed buffalo. The animal is killed only insofar as he is needed. And he is then worshiped and respect is given to him. There is an attitude of gratitude. The great festivals are festivals in honor of the principal food animal. And there again is the business of accord with the natural world.

*Once having traversed
the threshold, the hero
moves in a dream
landscape of curiously
fluid, ambiguous
forms, where he must
survive a succession of
trials.*

Joseph Campbell,
*The Hero with a
Thousand Faces*

*Joseph Campbell, a portrait of the scholar as a young man at the University of Paris,
1928.*

2

The Road of Trials

From 1922 to 1927 Joseph Campbell lived an eclectic life as student, athlete, and traveler. He studied under Raymond Weaver at Columbia, receiving a master's degree in medieval literature in 1926; played saxophone in a college jazz band; and ran world–class times in the half-mile for the Columbia track team and the New York Athletic Club. During the summers he traveled extensively with his family through Central America and Europe. On one of those excursions, a boat trip to Europe in 1924, he met the theosophical teacher Jiddu Krishnamurti, and became interested "in a vague way" in oriental studies.

In 1927 Campbell received a traveling fellowship from Columbia and went to the University of Paris to study the Arthurian romances, Old French, and Provençal. When he arrived he found himself in the midst of *"les années folles"*—"the crazy years"—of the Paris bohemians. As he was fond of saying later, "the whole world opened up" when he collided head on with the modern art of Picasso, Brancusi, and Klee, and the literature of Joyce, Yeats, and Eliot.

After receiving an extension on his fellowship, he transferred to the University of Munich in 1928 to resume his studies of medieval literature but in the original German texts. Once again his interests diverged, this time from Indo-European philology to Sanskrit, medieval literature to Hinduism and Buddhism, and the works of Freud, Jung, and Thomas Mann. The postgraduate years in Europe were a confluence of the major intrigues of his life: myth, dream, and art, psychology, literature, and anthropology.

BROWN: Did you play sports in prep school?

CAMPBELL: Oh, we *had* to. Later, when I taught my first year at that school, I understood that when you're teaching a bunch of boys you've got to wear them out. They've got to participate in athletics. So you send them out in the fields where they can knock each other around. In primitive societies the violence delivered to young men in their teens is prodigious and it is taming them. The young male is a compulsively violent piece of biology and you've got to integrate that.

People talk about looking for the meaning of life; what you're really looking for is an *experience* of life. And one of the experiences is a *good fight*. Remember that old Irish question: "Is this a private fight or can anybody get into it?" It heightens your experience of being alive, being in a good fight. And that's the advantage of the experience in athletics—there's organized violence and it does everybody good. And those who can't even wiggle a finger can at least properly sit and look at it and get a certain satisfaction out of seeing people knock each other around.

Campbell (third from right) playing an exuberant saxophone in a Columbia college jazz band, 1921–1922.

The American Mile Relay national champions of 1925: Joseph Campbell, John Holden, Allan Helfrich, and Joe Turney, at the San Francisco AAU championships. Of his days as a premier runner, Campbell said, "I think I learned more about living then, what it takes to win, and what it takes to lose."

So I played football and hockey. I didn't like baseball so I didn't play baseball. But I was a hockey goal guard and in football I played guard. Guards were heavier in those days. When I was a kid I weighed 180 pounds, so I was a good guard.

And then I went to college at Dartmouth. My first year there I played tackle and then I went to Columbia and I played end. The history of my experience at Columbia was rather funny because I came late to the training season and was scheduled for end. At the first scrimmage, on about the second pass, the ball went over the quarterback's head and I picked it up and ran for a touchdown the length of the field! So they put me on the first squad. But I was never much of a football player. I don't think I ever got into a decent game.

Track, though, came as a surprise.

I never had the ability to let someone be ahead of me. We had to take Physical Ed., as they called it. The indoor track must have been ten laps to a mile. When we started out running there

THE NEW YORK TELEGRAM,

Columbia Has New Athletic Star

JOE CAMPBELL NEW LION HERO

Half Miler's Fine Running at
Penn Relays Puts Columbia
on Map in Track Athletics.

By H. V. Valentine.

The sturdy form of Joe Campbell, of Columbia University, stands head and shoulders above the bevy of "heroes of the minute," ground out by ten hours of relay racing at Pennsylvania's great athletic carnival at Franklin Field, Philadelphia, last Friday and Saturday.

Campbell's great running in the two relay races that brought so many championship to Columbia, was the high spot in the tremendously impressive showing on the part of metropolitan district foot racers in the Quaker City's annual classic.

If the Columbia undergraduates do not carry Joe around the campus on their shoulders today they ought to, for his fleetness of foot and stoutness of heart ... soul-stirring struggles on the Franklin Field path shed more track glory to the Morningside Lion than that worthy monarch has known in years.

The race that Campbell and Eddie Swinburne, of Georgetown, another New York boy, put up in the last leg of the sprint medley championship on Friday will not be forgotten soon. This one had 10,000 spectators ... on their feet yelling like mad. It was ... in the last five yards, where the Blue and White's new track here displayed a slight edge in strength.

Compared to the medley struggle the two mile championship race on Saturday was a "pipe" for the Morningsiders. Once Gus Jaeger, Jimmy Brick and Johnny Theobald had stuck to the Boston College pace, to send Campbell away within twelve yards of "Babe" Daley, the game but none too strong B. C. anchor, the result was a foregone conclusion.

Campbell's teammates had to average 1 minute and 59 seconds to keep their alma mater in the running, and they deserve a full measure of credit for making good.

Columbia's double barreled victory in the major championship events flattened the experts' dope completely. Georgetown was figured to take the sprint medley race by a block and the fine reliance of the Boston College two-mile team was expected to offset Campbell's brilliancy in the final leg. It is believed that the Georgetown team would have done better in the medley had Jimmy Burgess not run the first leg. Jimmy never runs as well in front as he does behind. In Friday's race the former national champion pulled out about five yards lead on runners to whom he could allow fifteen yards start, running from behind.

CINDER STAR

JOE CAMPBELL

Stars middle-distance runner of Columbia University who bids fair to garner quite a few points for the Blue and White this season. As anchor on the mile relay quartet, it was Campbell who brought victory to his school by a thrilling finish at the recent Penn games. Campbell is captain of the team and one of its mightiest twinklers.

SPRINT MEDLEY BIG THRILL, SAYS ROBBIE

Last Leg of Relay Won by Columbia Bright Spot of Day, Writes Penn Coach

EXPECTS NEW 880 RECORD

By LAWSON ROBERTSON
Penn Track Coach

THE thirty-second renewal of the ... great track meet in the world measured by number of events, got off to a flying start yesterday to the tune of many a busted record and a couple of dizzy half-mile performances turned in by Swinburne, of Georgetown, and Campbell, of Columbia.

Of course, other sterling races were run and the decathlon decided for another year, but to my mind the last leg of the sprint medley relay was the bright particular spot of the afternoon.

I caught Campbell of the Morningsiders in the rather phenomenal time of 1:53 for his two laps which is surely moving for this time of year and seems to have established this young man over-night to the forefront of the athletic firmament.

The Georgetown team in this event consisted of Jimmy Burgess, former national quarter-mile champion, who ran the 440; Vernon Ascher, also former national quarter-mile champion, and Ray Hass, Intercollegiate Hurdle Champion, who ran 220 each, and Swinburne, member of the Georgetown World's Record Two-Mile Relay team, who ran the half.

Columbia Comes Through

Such a team on paper sounds like an unbeatable combination and they panned like potential crackers of the record for the distance before the race.

Columbia is the present scene of a remarkable rejuvenation and renaissance and not satisfied with winning the intercollegiate basketball crown and drawing first blood in the intercollegiate baseball race by smacking Penn for a loss last week they up and plucked themselves a whole sugar plum from the track bush yesterday.

Swinburne, Campbell and the great Lennes, of M. I. T., started with but a few strides separating them and staged a thrilling triangular duel with Lennes lost in the mad dash at the tape. The time was only a second slower than the record.

Newspaper clippings from the "cinder star" 's scrapbook, a gift from his father upon graduation from Columbia.

was always someone ahead because after I'd lapped the field they were still ahead of me. When we finished the man in charge called me over (he happened to be the track coach) and he said, "Have you ever thought of running?" I said, "No." He said, "Well, you can run a faster half-mile than anybody on the campus. Why don't you come out for track?"

So that started. And actually that was one of the great experiences of my life.

BROWN: You had quite a career in track. What did those years of competition teach you?

CAMPBELL: The young men there in my years of running, and the attitude they had toward each other in competition, was beautiful. It was a beautiful manhood.

I got up there in the high brackets, you know. I could run as fast a half-mile as anybody in the world at that time. My years of running were exactly between the 1924 and 1928 Olympics. I had only three years of running so I actually went back for my graduate degrees because I had another year of running!

That was a beautiful, beautiful period. In New York we had indoor track meets all through the winter. After the 1924 Olympic Games the athletes who had been winners over there were over in New York. Men like Paavo Nurmi. I've seen him run and run and run. Just gorgeous. A beautiful man. I think that meant more to me than anything else in my college years—the track. I think I learned more about living then than any other time in my life, what it takes to win, and what it takes to lose. All of that.

RICHARD TARNAS: It seems that a lot of people are moving toward their own kind of physical and spiritual disciplines nowadays, like in body work or like Michael Murphy with his ideas of running in altered states and higher awareness. Different people from different disciplines seem to be coming to a similar conclusion.

CAMPBELL: I've seen it all around.

TARNAS: The idea of becoming the bliss and actually living that layer of being: How do we find it in our own culture?

CAMPBELL: That's our problem. In the West the different departments of life were separated from each other so you lose the holistic approach. You speak of the jogging theme that's going on. People are beginning to realize that there is a kind of mystical bliss that comes when the body is overtaxed. I experienced this when I was running in college and a couple of years after college. As I look back now there were a couple of moments in the last eighty yards of the half-mile when I was running in championship time . . . you know, you're spaced out then. If anyone would ask me what the peaks were, the high moments of my life experience— really, *zing!* the whole thing in a nutshell—those races would be it. More than anything else in my whole life.

Some of the things that are happening now in the West are a result of the oriental martial arts and Asian disciplines that are coming in. The handling of the body in combat or in competition is a function, really, of a psychological posture. There has got to be a still place in there and the movement has to take place around it. I lost two races that were very important to me because I *lost* the still place. The race was so important that I put myself out there to *win* the race instead of to *run* the race. And the whole thing got thrown off.

Well, this is a way of presenting of yourself and finding of yourself in relation to *action*. My wife, Jean, is a dancer, and dancing makes athletics look like an easy job. But there, too, centering is the whole thing. When you see someone come on the stage who really knows where she is, it's a different experience than someone whose body seems to be different limbs attached to a torso. It's a fantastic thing. This, I think, is coming in through the influence of the oriental teachers.

TARNAS: Some of these forms and disciplines begin to look very much like the Kundalini awakening, where people are allowed their own experience of surrendering to their own quiet place within themselves. Then something from inside begins to come out, a kind of bliss consciousness or high energy form seems to come through people. It's very similar to the ideas in yoga that India has had for thousands of years. But now we're coming into it in our own way.

CAMPBELL: In Kundalini yoga there is a systemization of the possibilities of transpsychological transformation. And the first of the three levels, the chakra of the pelvis, represents the usual transformation from just tenacity to life, to erotic, to aggressive. But then at the level of the heart comes the transformation into the spiritual consciousness. This is the field of the virgin birth. And it's the symbol in the lotus of the heart center, of the lingam yoni, the male-female organ, in gold, the new transcendent life. And then the upper chakra takes these energies and transforms them into spiritual states.

If there's Kundalini transformation, it certainly is similar. No doubt about it.

DREESSEN: In the Aikido tradition and discipline we use some key phrases: Be here now for yourself. Open up to it. Let it happen. It's very subtle, very difficult. I think the whole practice of martial arts is to let go of concern. Be here now for yourself, then there is a release mechanism and that deep inner personal acceptance. And then, wow, it comes.

BROWN: There's a difference between the visual process in the winning of a race, for example, and the running of the race.

Yet, if you ran not to win but you saw yourself winning while running—in your mind while it was happening—would this kind of process have any relationship to the Kundalini phenomenology you're talking about?

CAMPBELL: It's a shift of emphasis from here to there, to what they call in the Orient the *chi*. The energy comes from the lower center—that's the Wisdom Sheath center. That's the sheath of the body's intentions, and nature's intentions, and you're settled in there and your manifestations—that's just the growth of a tree. Your winning the race is a manifestation of the potentiality of the energy and powers of the body. As soon as you begin relating to other powers, that stuff up here, you soon lose your center; you lose energy that way.

BROWN: I've heard you say in your lectures and seminars that some of the same feeling goes into your preparing yourself as if—

CAMPBELL: —As if it were a track meet. Well, it *is* [laughs]. I tell you, the two-hour lecture *is* a track meet!

PHIL COUSINEAU: Speaking of track, how did you become friends with Jackson Schultz, the Olympic runner?

CAMPBELL: Jackson Schultz was a sprinter—a gorgeous runner with a smooth running style. He ran the 100 and 200. I roomed with him on two major occasions. In 1925 I was on the New York Athletic Club team that came to San Francisco for the American Athletic Union championships and Schultz was my roommate then. The year before Schultz had won the 200 meters in the Paris Olympics and had gone around the world with a couple of other athletes, and all he could talk about was Hawaii. In those days it was a four-and-a-half-day train ride from New York to San Francisco. And there I was with Schultz talking about Hawaii. I thought, Well, why don't I just drop this team and go to Hawaii? And he said, "Go ahead."

So this was how I first visited Hawaii. When Schultz had been there he had met the Kahanamoku family. What he did was wonderful. He wrote to people in Hawaii to meet me. When I

Joseph Campbell (bottom) and friends on Waikiki Beach in the summer of 1925. While there, Campbell learned to surf with the "father of surfing" himself, the legendary Duke Kahanamoku.

came out on the boat after my four-and-one-half days, it docked off in the water waiting for the quarantine officials to come out. You could smell the islands with the flowers and all. God, you were just captured. The boat moved into the dock, where the Royal Hawaiian band was playing "Aloha." And there was a little pennant above the crowd that read: "Aloha, Joe Campbell."

Well, we had won everything in San Francisco, and so I thought, This is an adequate reception! But of course it was the chap who had come to meet me who had the pennant. I went ashore and met Schultz's friend and he brought me to a hotel, the Hotel Courtland. Many years later I learned that it was one block from Jean's residence. She was a little girl taking hula lessons in the very hotel where I was living!

All I did that summer was wait for the trolley—that "Toonerville" trolley they had to go to Waikiki—and spend the day on Duke Kahanamoku's surfboard. Now it's in the Bishop Museum. It was as high as I could reach with my hand, made of koa wood. Well, I was a track man. I didn't have anything up here in the chest, so I couldn't even propel it in the water. But it was the surfboard that was given to me by David Kahanamoku, so I would lug it down to the water, get on the thing, and swim it out to where the waves were, and then for the rest of the day lie out and try to catch a wave!

One fine day David came out on the board and he said, "You no catch a wave," and I said, "I can't get this thing going." So he says, "All right, I'll give you a little push." So I got a push from David, and I tell you being on that surfboard was like being on the *Queen Elizabeth II*. That was my one great ride.

I went to Europe as a student for my graduate work in 1927. The next Olympics was 1928 and Jackson Schultz was over there. So I roomed with him for my first several weeks in Paris, and then when he came back again for the Olympics I saw him some more.

It's funny. When you get on in years and look back and realize the role that certain people have played in your life, it's surprising. And Schultz, I think, was one of the major people. Sometimes it's just that little kick that brought you onto this path instead of that one.

I haven't seen him since those days. He was a fine man.

⚇

COUSINEAU: You once said that when you were a young man you wanted to be a synthesis of Leonardo da Vinci and Douglas Fairbanks. Were they your next heroes after Buffalo Bill?

CAMPBELL: When I was a kid Douglas Fairbanks was a magnificent performer and a beautiful man doing fantastic things! There was one great show where Fairbanks was a pirate, and somebody was chasing him up the mast of a boat. Then he takes his knife and puts it in the sail and he comes *down* that sail like this— I'll never forget this! Where does he get this? Well, a guy who can do that kind of thing . . .

In respect to the world of the intellect I was never interested in small, specialized studies. I think they tend to dehumanize you. In his wonderful, majestic translation of everything into human values, Leonardo da Vinci seemed to me to represent what I was looking for.

When I was in prep school I was interested in biology and mathematics, and that was also true in my freshman year in Dartmouth. But in the interval between my freshman and sophomore years somebody gave me Dimitri Merejkowski's *The Romance of Leonardo da Vinci.* That is what turned me on. My God, I discovered that I didn't know anything about the world of art and culture and civilization. I knew about American Indians but not about art and civilization. My whole world shifted with that book.

COUSINEAU: What did you mean when you said that in your studies of the Celtic Arthurian romances you understood your Irish Catholic background in a new way?

CAMPBELL: The Arthurian romances are right out of the Celtic world. They are transformations of Celtic heroes into medieval knights. Every single one of them has a Celtic background. My affinity for the material I'm sure has to do with my actual inheritance. And then the fact that James Joyce grabbed me. You know, that wonderful living in a realm of significant fantasy, which is Irish, is there in the Arthurian romances; it's in Joyce; and it's in my life.

COUSINEAU: Did you find that you identified with Stephen Daedalus, the young romantic rebel who lived in "silence, exile, and cunning" in Joyce's *A Portrait of the Artist as a Young Man?*

When you open A Portrait of the Artist as a Young Man, *my copy I bought back in Paris in 1927, on the title page we see in Latin,* "Et ignotas anuimum dimittit in artes," "*And he turned his mind to unknown art.*" *The name of the hero is Stephen Daedalus, who created wings of art by which he flew.*

Joseph Campbell

27

James Joyce in Dublin at age twenty. Campbell was nearly the same age (twenty-three) when he discovered Joyce's groundbreaking novel Ulysses *in Paris in 1927. "His problem was my problem, exactly. And the problem is when you're deeply built into the system and you're losing your faith. It's no fun."*

CAMPBELL: His problem was my problem, exactly. And the problem is when you're deeply built into the system of the church and you're losing your faith. It's no fun. I mean, it started when I was studying biology. There's absolutely no relationship between the biological evolution of the human species, the animal and plant world, and what you get in the Book of Genesis. And in those days we were supposed to be believing in this stupid literacy of a text that goes back to the first, second, third, and fourth millennium B.C. And how can you go through life with that?

Well, I couldn't anyhow.

And yet this other thing had been built in. The problem was to work it out without losing the symbols. Joyce helped release me into an understanding of the universal sense of these symbols, the deep human sense. Not the anecdotal historical symbolization of the sense of these great universal symbols that come to us through our Christian heritage. But on the wings of art, an opening out of a mythological reading of these symbols.

So Joyce disengaged himself and left the labyrinth, you might say, of Irish politics and the church to go to Paris, where he became one of the very important members of this marvelous movement that Paris represented in the period when I was there, in the '20s.

The thing that saved me was the Upanishads, Hinduism, where you have practically the same mythology, but it has been intellectually interpreted. That is to say, already in the ninth century B.C. the Hindus realized that all of the deities are projections of psychological powers, and they are within you, not out there. They're out there also in a certain way, in a mysterious way, but the real place for them is in here [points to heart]. Boy, that saved the whole day.

☷

BROWN: When did that realization first dawn on you?

CAMPBELL: Now when did I . . . In 1924 when I was around nineteen years old. And it came in a very interesting way. I was on a boat trip with my family to Europe. We used to take the slower boat—not the big ones that get you across in about five days, but the ten-day crossings—because it was such fun on those boats, first-class boats like the *President Harding,* President this, that, and the other.

On the return trip from Europe, in 1924, there were three dark young men seated in steamer chairs on the deck. I noticed that there was a young woman who knew them. I had never seen such people before because we never saw Hindus over here at that time. Never. They all ended up in England; they never got to the United States.

Jiddu Krishnamurti, 1935.

It happened that one of them was Jiddu Krishnamurti, and the others were his brother Nityananda and his secretary at the time, Rajagopal. This was my introduction to the world of India. And the young woman who introduced me gave me Edwin Arnold's *The Light of Asia,* which is the life of the Buddha from the sutras. And that was the opening up, and it was like a *light* going on.

When I went to Europe as a student of literature, philology, romance literature, and then to Germany and started my Sanskrit, there was all this stuff again. I really got into it in those years. But it had started with what I learned from that little book about the Buddha.

Strange, just a little touch like that and everything changes.

I had the earlier change with *The Romance of Leonardo da Vinci.* My whole world shifted with that book. Then later this little one on the Buddha added another dimension. You know, you have to have some kind of silly thing out in front of you to keep you on the line, something difficult to do.

BROWN: How did your years of study in Europe influence you when you were awarded a traveling fellowship from Columbia?

CAMPBELL: I was over there first in Paris and then in Munich, one year in each, *and the whole world opened up.* Those were the late '20s—'27, '28, '29, and you'd be surprised [laughs]. I mean Americans now are so aware of what's going on in the rest of the world that you can't realize what it was like when I was a young

Joseph Campbell and his sister Alice in Chartres, France, in 1928, the parish he considered his spiritual home.

Self-Portrait in His Atelier. Photograph by Romanian sculptor Constantin Brancusi, c. 1933. The painter Henri Rousseau once told Brancusi, "Well, old boy, you've made the ancients modern."

man there. The discovery of modern art happened when I was in Paris.

I'll never forget the moment, going into a grand gallery in the Bois de Boulogne. They had built a big exhibition place for the "Indépendents," the "Intransigents"—artists who were not showing in the official galleries. And these happened to be men like Picasso, and Matisse, and Miro, and Brancusi . . . and the whole lot.

I remember seeing Brancusi's *Bird in Flight* the first time it was exhibited, and walking around it was Raymond Duncan dressed like a Greek. Well, I had come over from good ole rural America, you might say, and this whole world of far-out, avant-garde, well . . . *bohemians* was totally new. And my opening up to the world of art and *its* relationship to my life took place there.

CAMPBELL: The whole discovery came to me in that moment at the University of Paris. I had gone over on the straight and narrow path of scholarship. I was living in a little room on the Rue de Staël, which is way down at the other end of the Boulevard Montparnasse. And here was the university over on the "Boule Miche." So what did I have to pass going from my little room to the university? I had to pass Montparnasse *et* Raspail. And in those days there was La Coupole and Le Dome and everything—all these bizarre places. Now I had just come from the United States, and my dear friends in those days we'd never seen anything like that. We had no idea what modern art was about. And there was also a big blue book in all the bookstores. *Ulysses!* Nobody in the United States had one. I had to smuggle my copy back into the country.

So I went in to one of the bookstores and said, "Avez-vous *Ulysses*?"

"Mais oui, monsieur."

And when I came to chapter three, "Ineluctable modality of the visible; at least that if no more, thought through my eyes. Signatures of all things I am here to read," I thought, Good God, what is this? I thought I had got my degree. But I don't know what he's talking about.

So I went around to the Place de l'Odéon, and there was Shakespeare and Company, and there was Sylvia Beach. I went in as an indignant young academic and asked, "What kind of writing is this?" and so forth. Well, she told me what kind of writing it was and she sold me a lot of books. That changed my career.

Now when you've gone through *Ulysses* three or four times and you know where you are, it's very exciting because it's all protein. There's no fat, there's no carbohydrates. You've just got the sheer experience right in front of you and it is a delight to read it over and over and over and over. I've never had that with any other author, that kind of experience. I bought this book in Paris in 1927 and I've been reading it ever since. And it's a delight every time.

Shortly after that I met a young sculptress from New Orleans named Angela Gregory who was working with Antoine Bourdelle. And you know how sculptors are. They are always wanting someone to pose so they can do some work. So she asks me if I would sit down and let her do my head.

"Oh, sure," I said. So I went around to the studio and there

Bust of Joseph Campbell, age twenty-three, 1927, by Angela Gregory. "You know how sculptors are," Campbell once said. "They are always wanting someone to pose so they can do some work. So she asks me if I would sit down and let her do my head. 'Oh sure,' I said."

The secret of art is love. . . . Art brings out the grand lines of nature.

Antoine Bourdelle

French sculptor Antoine Bourdelle beside his monumental work, Hercules. By using the archetypes Bourdelle felt that the artist recreates the world. "The secret of art is love," he said. "Art brings out the grand lines of nature."

was this magical man, Antoine Bourdelle. He was in his middle eighties or so. To hear that man then talking about art and what art was about! One phrase of his got into my mind and it's been there as a kind of a guiding phrase ever since: *"L'art fait ressortir les grandes lignes de la nature."* "Art brings out the grand lines of nature." And this is what myths are also about.

So I'm sitting in the Sorbonne there working on Provençal, Old French, the Celtic influences on Arthurian romance—I think, Good God, I don't even know how to order a decent meal in a restaurant. It was embarrassing. Here I am learning all this stuff. Finally one day in the Cluny Gardens near the university, a flash went up and this is what carried me off the straight and narrow into the woods: my theme of following your bliss into the forest adventures. I had no idea where I was going, but there was Joyce.

Later Sylvia Beach sold me [the journal] *transitions,* where some of the earlier versions of *Finnegans Wake* were appearing under the title "Work in Progress." To give you an idea of the difference, the first sentence was, "River run brings us back to Howth Castle and environs." And then when I bought *Finnegans Wake* years and years later, it began, "riverrun, past Eve and Adam's, by swerve of shore to bend of bay, brings us by a commodious vicus of recirculation back to Howth Castle and Environs." This is what had happened to Joyce in twenty years.

Well, old French seemed rather dull at that time. This was a world of *translating the learning,* because no one in the world knew more than what James Joyce knew of what I was trying to find out. To translate knowledge and information into experience: that seems to me the function of literature and art. And it was with that I made the step not to becoming an artist but to try to find what the *experience* would be in the material that I was dealing with. And Joyce certainly helped.

Then I went the next year [fall of 1928] to Munich. There I discovered what we didn't know in the United States at that time: I discovered [Sigmund] Freud, I discovered [Carl] Jung, I discovered Thomas Mann, and I started my study of Sanskrit. One of the wonderful things about coming all at once out of the realm of Columbia University into the world of what one of my professors called "the castle of German scholarship"—and Sanskrit at the same time—was an awakening that you can't imagine. And there it was that I found what the depths were in the richness of the world that I had been dealing with in dealing with Arthurian romance, and the Celtic material that I had loved ever since early boyhood, and the American Indian myths where the same motifs existed.

The thing I learned as a boy when I was excited about the Indians, and was up in that wonderful forest country of the Poconos in Pennsylvania, was that the function of myth and the function of Indian lore was to put man in accord with nature. And the function

There is one phrase in Finnegans Wake *that seems to me to epitomize the whole sense of Joyce. He says, "Oh Lord, heap miseries upon us, but entwine our arts with laughters low." And this is the sense of the Buddhist bodhisattva: joyful participation in the sorrows of the world.*

Joseph Campbell

of art is to bring out the grand lines of nature. So it is one grandiose song that I found.

☒

COUSINEAU: What role did the learning of languages play in your years as a young scholar in Europe?

CAMPBELL: Oh, now, these are the things that I really want to talk about. I think our educational system, at least when I was in school, was just no good. We spent so much time learning languages—French and Spanish were what we had learned—languages you never heard spoken and the person teaching you couldn't speak the language you were learning! You were learning *je suis, tu es, il est, elle est,* that sort of thing, but nothing of the swing of the language.

When I went to Europe as a student I had been studying French since *kindergarten* [but really had no grasp of the language]. I went to the *Alliance Française* [in Paris] and in three months was speaking and reading French and understanding it. I had never studied German. But when I learned that all the real learning in Europe was in Germany, I wrote to Columbia and asked if they'd give me a fellowship to go the next year to Germany. They said, "Yes, go ahead." So I had to learn German. In three months I could read and talk German. When you're in the place, saturated, and it's in the melody of your life, the languages come through. When I graduated from prep school I thought, God, I hope I never have to study a foreign language again. But going deeper into that world was a rapture. Every language carries a whole range of experiences that are peculiar to it.

I'm having a very interesting experience right now. A couple of my books are being translated and published in German. One, *Myths to Live By,* is a rather popular and easy book. I had the experience about a month ago of reading the German translation of that thing, and boy, was that a different book! So many of the ideas that have come out of the German slide back into German very easily. But they acquire something different just in going back into German, which is a poetic language, a mystical language, whereas English is a practical language. Quite a different realm of dimension. *Suddenly* my writing was saying what I had really meant to say, and I hadn't realized it. I read back into English again and back into the German, and the realms of association and implication of the words was exciting. The discovery of German was a real event in my life. The whole poetic majesty of the language is something that just caught me. I love it.

I had gone over there to work on medieval philology, old French Provençal, and the Arthurian romances and troubadour poetry, but, my God, everything opened out in all directions. Then in Germany came the Sanskrit and that wonderful philological background of the German scholarship—there's nothing like it in the world. The Germans were the first to find out about these things. Goethe was already there 150 years ago, and the Romantics around that period were, as they say now, "into it." But we have so much more material now than those people had in those days.

When I was a student in Germany the metaphysical aspect of what I was studying broke open for me. I'd been working on mythology, and particularly medieval mythology, just in the way of a Western scholar. Then I ran into Goethe, ran into Thomas Mann, ran into Jung, and suddenly I realized the mythic dimension of these things, not simply the academic circus. Consequently I have a very deep feeling for that country.

CAMPBELL: In 1936 there was a very amusing occasion. Thomas Mann was invited to give the talk at the party in honor of Freud's eightieth birthday. Now how anyone could have thought that an artist could talk about anyone but himself, I can't imagine. And it *was* amusing.

Thomas Mann started by saying he didn't understand why he had been invited to do this because he was an artist, a creator, and not a scientist, not an analyst. So he said, Well, perhaps what people wanted was a saturnalia, a topsy-turvy evening where the one who usually is the object becomes the subject and instead of a talk based on practical science, and so forth, we have one of dream-like penetration. Now you know in a saturnalia everything is topsy-turvy. The servants are commanding their employers and a clown

I had the pleasure of meeting Mann three times, and being with him for a long period at one of those meetings. He was a man in form, and was very formal in his manner. But it was with ease. Like writing sonnets or Japanese tea ceremony, you have to know the form, and so master the form that you can be at ease with it. This is an important point in art. You don't have an artist who doesn't have a technique.

Joseph Campbell

Thomas Mann, early 1950s.

is appointed the judge of the city, and so forth, and everything is sort of upside down. So this was a warning that Mann was going to be a little rough.

The paper that was published of this talk is called "Freud and the Future." And it had almost nothing to do with Freud. Mann began by saying that the real achievement of Freud was that he had, through his researches, reproduced in medical terms all of the findings of the German Romantic philosophers of the nineteenth century, even though Freud had never read any of these. He did not know not Schopenhauer, says Mann; he did not know Nietzsche; he did not know [Søren] Kierkegaard; and yet out of his own ignorance on his own boat he had reproduced the whole thing.

Then he said, Now if you will pardon me for talking about myself, I will show that in my works, long before I heard of Freud, I was already working in this mode. And then he spoke of his own early short story, "Die kleine Herr Friedman," "Little Mr. Friedman." This was published in 1886 or 1897, three or four years before Freud's *Interpretation of Dreams*. And it's a fact that in that little story you get a good deal of Freudian information, or the information that Freud produced also in another language and with a totally different slant.

About halfway through the lecture Mann mentioned the unutterable name—Jung—and how Jung inspired the works that he was doing now, which was his *Joseph* novels. He had just then finished Volume III.

I can't imagine what went on in that room while he was doing this. Now, I bring this up because it is a very good lead into the whole context of what was going on in the realm of unconscious research in the first half of the century. This was a wonderful period in the arts. Joyce and Mann, completely ignorant of each other, simultaneously went through a transition in their novels, in their writings, from what might be called nineteenth-century naturalism through the psychological accent given in their works to a breakthrough in myth.

Then the First World War comes along [1914–1918] and immediately after it these epochal works appear. Joyce's *Ulysses* in 1922; Mann's *Magic Mountain* in 1924. And both of these pretended to be naturalistic works. But they were structured on a mythological base. And the mythological structure was given to you in a cue in the title: *Ulysses* and *The Magic Mountain*. Then they slide right into the whole sea of myth in their next great works, Thomas Mann's *Joseph* novels and James Joyce's *Finnegans Wake*.

The contrast between Joyce and Mann is interesting. Joyce was an Irish Catholic, and Thomas Mann had been brought up a German Protestant. Insofar as you take the religion seriously, you're living in immediate relationship to myth; and the problem then is to relate your experiences when you move into the world to this mythological ground, to see the world in terms of those structures which have been put into you in the beginning.

Thomas Mann comes the other way around. One of the characteristics of Protestantism, I would say, is that it rejects the ritual and mythological interpretation and accent in the religion; and so Mann comes gradually into a realization of the mythological depths and what they implied. It took him a long time. This gave

I happened to know the woman who was responsible for bringing the Mann family over here, Mrs. Eugene Meyer. She was the wife of the owner of the Washington Post *in those days. When I recognized that Hans Castorp's dream was a repetition of the last paragraph of Nietzsche's* Birth of Tragedy, *I asked Mrs. Meyer if she had recognized this and if Mann had ever spoken to her about it. She said, "I'll ask Tommy next time I see him." About three weeks later I got a letter from her saying, "I asked him about the scene from* The Birth of Tragedy *and he was stunned. He had never realized what he had done."*

This is known as cryptamnesia; the brain doesn't forget things, but your attention may be so far away from that that you will have forgotten, but there it is. And if you read the last paragraph of The Birth of Tragedy *you'll be stunned too.*

Joseph Campbell

Joyce a kind of advantage in that he was a professional in mythological thinking, right from infancy, and Mann comes gradually into it. And this makes the two of them an extraordinarily interesting pair to bring together.

CAMPBELL: In *The Magic Mountain* Thomas Mann is continually explaining the implication of his mythology. He gives you the image and there is an interpretation that's given you one way or the other. Joyce does nothing of the kind. Joyce just gives it to you—*bing!*—like that, and you've got to work into it. So I have always found in my own reading and thinking about these matters that these two men complement each other in an extraordinarily interesting way. Their approach to art is also interesting.

In their backgrounds are the German philosophers of the nineteenth century. Wagner, of course, was a very important influence in the years of their growing up. Both of them took some themes from Wagner. One of the musical devices Wagner used is that of the leitmotif, the returning echo; the cliché that is associated with a certain body of meaning and system of associations that recurs, and every time it recurs the whole meaning of it comes back again in new relationships. For Thomas Mann this was a device, and anyone who has read Mann's *Buddenbrooks,* for instance, or any of his early short stories, has recognized this. When he mentions a character he will always mention some little context of adjectives or commentary that he has mentioned before with respect to this character. So the whole thing comes in again as the leitmotif. Joyce, who was a very musical person, also used the musical device as a recurrent refrain. (One of the great disappointments of his life was that in a singing contest in Dublin, he didn't win. John McCormack won.)

Now the trick for the artist is to present his material so that it doesn't put a ring around itself and stand there as separate from you, the observer. And that *Aha!* that you get when you see an artwork that really hits you is, "I am that." I am the radiance and energy that is talking to me through this painting. In purely empirical terms it's called participation. But it's more than that. It's identification.

Now what Mann tried to do when he turned to mythology was to reinterpret Genesis in terms of the elementary ideas that are implicit in the ethnic ideas of the Bible. It's a very important work and it's the only way to translate the Judeo-Christian heritage into a heritage for mankind instead of for a certain group.

Do you get my point? It's a big one. This is what Mann is working on, this is what Jung is working on, this is what Joyce is working on, this is what everyone is working on who is trying to retain the positive values that are in this heritage, and at the same time move into a global period of life where we don't isolate ourselves and say everybody else is worshiping devils.

Now what we must come to find is how the artist, how Joyce, how Mann, has broken through and rendered this mystery. One way is through the rhythms of their prose. This is a problem of poetry. The poet is breaking you past the image; breaking you past the words so that things should point past themselves. Rhythm has a lot to do with this.

And so here is the secret of Mann's art. The absolutely ruthless eye, which sends the arrow of the correct word to name the fault and on the arrow is an ointment of love. This he calls *erotic irony*. He also calls it plastic irony, and it's the secret to Thomas Mann's art.

Now the function of art, and it was Shakespeare who said it, is that "Art holds up the mirror to nature." Art holds, you might say, a holographic mirror up to nature so that you can see that in this object is the totality. Each is a totality in itself. And this is the way these men deal with their characters.

It was Schopenhauer who was the first to bring oriental terminology into Kantian thinking. Here, at the beginning of the nineteenth century, we have this synthesis of the two philosophies. It then became possible for writers like Mann and Joyce to take in the whole enrichment of the oriental understanding of transcendence and the Maya aspect of personality, how it's all an illusion based on the mirror images of time and space, and render it purely in occidental terms.

This notion of what might be called psychological or spiritual morphology informed all these works. Yeats has the same thing in his thinking and writing. At the same time you have Schopenhauer opening up the whole story of the unconscious and Freud then coming along and turning it into medical terms.

This is a great, great moment.

Karlfried Graf Dürkheim, German psychiatrist and author. "To me he is the polestar."

TARNAS: That reminds me of one of your favorite expressions, being "transparent to the transcendent."

CAMPBELL: A couple of years ago I learned of a great German psychologist. His name is Karlfreid Graf Dürkheim and he has a center in the Black Forest, the Schwartzwald, not far from Freiburg. So I went back to Germany last September [1981] after fifty-two years (that was a gamble!), and I had the pleasure of an hour with this wonderful man who is just about eighty-five years old now. He said the whole problem of life is to become "transparent to transcendence": so that you realize that you are yourself a manifestation of this. That you live the myth. That you live the divine life within you. Yourself as a vehicle; not as the final term but as a vehicle of consciousness and life. This is the great theme that I find there.

"Transparent to transcendence." When that came into my vocabulary it just seemed to be the only thing necessary. My definition of myth now is: a metaphor transparent to transcendence.

To me he is the polestar.

TARNAS: Could you talk about exactly what transparent to transcendence means?

CAMPBELL: Mythology opens the world so that it becomes transparent to something that is beyond speech, beyond words, in short, to what we call transcendence.

If the metaphor closes in on itself and says, "I'm it, the reference is to me or to this event," then it has closed the transcendence; it's no longer mythological. It's distortion. It's pathological.

The energies of the universe, the energies of life, that come up in the subatomic particle displays that science shows us, are operative. They come and go. Where do they come from? Where do they go? Is there a where?

The ultimate ground of being transcends definition, transcends our knowledge. When you begin to ask about ultimates you are asking about something that transcends all the categories of thought, the categories of being and nonbeing. True, false: these are, as Kant points out in *The Critique of Pure Reason,* functions of our mode of experience. And all life has to come to us through the aesthetic forms of time and space, and the logical ones of the categories of logic, so we think within that frame.

But what is beyond? Even the word *beyond* suggests a category of thought! So transcendence is literally transcendent. Of all knowledge. In the Kena Upanishad, written back in the seventh century B.C., it says very clearly, "that to which words and thoughts do not reach." The tongue has never soiled it with a name. That's what transcendent means. And the mythological image is always pointing toward transcendence and giving you the sense of riding on this mystery. And in Aikido or winning a race, you are riding on that. That's the mysticism of athletics. And the mysticism of love is the riding of the two—they really are one!—only they look like two. And the experience is the experience of a truth. An intuitive experience that disregards time and space.

Schopenhauer has a wonderful paper he calls "The Foundations of Morality." That's the one where he asks, How is it that a human being can so participate in the danger of another, that forgetting his own self-protection, he moves spontaneously to the other's rescue? How come, when the first law of nature is self-preservation, that is dispelled?

His answer is that this is a metaphysical impulse that is deeper than the experience of separateness. You realize you and the other are *one*. And the experience of the separateness is simply a function of the way we experience in the field of time and space. This is the realm to which myths apply, the realm that is a fundamental reference, and it's no realm at all. When the Zen masters talk about things on this level, they say, "That which is and is not that." They just erase the word immediately. Or the void of *sunyata,* the void that is no void but a pleroma, a fullness; you go past the pair of opposites.

Within the field of normal life concerns we don't have to worry about those things. But when you really are at the fighting point, the sharp life point, and a life crisis comes and it's major, you'd better get in that position or you won't be able to take it.

My friend Heinrich Zimmer used to say the best things can't be said. This is one of them. The second best are misunderstood. That's because the second best are using the objects of time and space to refer to transcendence. And they are always misunderstood by being interpreted in terms of time and space. The third best: that's conversation. We're using the third best in order to talk about the first and second best.

ARRIEN: I'm thinking now of that really beautiful Basque myth about the mermaid who would swim only in the lighted waters of the sun and gradually the sun fell in love with her. He stuck out his tongue, which was a beautiful rainbow, and pulled her up to him. And when they unified there were seven teardrops of joy. Then he spit her back and she became a huge shooting star that grew and grew to become the moon.

Now during twilight you see neither the sun nor the moon because once again they are unifying. But you see all their children, which are the stars.

CAMPBELL: That is a sweetheart [laughter].

ARRIEN: That's transcendent!

CAMPBELL: It's a beautiful one. Where does that come from?

ARRIEN: That's Basque.

CAMPBELL: A Basque myth? We always knew they were wonderful people! Isn't it wonderful when you hear a little myth like that? I've never heard it before, but you know it's mythological. You could have heard it from three or four other cultures, only you didn't. You didn't but you could have. It's talking from a certain center of the imagination and symbolization that has a quality that is the mythological quality and it does not come out of intentional fiction. It comes out of some kind of metaphorical way of speaking about a beautiful life truth of some kind.

AUDIENCE QUESTION: You talk about being transparent to transcendence, but I think that the issue is that some people don't see themselves as being transparent. They see themselves as being opaque, and that's ego inflation. And that's where they get confused and that's also the problem.

CAMPBELL: I always get a message from somebody, and this is a good one. Yes, it's lovely. "I'm not quite transparent." It's the "who" that is the I. The thing the Hindu teachers tell you is you can't say *atman*—the transparent Self—as long as the "I" that you're referring to is the phenomenal one. Then it's better to be irreverent.

So you might say that Judaism and Christianity are popular religions. They're religion on the popular level for the people who are not yet ready to recognize the transcendent within themselves.

They ought to be a little more available than they are to the opening of the door to transcendence.

BROWN: What role does psychology play in contemporary myth? And how can myth help a psychiatrist or someone who goes in for therapy?

CAMPBELL: What the psychologist is finding out about the structure of the human psyche: that is what is most relevant to mythology. Because mythology has to do with relating that psychological structure to the circumstances of objective life in the world today. It gives you a clue. It's a signals system. The images of myth are not fact, they are metaphors; and the reference is to transcendence. They take the facts of life and relate them to the psyche. This double relationship is then shown to the mystical function to rest on—what do you want to call it? The void? The Fullness? The pleroma? Those are words that point past what can be conceived of, and they make the point that this whole marvelous universe that we now know of, billions of galaxies, is on the void.

No one knows where those little subatomic particles come from or go to, that flash on the screen. Lives also come and go and they are spirits within the field of time and space in causal relationships. That's what we find.

The myth has to deal with the cosmology of the day and it's no good when it's based on a cosmology that's out of date. And that's one of our problems. I don't see any conflict between science and religion. Religion has to accept the science of the day and penetrate it to the mystery. The conflict is between the science of 2000 B.C. and the science of 2000 A.D. And that's what we've got in the Bible, which is based on a Sumerian mythology.

DAVID KENNARD: What happens to a nation that has absolutely no mythology at all?

CAMPBELL: It's not a nation. It's a congeries of disparate people. Not even a civilization.

KENNARD: But are there any of today's nations—

CAMPBELL: I'm not a sociologist. I don't keep up with the most recent things. So I just don't know.

BROWN: What do you see is the difference between Freud and Jung's point of view of the unconscious?

CAMPBELL: When Freud learned from Jung that there was a relationship between mythology and psychology (and you get

Carl Jung before the carved door of his home in Kusnacht, Switzerland. The Latin inscription carved in stone above the door is from Erasmus: "Called or not called, God shall be there."

this from their letters that have been published), Freud then started to study mythology from a standpoint of his psychology.

The Freudian unconscious is a kind of scrap basket of repressed experiences that you can't tolerate, that you don't know how to assimilate. Consequently for him it's a function of your biography, do you see? So that your unconscious is a function of what you experienced before you even knew you were experiencing. We can't, we don't have the same symbol system.

The Jungian unconscious is based on a biological point of view. The energies that inform the body are the energies that inform our dreams. But these dreams are inflected by our personal experiences. The Freudian unconscious, which Jung called the personal unconscious, is basically biographical, not biological. So Freud was trying to interpret the totality of mythological forms in terms of a historical crisis in the past. That's patricide, you know, in *Totem and Taboo*. In other words he interprets the symbology in terms of historical and biographical events.

Jung sees that, yes, that's one aspect of the psyche, but the other aspect is the energies of the organs which are the same in all of us. Moving us. That's what is called the collective unconscious; that's the unconscious that each of us shares. Mythic symbols come out of that depth, not out of the personal depth at all. Every mythology is, of course, oriented to a historical situation; it comes out of this people, this province, and that one and the other. And so there is that local inflection. But what is inflected are the deep energies of the total id.

CAMPBELL: Adolf Bastian, a German anthropologist, has meant a great deal to me with just this main idea. He died around 1925. These common themes that come out of the collective unconscious he calls elementary ideas. But they always come to expression in specific social environments and it's historically and geographically differentiated. He called those differentiations *Elementargedanken,* or ethnic or folk ideas. When you are in your youth the folk idea guides you into the society you are inducted into for life. But there comes a time when life dismisses you and then the folk idea unshells, you might say, the elementary idea, which guides you back.

In India, in art criticism, these same two aspects of images are recognized. The folk aspect, which simply has to do with people and things in stories and time and space is called *desi*, which means local, popular. On the other hand the elementary ideas, when the deity is represented, are called *marga*, the path. *Marga* is from a root word, *mrg*, which refers to the footprints left by an animal, and you follow that animal. The animal that you are trying to follow is your own spiritual self. And the path is indicated in the mythological images. Follow the tracks of the animal and you will be led to the animal's home. Who is the animal? The animal is the human spirit. Where is its home? It's in your own heart. So, following the elementary idea, you are led to your own deepest spiritual source.

So the *desi*, the folk, guide you into life, and *marga*, the elementary, guide you to your own inward life. Mythology serves those two purposes that way.

The elementary ideas do not change. Where do they come from? They come from the soul. The origin is the soul of man. *Marga*.

The problem is not to lose touch with them. And when the folk ideas that relate to a certain social order and structure are no longer functioning for that structure because another structure has come along, we are in psychological disarray. This is one of the problems today.

These days the social system and the social ideals and also the physical environment is changing so fast that there is no opportunity for a constellation, for a crystallization, to develop. Just in my own lifetime the transformations in terms of ethics and how people are expected to behave—well, it's prodigious.

CAMPBELL: One afternoon when I was a very little boy, down here on 98th Street and Riverside Drive [in New York City], my uncle came in and said, "Joe, we're going down to Riverside Drive to see a man fly an aeroplane from Albany to the Battery."

And this was the longest flight ever. It was Glenn Curtiss flying a sort of flying bicycle down the Hudson River.

I remember standing along the street with all the people standing on buildings watching this thing happen. As the sun went down it was twilight and then we saw this thing coming, and everybody shouted, "There he is! There he is!"

That was when I was a little boy and then the year I left Columbia to go to study in France and Germany [1927] was the year Lindbergh flew across the water in that little thing [*The Spirit of St. Louis*]. You should see it in the St. Louis airport.

And now they are on the moon. My God! Just in terms of mechanics it's a terrific job, not only the actual act but the notion of consciousness, the notion of man's relation to the universe is transformed by this.

So we're in the middle of a big change.

CAMPBELL: I had the real pleasure, many years ago [1954], of having an invitation to tea, my wife and I, with Dr. and Mrs. Jung. And this was at his place outside Zurich called Bollingen, after which the Bollingen Foundation was named. It's at the far end of Lake Zurich.

So we stopped at a lovely little hotel and viewed that part of the area. And when it came time to go to Jung, we got in our car and drove down the road looking for Bollingen. I had driven a couple of miles when we asked one of the peasants at the side of the road, "Bitte, wo ist Bollingen?"

"Bollingen ist hier entlang."

Back I go this way and I see another chap and then I say, "Bitte, wo ist Bollingen?"

"Bollingen ist hier entlang."

So this is the way I finally came to the place where it was and it was a little road that ran off. We turned across that road and across the railroad tracks. Now the Swiss trains are silent and fast and when we crossed that rack—*poof!*—behind us went the train. I said to Jean, "We've gone through the Symplegades! We've gone through the Klappfelsen! We're in the Holy Land now."

And Jung asked himself by what mythology he was living and he found he didn't know. And so he said, "I made it the task of tasks of my life to find by what mythology I was living."

Joseph Campbell,
Esalen, 1982

47

We drove up to the place where Jung's little castle was that he had built with his own hands, this stone castle that was part of his opus to find what his mythology was. We drew up there and got out of the car and began walking up the path, but so many people had walked there that the path was worn too deep to reach the door. I didn't know how to get in.

Well, Jean knows how to do things, so finally she found the bell and rang it, and we came in and were greeted by Dr. and Mrs. Jung. We had tea there, and now this is the man's character: No "Herr Doktor Professor." He was just a genial host. I had no trouble with him because by that time I had published four volumes of Heinrich Zimmer's work. Zimmer was a friend of his, and Jung had published one of Zimmer's German works. So we were coeditors, you might say, of Heinrich Zimmer.

Now I was about to leave for India and so Jung said, "Well, you're about to go to India. Let me tell you about the meaning of the syllable OM."

I thought, Well . . . !

He said, "When I was in Africa a group of us went for a walk and we got lost. Pretty soon we realized that there was group of young warriors around us, standing on one leg, holding spears, with things through their noses. We didn't know who they were. They didn't know who we were. Nobody could speak anybody else's language.

"And," Jung said, "after a rather embarrassing and troublesome moment, we all sat down. We all looked at each other and when we all felt comfortable that everything was all right, what do I hear? I hear OM. OM. OM.

"Then," he said, "two years later I was in India with a group of scientists, and if there's any group of people that is not susceptible to the experience of awe, this is it.

"We went up to Darjeeling and went to Tiger Hill. To get there you have to leave early in the morning, before dawn, and are transported up the hill. You don't know what you're going to see. It's dark. Then the sun comes up and infinitudes of snow-capped Himalayan peaks burst into rainbow colors. And what did I hear from the scientists? OM. OM. OM."

Then Jung said, "OM is the sound nature makes when it's in harmony with itself."

I thought, That was all right. And so I went away to India.

Jung was a beautiful man to be with. That's all I can say.

ARRIEN: You speak of the mythology of youth as the mythology of moving into the world. But if in your youth you chose something that you wouldn't have chosen at age thirty-five, do you go back and choose that? Do you stick with your original decision? Or move to the inward journey?

CAMPBELL: Is there any single rule [laughter] that would work for everybody? If there was it would be so easy to answer that question. The point is that every individual has his own very special problem in this mid-life or late-life crisis about what he has been doing. How deeply has it really involved him? Has he had other outside marginal interests of any kind whatsoever? What were they? All these are very special problems.

Now there's a moment in Jung's life when he had finished his work on his first great book, the book that Freud would not accept, *Symbols and Transformation*. This had to do with the imagery of a woman who was in deep psychosis. He began recognizing the analogues between her hallucinations and basic world mythological imagery. And Jung said when he finished work on the book he realized what it meant to live with a mythology and what it meant to live without one. And he asked himself by what mythology he was living and he found he didn't know. And so he said, "I made it the task of tasks of my life to find by what mythology I was living."

How did he do it? He went back to think about what it was that most engaged him in fascinated play when he was a little boy. So that the hours would pass and pass.

Now if you can find *that* point you can find an initial point for your own reconstruction. Go back and find what was the real fascination.

So Jung went back to boyhood and found that he loved to play with stones, making little villages. Then he went and bought himself a piece of property and began, with his own hands, building that amusing little castle that he had there in Bollingen on Lake Zurich.

Now each one has to work it out in his own way. But if a person just refuses to think that he has an inside problem, he's not going to work the thing out. Nobody can do it for him.

You have to learn how to recognize your own depths.

It's not the agony of the quest; it's the rapture of the revelation.

Joseph Campbell

Professor Campbell teaching at Sarah Lawrence in the 1960s. "What it was, was The Hero with a Thousand Faces. *What it is, is my first lecture to my students at Sarah Lawrence."*

☙ 3 ❧

The Vision Quest

Two weeks after Campbell returned to New York, in October 1929, came the Wall Street Crash. Unable to find a job, and unwilling to resume the PhD program at Columbia, Joseph Campbell retired at the age of twenty-five to a friend's cabin in Woodstock, New York, with his sister, Alice, a student of the Russian sculptor Alexander Archipenko, to read and to try his hand at writing fiction. For the next couple of years "the callow young author," as he described himself, read voluminously and wrote unsuccessfully.

Finally, in 1931 he traveled in the family Model A Ford to California to look for a job. Through the young nutritionist Adelle Davis, he met John Steinbeck and the biologist Ed Ricketts, who rekindled his interest in the relationship between mythology and biology. He sailed with Ricketts up the West Coast to Alaska on the Inside Passage, where they collected intertidal fauna and Campbell played the balalaika with Russian goldminers.

In 1933, he accepted a teaching job from his old master at Canterbury prep school, but resigned at the end of the term and went "back on the Depression." Serendipitously one of his short stories sold, a now long-lost piece called "Strictly Platonic." On the $300 windfall he earned from the story he returned to Woodstock for two more years of self-imposed exile, studying in depth the authors who had galvanized him in Europe: Joyce, Spengler, Mann, Freud, Jung, Frazer, and Frobenius. In spring of 1934 came a job offer from Sarah Lawrence College, which he immediately accepted. There, for the next thirty-eight years, he taught enormously popular classes in comparative literature and mythology.

CAMPBELL: I think the most important period of my scholarship and study followed my return from Europe. I came back to the United States about two weekends before the Wall Street Crash. And there wasn't a job in the world. I went back up to Columbia to go on with my work on the PhD and told them, "This whole thing has opened out."

"Oh, no," they said. "You don't follow that. You stay where you were before you went to Europe."

Well, I just said, "To hell with it."

My father had lost all his money but I had saved some as a student. I used to play in a jazz band and so I piled up money during a few years. And on that, you might say, I just retired to the woods. I went up to Woodstock and just read, and read, and read, and read, for *five* years. No job, no money. I learned then that you don't need money to live if you're a young man who didn't get himself involved sooner than he should have, before he had the ability to support what his involvement might be.

So during the years of the Depression I had arranged a schedule for myself. When you don't have a job or anyone to tell you what to do, you've got to fix one for yourself. I divided the day into four four-hour periods, of which I would be reading in three of the four-hour periods, and free one of them.

By getting up at eight o'clock in the morning, by nine I could sit down to read. That meant I used the first hour to prepare my own breakfast and take care of the house and put things together in whatever shack I happened to be living in at the time. Then three hours of that first four-hour period went to reading.

Then came an hour break for lunch and another three-hour unit. And then comes the optional next section. It should normally be three hours of reading and then an hour out for dinner and then three hours free and an hour getting to bed so I'm in bed by twelve.

On the other hand, if I were invited out for cocktails or something like that, then I would put the work hour in the evening and the play hour in the afternoon.

It worked very well. I would get nine hours of sheer reading done a day. And this went on for five years straight. You get a lot done in that time. When the job at Sarah Lawrence came, until I started writing, I continued that schedule over the weekends, when I was at home.

Reading what you want, and having one book lead to the next, is the way I found my discipline. I've suggested this to many of my students: When you find a writer who really is saying something to you, read everything that writer has written and you will get more education and depth of understanding out of that than reading a scrap here and a scrap there and elsewhere. Then go to people who influenced that writer, or those who were related to him, and your world builds together in an organic way that is really marvelous. Whereas the way these things are taught normally in college and school is a sampler of what this one wrote and that one wrote and you're asked to be more interested in the date of the publication of Keats's sonnets than in what's in them.

And so with those women students at Sarah Lawrence to help me, I broke completely away from the academic approach to these subjects.

It was a grand, grand experience. I was a little nervous at times. I remember having a one dollar bill in the top drawer and knowing I would not die as long as that dollar bill was there. And so various things turned up. I spent the year before I got the job teaching at Sarah Lawrence minding a dog for some people who had built a house at Woodstock, a beautiful little house. It was a great big dog, a kind of a cross between a police dog and a Doberman pinscher, whose name was Fritz. I spent a year with this animal and I learned a lot about dogs. He fell in love with a cat down the road and I tried to condition his reflexing so that he wouldn't go down to the cat, and, of course, he found ways to get down there.

That was one way of living life, on no money.

TARNAS: I'd like to hear about the advantages of *not* having a PhD [laughter].

CAMPBELL: Well, it's not an advantage to be without a PhD. But it's an advantage not to have taken a PhD because of the things that they do to you to get you into the slot that they want you in, just at the time of your life when the stars are opening and your mind is opening to new thoughts, new things, they put you under the supervision of some professor who had his excitement—if he ever had it—a lifetime ago. Now he's interested principally in the footnotes that you are handling. You know, it's dreadful!

And so I have a theory that, yes, PhDs are all right in certain areas; but in the areas of the liberal arts, of culture, it's a sign of incompetence to have a PhD [laughter].

I mean it. The time when you should have been finding your thoughts, should have been opening up and being excited at the stuff is exactly the time they bring the axe down on you.

I can remember a wonderful professor at Columbia named Raymond Weaver. He's the one who rediscovered and reedited Melville back in the '20s. And he had no PhD. When I decided I was going to go on to graduate work he said, "Well, be careful because they're going to flatten you out." And while I was working on it an invitation came to accept the teaching position out in the Middle West. When I spoke to him, he said, "If the PhD doesn't flatten you out, a job like that will."

And those remain in my mind as very important clues for a learner from a marvelously civilized man.

CAMPBELL: So I quit the PhD because they didn't want to hear about Sanskrit, they didn't want to hear about modern art, they wanted to hear about the relation of Celtic myth to Arthurian romance. And I got over that.

I remember that I just didn't have anybody to tell me what to read and so I began pulling these things together. The realization I discovered during those years—Oswald Spengler's *The Decline of the West,* and the marvelous work of Leo Frobenius, seeing these men talking about historical forms, and seeing how it all went together with Jung and Freud and Mann and Joyce. Then I discovered Robinson Jeffers out there in California. Those were great

Sarah Lawrence College in the 1960s. "It had been founded as a women's college with the idea that women did not need or really want, nor were they properly served by, a spin-off on the male curriculum on the model of a male college."

illuminations. And I didn't have to write a thesis. I didn't have to write anything. All I did was underline sentences and take notes. It's funny, I spent about forty years taking notes—I have fourteen file drawers packed full of notes—and I never bother with them now anymore. The thing comes in that way.

So when you don't have a job and you are doing your own reading you've got deep psychological questions. As deep as those of a little boy. And I thought, I don't want a job. So an invitation came from Sarah Lawrence to see if I wanted a job and when I saw all the pretty girls I said, yes, I want a job. Then a funny thing happened when I got the job—namely, all my psychological problems disappeared.

BROWN: Did you have some sense that you were headed for a job as a teacher?

CAMPBELL: What happened with my mind was that I was enjoying so much just reading and doing what I wanted, without any goal out ahead other than that to which my reading was taking me. It was all this stuff that I'd found in Europe that was beginning to come together in the way that I can see it now. I didn't think I wanted a job or anything of the kind. And then came that one day when in the mailbox was this little letter from Sarah Lawrence inviting me down for a job. One of my professors at Columbia, W. W. Laurence, from three years before, had recommended me as someone who would possibly be okay for this.

Since I hadn't *ever* earned any money in my life, when I was asked, "Mr. Campbell, what kind of salary do you want?" I said "Oh, I don't know. How about two thousand dollars?"

And Constance Warren, the president of the college, said, "We don't pay that little." So they paid me two thousand, two hundred. When I hear what people start on now, just falling out of the cradle, I can see that those were interesting times.

The wonderful thing about Sarah Lawrence—and the reason I really took the job—was that the college had been founded only few years before for young women. The college had just started so I didn't have to fit into a slot. You know, teach this and you're going to teach that, too. It had been founded as a women's

A perfectly marvelous faculty was assembled. You have to have men and women of considerable sophistication to follow a student's lead and to be able to carry that person into the mainstream of the humanities out of his or her own impulse. That we did.

Joseph Campbell

Professor Campbell, second from right, at a faculty meeting in the 1950s.

college with the idea that women did not need or really want, nor were they properly served by, a spin-off on the male curriculum on the model of a male college.

So the idea was that we should follow the interests of the students. Now that was a very interesting time. There was a big resource pool of academic people out of work. There were people coming over from Central Europe, with Hitler over there, and so a perfectly marvelous faculty was assembled. It really was. You have to have men and women of considerable sophistication to follow a student's lead and to be able to carry that person into the mainstream of the humanities out of his or her own impulse. That we did.

Very soon the creative arts faculties built up. In those years, in the men's universities, if you wanted to study art you studied the history of art. Here we had studios. And the dance: Martha Graham teaching the dance at Sarah Lawrence! I mean, this is what we had, a marvelous, marvelous school. To move in there and be able to give the courses that dealt with materials that had meant something to me during my five years of reading and know that they would meet the needs of other young people was a real privilege, really great.

So I took the job and was there for thirty-eight years. It kept getting to be more and more instructive to me. I had to cut it down to only seniors so that I wouldn't have to make a selection, because I could teach only a certain number of people—we never had mass classes. I had to have interviews with every one of my students every fortnight and so couldn't teach more than twenty people. I could see how it enriched all of their understanding of the work they were doing.

As a male studying mythology I had certain interests of my own. But at that college not only did we follow the interests of the students, we *found out* what the interests were. In the half- to three-quarter-hour conference with every one of my students I came to know personally what they were getting and what they wanted. I was forced by my female students to consider the material from the point of view of the woman. And that point of view had to do with: What does the material mean to *life?* What does it mean to *me?* I don't care why this myth occurred there, and then over there, but not over here. What does it mean to *me?*

When I was teaching I would say I had almost a 50/50 split between Christians and Jews, and now and then Buddhists,

Professor Campbell teaching a class of rapt students, 1950s. "I was forced by my female students to consider the material from the point of view of the woman. And that point of view had to do with: What does the material mean to life? What does it mean to me?"

Zoroastrians, and people of other kinds. And my first thought was that I am going to relieve them of their religion. But I found very soon that the result was exactly the opposite. That suddenly these religions, which had been presented to them as "God is out there," had new messages. And I have known and met those students since (this started forty years ago) and they're all mothers of children now. They tell me time and time again what the value of this thing opening out is. You don't lose your religion. You stay with what you've got, but certainly it can talk what I would say would be its original language before the clergy closed it off.

In my thinking about the determination of the direction of my own thought, I have to give the credit to my students. What they did was in the way of keeping me on a beam that was a beam of the vitality of the subject.

I think it's a shame what's happening now with the coed movement. This differentiation, which is so important to human life; the difference between a male and female is being wiped out. All differentiations are being wiped out. You're almost not allowed to even have a club now. Anything like a differentiation is called "elitism" and it's not enjoyed.

But having had my five years of doing my own reading, and then thirty-eight years of supplying young women with the vitality of the subject that I had found for myself—it was marvelous, marvelous.

ARRIEN: When I think about how much you learned about women after all those years of teaching—

CAMPBELL: I taught them for thirty-eight years and I still wouldn't want to say that I knew what they're all about!

ARRIEN: Not many people can say that they taught all women for thirty-eight years. How many on this planet, in this culture, can say that?

CAMPBELL: I learned more than I taught. But it wasn't about women!

ARRIEN: What was it about?

CAMPBELL: It was about teaching. Their attitude was very different than mine. And if my works are around and regarded as helpful and important, it's because of those young women. I know it. Now *that* was a great privilege.

BROWN: Did you have to deal with projection from the students?

CAMPBELL: I knew what the projections were, so that I knew it had nothing to do with me or them. It was just something going on. So I always called the students by their last name until I began to think of myself as a grandfather. Then I could begin to call them by their first names. The thing was to keep a good cool front.

Now with a girl like Marilyn Monroe, the beauty is a kind of screen in front and they feel nobody's getting through to them. I had about four students like that, and when they came into the room I had to go to work just to talk to them properly! And you know then that you're just in the presence of something that is almost divine. And that's no good to you as a teacher; that's a curse. It's fascinating.

BROWN: Joe, I know one of your students who is in her forties now who swears she's never loved any man as much as you, even though she's been married three times.

CAMPBELL: Well now, that's sweet of her.

BROWN: Each time to a very adequate man, she tells me. But always working in the background is Joe Campbell. What do you think about that?

CAMPBELL: That the serious side of teaching women comes from the fact that they did not let me, in teaching this subject of mythology, get off into all kinds of academic corners. They always wanted the material to relate to themselves, to *life*. And I attribute the popular aspect of my writing to that training I got from these students. They were wonderful.

BROWN: How could you be sure they were getting the message?

CAMPBELL: My friend Heinrich Zimmer used to say that "the radio station WOB, Wisdom of the Buddha, is broadcasting all the time. But you've got to have a receiving set. And until you have the receiving set, well, you're not getting the message." You can't teach Buddhism. You can't teach illumination. You *can* give different clues to how to get it. But if a person isn't willing to paddle his own canoe he's not going to get across the river.

Some people are just unable to experience the radiance, but they can listen to a lecture. I think it was Oscar Wilde who said if an American was given a chance to choose between going to heaven and hearing a lecture about it, he'd go to the lecture. And so if you're unable to experience heaven you can take a lecture about it. And maybe that will save you.

They say you can lead a girl to Vassar but you can't make her think! They didn't say that about Sarah Lawrence!

JAMAKE HIGHWATER: Somewhere in your work you mention the fact that you thought that very early on humankind was actually in a perpetual dream state. What I'm wondering about is if this dream state, this art world which we all, I think, have such enormous regard for, has not in some way been dismissed as secondary, and that what your work really does is try to bring us back to the fact that this is not secondary, that this is primary. This is what it is to be alive. And isn't that what finally makes the *Iliad* and the *Odyssey* viable and important to us today? The symbols might be different and the images may be different, but that which motivates those epics is still within us.

CAMPBELL: That whole problem of breaking out of the field of waking consciousness into a field of dream consciousness is a basic problem of ritual.

I would say the main function of rites is to orient an individual to the dream consciousness level, which is the productive level, the second level area in *AUM*, as it is interpreted in one of the Upanishads. Dream consciousness is further in, and it's a creative consciousness, whereas waking consciousness is a critical consciousness. It's a totally different logic. In the dreams you are the dream.

The most primitive people of the world, and they are almost extinct now, are the bushmen of South Africa, who are hunters on the plains. The pygmies are really gatherers mainly in the jungle. They spend their nights in dances and the men dance and the women simply sit in the center and clap and guide them a little bit. But the men are going round and round in a very stiff manner with the expectation that they will flip out and go into a trance state. Among these people there are always those who undergo a psychological crack-up, what's known as the shaman crisis, where the person goes down into the unconscious. Between the complete flipping out and the moment of loss of balance they are in a position to cure. And then they go into this state.

Now we have descriptions that have been given by some of these men of what they experience in the trance state. And it is a whole mythology. Climbing the sky on those strands that the sun sometimes sends down, spider webs and things like this, and of who they meet up there. It's a whole mythology that comes right out of an inward experience and then becomes the mythology of the people. Not everyone goes into these trances but they get the news of what's inside themselves from these ones who do go into trances.

And then you have the shamanic experience of the North-

Therefore, in sum: The "monstrous, irrational, and unnatural" motifs in folktale and myth are derived from the reservoirs of dream and vision. On the dream level such images represent the total state of the individual dreaming psyche. But clarified of personal distortions and profounded by poets, prophets, and visionaries, they become symbolic of the spiritual norm for Man the Microcosm. They are thus phrases from an image-language, expressive of metaphysical, psychological, and sociological truth.

Joseph Campbell,
Commentary to *The Complete Grimm's Fairy Tales*

The Flyer. *Watercolor by John White, from Virginia series, England, c. 1585–1590.*

Siberian Tungus shaman. Engraving by Nicolas Wilsen, Holland, 1705.

ern peoples, the Siberians, and down in South America. And what it's associated with in the North and the Americas is the *song*. Every shaman has his song that takes him away. There have been descriptions of how a person first hears his or her song, walking along a seashore or being in a forest. There's this experience and from then on he's overtaken.

There's an interesting paper, *The Shaman from Elko,* in the *festschrift* novel volume for Joseph Henderson, a psychiatrist in San Francisco. It's an account of a woman in West Virginia, in the coal mining areas there, who in her late sixties had the dreadful feeling that she had lost life, that she had never lived life, that there had been a life for her that she had not lived. And in the analysis they found one time when she was a little girl, about thirteen years old (that's about the time for the experience), she was walking in the forest and she heard a strange music, a strange song. But she didn't have in her culture the assistance to help her do something with that and so she lost it. And then throughout her life she had the feeling that she hadn't lived her life. The thing about the shaman crisis is that if the individual does not follow the song he will die, he will really die.

This is a strange psychological thing.

STANISLAV GROF: In this society many of the states the shamans go through would be labeled as psychotic. The career of many shamans start by the powerful experience of unusual states of consciousness with the sense of going into the underworld, being attacked, dismembered, and then being put back together, and ascending to the supernal realm. If you look at these experiences and give them psychopathological labels, those in our culture undergoing a shamanic transformation wouldn't typically be allowed to complete it.

HIGHWATER: How would we apply that kind of knowledge, which is so remote from this moment, in this dominant society? How would we apply it to life as we live it today?

CAMPBELL: I think the thing in our own experience is the person who in youth has the sense of a life to live, and then Daddy says, "No, you'd better study law. Because there's money in law."

No, I mean it! I think this is exactly the counterpart. And you meet those people later on, and they are the ones who have climbed to the top of the ladder and found it's against the wrong wall. They have not lived their lives.

HIGHWATER: My people say it in a different way, but which is exactly the same. They say, "Do not be afraid of what you're becoming."

CAMPBELL: That's right.

BETTE ANDRESEN: You talk about the decision to follow your bliss or your song during the crisis of youth. How about somebody who didn't have this courage at that time? Is that perhaps a mid-life crisis? And is it too late if you miss the boat at thirty-five?

CAMPBELL: According to the Gospels it's never too late for salvation! That was a nice question she put to me.

ARRIEN: It was. And not only was it a nice question that she put to you, it's going to reach a lot of people who have this same crisis.

CAMPBELL: Exactly.

ANDRESEN: I know so many people who are in the same boat I was in a few years back. They need that validation that says follow your bliss. But I can remember being told in Sunday school that if the road is hard and rough and you're suffering, then you're on the right track.

CAMPBELL: That's the wrong one.

ANDRESEN: It *was* the wrong one and, I mean, it was painful.

CAMPBELL: I got this from the Sanskrit idea, that transcendence is transcendent. Now there are three words that come *close* to it: *sat-chit-ananda,* that is: *sat* is being, *chit* is consciousness, *ananda* is bliss. So *ananda* is the only thing you can be aware of. Follow it and it'll be all right. The probability is that when you follow it everything will work out, even if you think it won't.

ANDRESON: I understand that more and more because as I do that, as you say, doors that were never there open—

CAMPBELL: It really works. They open.

ANDRESON: So is the mid-life crisis which a lot of people are experiencing in their early thirties or maybe mid-thirties—is it that they are finally realizing that the ladder *was* up against the wrong wall? That perhaps this is the last chance?

CAMPBELL: I would think that likely, but the mid-life crisis like any other late-life crisis, is that of unshelling a system of life and immediately moving into a new system of life. Because if this life is unshelled and you don't have a new intention, there is a total disorientation.

This, I think, is the big problem in retirement. And it's going to be more of a problem now that retirement's being made earlier and earlier and earlier. The life in which you have involved yourself fully has suddenly been moved. And so what? I'm told that the life expectancy of a blue-collar worker after retirement is around five years. That means that his body says, "You've got nothing for me to do, so let's say goodbye."

Following your bliss just seems to me to be the clue to believing what might be called the *mythologically inspired life.* I've had the experience of teaching young women for many, many, many years, and occasionally you would see someone wake up right there in front of you. A wonderful moment in a pedagogical experience. And then you meet the person five years, ten years, twenty years later at the alumni reunions, and you can see the difference between the woman who had been able to follow her star and the woman who had married into an archetypal marriage situation, where now she is the wife of the family and doing all the chores that have nothing to do with what she originally intended for her life! You can see it when you meet them—the vitality that's in them. Those who are fortunate enough to be artists and move into a field that is always evoking the life of the imagination are the ones who have the easiest time, I guess, but that's not the only way to live your life of bliss.

ARRIEN: That is so important. Many people don't follow their song through those different transitions. They want to follow the song and yet they're socially pressured by their conditioning.

CAMPBELL: Social pressure is the enemy! I've seen it happen. How in heaven's name are you going to find your own track if you are always doing what society tells you to do? I also spent a year teaching in a boy's prep school and that was a crowd that was trying to make up their minds, you know? I've seen them since and those who followed their zeal, their bliss, they have led decent, wonderful lives; those who did what Dad said they should do because it's safe found out it's not safe. It's disaster.

CAMPBELL: The image that comes to my mind is a boxing ring. There are times when . . . you just want that bell to ring, but you're the one who's losing. The one who's winning doesn't have that feeling. Do you have the energy and strength to face life? Life can ask more of you than you're willing to give. And then you say, "Life is something that should not have been. I'm not going to play the game. I'm going to meditate. I'm going to call "out."

There are three positions possible. One is the up-to-it, and facing the game and playing through. The second is saying, Absolutely not. I don't want to stay in this dogfight. That's the absolute out. The third position is the one that says, This is mixed of good and evil. I'm on the side of the good. I accept the world with corrections. And may this be the way I like it. And it's good for me and my friends. There are only the three positions.

I remember, as a kid, seeing a caterpillar into which an ichneumon wasp had laid its eggs and the eggs had hatched, and this poor caterpillar was being consumed from inside by maggots while it was still alive.

Yes. That's the way it is.

There's something rather, what can I say, exhilarating about putting yourself on the side of *life,* instead of on the side of protective *ideas.* When all of these protective ideas about life that you've been holding onto break down, you realize what a horrific thing it is, and you are *it.* This is the rapture of the Greek tragedy. This is what Aristotle called "catharsis." Catharsis is a ritual term, and it is elimination of the ego perspective: wiping out ego-system, wiping out rational structuring. Smashing it, and letting life— *boom*—come through. The Dionysian thing smashes the whole business. And so you are purged of your ego judgment system by which you're living all the time.

Now new notions of consciousness are beginning to come in with this holographic paradigm idea. We are all, in our consciousness, one. And we're one with the totality and potentially omniscient. But the brain brings us to focus here, so that we can live in this particular time and space. The brain is a constrictor. It contracts our knowledge. We know all these facts to help us, here. Then what happens when the brain is blown, let's say with LSD or something like that, *wow!* And you may never get your brain back.

We've got to live in terms of the here and now, the affirmation of this particular focus, but with the knowledge of the other foci, other possibilities, and the whole totality range, in order to work as artists in the sense of Mann and Joyce and Klee and Picasso, you're in a field of deep problems.

Why should these men have given their whole lives to working on problems like this if they weren't of life-shattering depth? This is the problem of the relationship of art to life.

Is it a killer or fosterer of life?

It's a fosterer.

CAMPBELL: The Communist thing in Tibet is a pretty nice thing to think about. I have a Tibetan friend [Rato Khyongla Nawang

Losang] and I spent three years helping him write his autobiography. He was in Lhasa when the Communists invited the Dali Lama to come to a theatrical production in their camp and leave his bodyguard outside. The Dalai Lama had just passed what we would call his doctoral exam, his *lharampa* exam, and this friend of mine was one of the examiners. The Dali Lama was living in the summer palace, the Nabolinka, about an hour and a half or so outside of Lhasa. So he's invited to go to the Communist camp. The whole population of Lhasa came out between the Nabolinka and the Communist camp so that he couldn't have gone even if he'd wanted to.

Meanwhile he's starting his escape. And the Communists then bombarded the Nabolinka and started the whole crackdown in 1959, machine-gunning people fleeing from the country and all that kind of thing. We don't think of that when we think of the power of things. We don't think of that when we think of the power of the will and so we read Lao Tzu; we still read the *Tao Te Ching,* even though Mao Tse Tung read those things too.

So there we are. There is this power. Now, in all my years of working with this Tibetan whose monastery was wiped out, his teachers tortured to death—I mean the torture system was terrific—I haven't heard him say one negative word about the Chinese or about what happened. This was Buddha consciousness, Buddha process. It hurt us; it hurt him; but life hurts. You don't say "No" to life.

Now that's big stuff.

And this taught me what religion is. I never heard any negative on his part, and I've known him now for seven or eight years.

It is from [Losang] that I have learned my deepest lesson— come on dove's feet— of what a life inspired by the teaching of the Buddha means.

Joseph Campbell,
Foreword to *My Life and Lives*

AUDIENCE QUESTION: Is there a danger that, if you accept violence, you could identify with the destroyer and not with the victim?

CAMPBELL: No, you have to identify with both. Say you're in the studio, painting a picture. You're at your desk, writing a book. You get out, you walk on the street, and you see somebody holding up somebody else, and you get into a fight. This is one of the problems, the difference between the position as artist and the position as personal life.

The metaphor I have in mind is a tennis game. If there's going to be a tennis game you've got to be on one side of the net. And you've got to play hard, and try to beat that person, or there's no game. But the referee doesn't care. And you shouldn't either, in your *other* aspect. This is what's known as good sportsmanship. You're trying to win, but suppose you lose?

There's an Eskimo saying, "To win a dogsled race, that's great. To lose, that's all right, too." There's the sense of the game. And then life is a game, you're the winner or the loser. And if you lose, you think of that winner, "He's a bad man." If you won, "Oh, how great am I!" It's too funny, it's too silly. We talk about the Nazis, and then we drop two atom bombs—one of them completely superfluous, the one on Nagasaki.

GROF: I would like to bring in material from a somewhat different area. I am a psychiatrist and I've been interested in unusual states of consciousness. In psychedelics, for example, you see that people have a lot of geometric visions, a lot of abstract visions, which can be very simple, or spirals, or phosphenes. But they also have some rather complex images that some people compare to arabesques, to elements in Muslim mosques or Gothic cathedrals.

If the process deepens further they start experiencing elements of the birth process, confronting death, powerful death-reversing sequences of the kind Joseph mentioned, that are enacted in certain aboriginal rites of passage. But then there seems to be another vast area in the psyche where people seem to move into mythological realms. But what's amazing is not only that this mythological realm literally erupts into the psyche but that it crosses the culture barriers. Somebody who might be Jewish or Christian at this point will start experiencing mythology of the pre-Columbian period.

CAMPBELL: People who have taken some of the psychedelic mushrooms that were used in Middle America have told me that they begin to have images that resemble those of the Aztec gods. Have you heard of this kind of thing?

HIGHWATER: Yeah, I've heard of it.

CAMPBELL: Of course, I haven't done it myself, so I can't say.

HIGHWATER: I've heard it, but I wonder how much of that may be autosuggestive.

CAMPBELL: But I was speaking about someone who's rather serious about this, Albert Hofmann, the man who synthesized LSD, and who was very much interested in this matter. The very special qualities of those Toltec deities—I couldn't believe it! At least this is a report from somebody who I regard as at least a reputable authority in these matters. I was trying to associate this with what you were saying—that certain psychedelics produce images of this type; others produce images of another type.

Among the Huichol Indians, for instance, the peyote is regarded as a good psychedelic entity; but then there is the counter one, the jimson weed, which is regarded as negative, and these two are opposed to each other. It must be the result of different images coming out of this experience from those that come out of the other one.

ROGER GUILLEMEN: But yet, if you study something like psychedelic experiences, you also have to consider green tea, which is loaded with caffeine or molecules like caffeine. And it's very well known that this has a profound influence on the function of some people. The mode of action is very well understood of these enzymes on the brain, which actually excite the functions of the brain so that this is a statement of fact.

So does this relate to the brightness of the young Japanese? It's hard to say, but I don't think you would get that kind of stimulation from milk or Perrier water.

HIGHWATER: I just meant that there have been a lot of discussions, as Campbell knows, about the iconography of Middle America and Andean America that may be identified with what was fundamentally a drug-oriented culture.

CAMPBELL: Oh, boy, they really were drug-oriented! [laughter].

HIGHWATER: Yes, so it's very possible that after all those visions there could very well arise some art. But I wonder if we would really like to impose the concept on the entire world of art of the Freudian notion that art is nothing more than a result of dietary disturbance or psychological disturbance.

I would like to think of art as so fundamental that it existed in concentration camps. Music was written in concentration camps, opera was written there. We have come to think of these things so much as a product of an elite leisure society. But, as you say, art seems to be such a fundamental human expression that it would seem to exist whether we are using jimson weed or not. These may be lubricants to a kind of experience, but perhaps what we're talking about predates both psychologically and biologically any of these effects.

CAMPBELL: Oh, I do think they do. In fact most artists have not been taking drugs. And those who did take drugs, you can see it in their art, in the very special effect that comes along. In English literature you have Coleridge as an example of someone who was doing a certain kind of work then started taking opium and he had a season of great productivity and then it all ran out.

GUILLEMEN: As Rimbaud seems to have.

CAMPBELL: Exactly the same.

GUILLEMEN: What we are talking about, or perhaps trying to discuss and dissect, is what was the very beginning—long before even some sort of a tribal movement would start, could start, giving the framework—of the very earliest manifestations of what was later to be called art. I would not be at all against the idea that by sheer empiricism one day the eating of this seed blended to another may well have triggered in this particular man a drawing of something new, which later of course became a part of that particular local culture.

Once you have that, all sorts of things can happen later on so that in later times you don't need the triggering mechanisms any more. Because it will come from the environment.

But at the beginning I don't see why it could not start with some happenstance like that.

CAMPBELL: The earliest evidence that we have of ritual life comes from the period of Neanderthal man. This would be about 150,000 to 50,000 B.C. The evidence is associated with two orders of phenomena. One is burial. Here, for the first time, we have evidence of a ritualized burial, with sacrifices and with the grave gear, which certainly indicates that the experience of death started something. The question is, What has happened to this body? It was walking around, it was warm, it lied down, it was cold. Where has it gone? This idea of where it has gone is the first clue we have to a mythological thought.

Then the next big period of evidence is that of the Cro-Magnon people in southwestern France and northern Spain. There are two orders of art there. There is the plastic art, which is represented by the little female figurine—just standing nude figurines, no face features, no feet either. They were probably made to stand up. In fact some of them were found standing up in little shrines. These are associated with the domestic areas, the legends under which people live. So here is the goddess, the figurine, the female power, all associated with the life of the people in their homes.

Then these great caves. Have you ever been in them?

Nobody would live in those. They are sheerly cold, dangerous, and dark. I remember when we were in the caves of Pech Merle, France, the concierge who was showing us through shut out the electric light and you've never been in a darker place in your life. You didn't know what direction you were facing in. Your whole consciousness was wiped out. It's in those caves that these animal figures appear. You find there is an order in the organization of these animals. We know that the animals are representing powers of some kind. These caves are almost certainly associated with the boy's rites, the men's rites, where they are turning boys into men, and they are learning not only how to pray to the animals and promise them compensation for their willing sacrifice, but they are also learning how to be men instead of mother's little boys. And they are having a hard time.

There is one cave—Les Trois Frères, in the Pyrenees—where the main chamber was entered through a long flume, which is almost like a great big sewer pipe, that runs on for a hundred yards or so. You have to crawl through like this, but I would be unable to do it because I have a kind of claustrophobia. I can't imagine what the experience must have been. But Herbert Kühn and a number of others went through this darn thing, and when you come out you are in an enormous chamber with hundreds of animal forms all over the sides. Right in front of you is this dancing animal master called the "Sorcerer of Les Trois Frères," with the antlers

The "Dancing Sorcerer" of the Magdalenian Cave Les Trois Frères. *Drawing after Breuil, Ariège, France. Paleolithic.*

and the owl's eyes and the lion's body. There's your animal master again, associated with food, animals, the mystery of death, and the participation in this order of life, which is that life lives on life, lives by killing, and the reconciliation of the psyche with this necessity. These animals were respected and sometimes regarded as higher powers than the human beings.

GUILLEMEN: Joseph, do you discuss this actually as the origins of mythology, or as a time when, as far as we know, humanity for the first time became somehow aware of the mythological dimension? Because there's this Jungian point of view that would see mythology as something that is really woven into the very fabric of reality. Or one that precedes reality in some sense, rather than somehow derives from the human experience.

CAMPBELL: I follow philosophers up to the point where their feet leave the ground [laughter].

What I'm talking about is first evidences. There is one bit of evidence earlier, and that comes from the period of *Homo erectus* (before *Homo sapiens,* before Neanderthal man) about 500,000 B.C. from the River Thames. A hand axe that's very long, too big to use, but is symmetrically beautiful.

This is what Robinson Jeffers called "divinely superfluous beauty," and is the first signal we have of a tool that's not simply a practical tool, but something that is a beautiful, beautiful piece of stone. No animal would do a thing like that. The only thing you can guess from it is for a ritual of some kind, a ritual associated probably with the sacrifice of animals.

Acheulean hand axe from Farnham, Surrey, England. Campbell called this image a prime example of the crossing of the threshold into the symbolic function of art, what California poet Robinson Jeffers called "divinely superfluous beauty."

GUILLEMEN: What you said about the significance of the arts, the liberal arts, as you call them, is exactly to be found in modern science. I feel terribly bad as a scientist that so few people nowadays recognize the extraordinary beauty of the reasoning in modern science. So very few people realize the extraordinary—I would like to use the exact word here and I'm afraid I am not going to find it—significance of scientific reasoning, which is just as *elating* for whoever is in the middle of it as in painting or the writing of a poem or reading or listening to a piece of music. It really will give you this very same sort of *elation*.

Scientific reasoning and the creations of science have just the same glory as the creations of art and I'd like to at least have that on record.

BROWN: One night Roger called me and took me to his laboratory at the Salk Institute. And for me that was like an experience of being sung a solo by Sutherland or Callas or anyone. You provided for me the equivalent of an opera by describing what you do. It was an art form and it's a beautiful art form.

GUILLEMEN: I'm so glad to hear you say that.

KENNARD: Can science develop its own mythology? As powerful as the mythologies of the past to sustain us through the times?

GUILLEMEN: That's an interesting question, which I somehow wanted to bring in with one word: prediction. Science can predict. Can mythology predict?

CAMPBELL: I think so. In intuiting the morphology of an organic process it would represent the intuition, the prediction that you are going to get old, that you are going to die.

GUILLEMEN: That's not fair [laughter]! That's not fair!

HIGHWATER: Dostoevski discovered the unconscious, right? There are all kinds of examples in which artists have predicted things. Weren't the Cubists really talking about what contemporary physics is talking about now?

GUILLEMEN: I think they are talking about the idea that there are many ways of looking at the same objects, rather than the empirical one of being a camera.

CAMPBELL: With classical structure the early temples were bodies. The classic temple is a physical temple: It's the outside—the inside is almost nothing in that little cellar out there. The glory of the physical form and the classical idea of the universe is not of a universe at all but of a multiverse, just as Jamake said, to the American Indian.

But the science of the Greeks and the Romans never got past the body. The atom was a little marble and the highest art form was the standing nude, and the culminating empire was one that could be viewed as a body. Spengler tracked that with the dynamics of the Gothic cathedral and the energy principle in our culture. The atom is now an energy and the flight into outer space is a consistent form of which art is one expression—not the predicting one, but one expression—and science another expression, all of it a single-sided structure of consciousness.

But if art, as Cézanne says, is a harmony parallel to nature, as I've said, then the exploration of nature should be no less exciting and no less spiritually rewarding than the function of art. I mean, it's the same field. When one's bliss is actually science, as it is for many young boys, it has to be. I can remember that when I was in prep school, biology was the thing that grabbed me, and now I think of mythology as a function of biology, a statement of the impulse system of the body and the organs. Not something that's made up in the head. What's made up in the head is the fiction; what comes out of [the heart] is a myth. These are totally different things altogether.

So I would just like to add my yea to what you've said about science. I think it's one of the calamities of contemporary literary criticism that these two worlds are totally separated.

GROF: There are even more areas where science touches on art. For example, in formulating some kind of hypotheses you would be drawing on a mythical form, the idea of evolution, and so on. Many of the major discoveries in science would be done actually in a dreamlike state, in a visionary state, after the scientist had done a lot of observation, collected that data, tried to analyze, and not been able to find a solution. The solution comes in a dream or upon waking in the morning, or in a disease, in fever. When all the rational forms are suspended the mythical form breaks through.

ARRIEN: Maybe what prediction is to science, the oracle is to mythology.

GUILLEMEN: But in the predicted power of mythology, how statistical is it? Will it really happen when the prediction is made?

HIGHWATER: Can you build a skyscraper out of wedding cakes [laughter]? It's just the same kind of question.

GUILLEMEN: The answer is definitely no.

HIGHWATER: The question has nothing to do with the whole

basis of mythology. The empirical question that you ask is a completely valid one, but mythology serves the ineffable, serves the unfathomable, serves the very things that we can't deal with in terms of aerodynamics. If we could deal with our entire experience in terms of the empirical or in terms of the practical, then there would be no reason for any of this discussion.

CAMPBELL: I may have an idea here. The whole space adventure interests me and has interested me from the beginning, enormously.

I can remember the space flight—I don't know which number it was, before the one with Armstrong stepping on the moon—when, as the astronauts were coming down, ground control in Houston asked, "Who's navigating now?"

And the answer that came back was, "Newton."

And that sort of blew me away. Immediately I thought of Kant in the *Prologemena to Metaphysics,* where he asked, "How is it that we can make statements for relationships in this state here, knowing with apodictic certainty that they're going to work in that state there?

And this was demonstrated in that particular moment. We did not know how deeply Armstrong's foot was going to go into the dust on the moon until we saw it happen. That was *a postiori* knowledge, that was knowledge after the fact. But the scientist knew exactly how much energy to expend from that tilted jet that tilted in a certain way to bring that little module down within a mile of a boat in the Pacific Ocean.

This just seemed to be terrific, that the laws of space as far as they go are right here in the head and can be worked out here.

So we, in a sense, are the children of space and have come out of one of space's productions, namely, the earth, spinning around the sun and we have come out of the earth and we are the earth, and we're the earth's ears and eyes and so forth. This involves a very important kind of realization.

Russell Schweickart's spacewalk. " 'And then,' he said, 'I had to ask myself what had I ever done to deserve this experience?' "

Now another thing that I've learned about space. About a year and a half ago I was on a platform with one of the astronauts [Russell Schweickart]. He told of a time when he was given an extravehicular action to perform, let's say to get out of the module when it's flying through space. And he's just in the space suit connected by the umbilical cord to the module and he was to do some photography, or whatever, around the machine with the counterpart work going on inside the module. But something went wrong inside the module so that he was left for five minutes with nothing to do.

Now those men were given a lot to do that kept them right on the ball so that they should not have the kind of experience that this man had at this time. He was out there alone in space, going *17,000 miles an hour.* There was not a sound; there was no breath of air; and up there was the earth; and out there was the moon.

Now just hold in your head for a minute what's happening to that guy.

"And then," he said, "I had to ask myself what had I ever done to deserve this experience?"

That is Odysseus hearing the sirens. And this is exactly the conflict field, you know, between this and the practical action he was capable of. He had to pull himself together to go back into that machine and return to work. There is the enormous difference between those two worlds. That really is enormous.

Woman, in the picture language of mythology, represents the totality of what can be known. The hero is the one who comes to know. As he progresses in the slow initiation which is life, the form of the goddess undergoes for him a series of transfigurations: She can never be greater than himself, though she can always promise more than he is yet capable of comprehending.

Joseph Campbell,
*The Hero with a
Thousand Faces*

Joseph Campbell and Jean Erdman at their honeymoon cottage in Woodstock, New York, 1938.

4

The Meeting with the Goddess

One of Joseph Campbell's early students was Jean Erdman, a dancer who was training with Martha Graham. She took advantage of Sarah Lawrence's avant-garde tutorial program by taking a private course in aesthetics with Campbell. Before long, Campbell later recalled, "It became evident to me that I was hooked."

When she left on a year-long around-the-world trip with her family, the smitten professor gave her a copy of Spengler's ponderous *The Decline of the West* to read on the journey, ensuring that she would have to see him when she returned, at least to find out what the implications of the book might be. The romantic ruse worked. They were married shortly after her return in 1938, and for the next fifty years worked within arms' reach of each other, vigorously pursuing their parallel careers: He read each day's work to her in the evenings, and she asked for his reflections on her pioneering modern dances. Their collaboration culminated in the founding of New York's Theater of the Open Eye in 1972.

In 1941 another of Campbell's students, Sue Davidson Lowe, introduced him to Swami Nikhilananda, the pastor of the Ramakrishna Vivekananda Center in New York City. Campbell spent the next few years working with Nikhilananda on the Sanskrit translations of the *Upanishads* and *The Gospel of Sri Ramakrishna,* the nineteenth-century Tantrist saint. In 1954, after completing three volumes of Heinrich Zimmer's lectures on Indian art and philosophy, Campbell traveled to India for six months with the personal guidance of Nikhilananda and Indian scholar Alfred Salmony, studying the holy sites while Erdman staged solo dance concerts.

BROWN: Jean, can you describe how your own art and your dance have come together and, in particular, how Hawaii itself influenced you?

JEAN ERDMAN: Well, I can tell you, I'm a child of Hawaii. I was born here. I'm the third generation of my family to be born here. It's wonderful to be back here because all the memories of childhood come flooding back. I never thought we'd move to Hawaii—I never thought Joe would want to move to Hawaii—but here we are. Joe always teased me. He said that my external soul was here at Mokuleia, which it is, I think.

I grew up doing what we all do here, which is dance. And we all danced the hula, and we danced in school. We also danced Isadora Duncan style, which, as you know, comes from her idea of imitating the ancient Greeks. So it was based on the natural body.

Both of those dances are performed in bare feet. When I went to New York and found the modern dance and Martha Graham, she was in bare feet so I'm a barefoot dancer. The world was quite integrated around my source. Of course the contrast between the Martha Graham style and my background was enormous, in terms of style; but that only helped me to find my own image, finally.

I found myself pondering what dance really is. I studied many different styles of dance, traditional styles, the Spanish dance, ballet dance. I spent a long summer on these studies. In fact it was the summer Joe and I spent at Nantucket near the end of World War II. Everyone was afraid to cross the water for fear of a German submarine. But we had the run of this beautiful house with roses on it. Joe was writing about the fifth version of *The Hero with a Thousand Faces,* and I was deciding what the art of the dance really should be, right? I was making comparisons of all these traditional styles and trying to find out why there had been this choice in the Spanish dance, which somehow achieved a certain feeling which

80

The Hero

*There is what I would
call the hero journey,
the night sea journey,
the hero quest, where
the individual is going
to bring forth in his
life something that was
never beheld before.*

Joseph Campbell

Blackfoot Medicine Man, Wun-nes-tow,
The White Buffalo, George Catlin, 1848.

The Death of Socrates, Jacques Louis David, 1787.

Joan of Arc at the Coronation of Charles VII,
Jean Auguste Dominque Ingres, 1854.

Sir Galahad, Arthur Hughes, about 1868.

Madame Marie Curie at the Institut du Radium in Paris, 1925.

"Sudama Approaching the Golden City of Krishna," from the *Bhagarata Purana*, Punjab Hills, India, about 1785.

Pablo Picasso at his villa, La Californie,
near Cannes, France, 1956.
(Photo © Arnold Newman.)

Georgia O'Keeffe at her Ghost
Ranch, 1968. (Photo ©
Arnold Newman.)

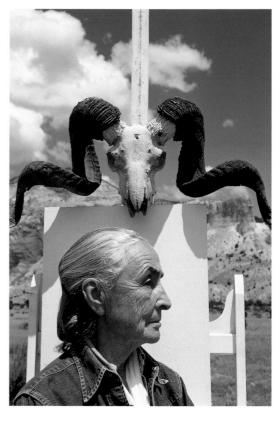

Jean Erdman and Joseph Campbell en route to Honolulu, 1946.

expressed them, expressed their culture. The same with ballet, and so on. So I realized that what choice one made, as to the limitations of movement, was going to be key to the expressivity of the dancer and the dance art.

When I started doing my own choreography, that was the way I worked. I worked in perfect silence because that was the only way in which the essential expressivity of the human body movement can be listened to and found—by listening to the dynamic rhythm of what one is doing. And also with a seed idea that had some kind of an image in it of the first dance that I ever did, that I still do, and have taught to other dancers, based on the archaic Greek image of the Medusa.

Now the Medusa, as Joe has told me, started as a lovely precept in the temple. She was so dedicated that her focus was only

Jean Erdman in a graceful "half-moon-shape" pose inspired by her work with Martha Graham, about 1936.

> *Jean is to dancing what Vivaldi is to music.*
>
> Alan Watts, *In My Own Way*

in one direction. She couldn't look any other way, so that whenever other movements came, she could only go from side to side. There was no *roundness*. The idea of seeing—finding out who she was as a god—was something that really caught her. And then she goes through this whole thing of facing this mirror image, as it were, and finally, after many movements through, there was a release from that. The pair of opposites is always there until one can find the center. Then in the center one can move and then go freely.

BROWN: How much influence did Joe have on your work? Watching you and imagining Joe watching you, and imagining you listening to Joe . . .

ERDMAN: It was wonderful because I would go for these emotional developments, these *transforming moments* in life. I used to call them "rooms," states of being. And Joe then would put the names to them. He named one dance "Medusa," but I had already done it from the point of view of an organic life. The major choreographic work was trying to pick out moves that would show the differences in these states of being. Every dance needs to have its own vocabulary. For every work you do you create the universe anew. You create the experience of time, and create the experience of space, and you create the experience of dynamic strengths and flow and control. That kind of energy, the energy process, is used in a separate way for each separate piece. I've had a marvelous time, a wonderful time, doing all this.

BROWN: How did you develop your own career after dancing with Martha Graham?

ERDMAN: I had a wonderful time developing choreography for both the company and the solo, and I actually went around the world as a solo performer with my own choreography. I continued doing performances in New York with my dance company until I got this inspiration to work with the Anna Livia Plurabella female figure in James Joyce's *Finnegans Wake*.

Well, my husband, as you know, had been working on *Finnegans Wake* when we first were married. I swore I would never read that book! Because I was on one arm and *Finnegans Wake* was on the other arm, and he spent just as much time with *Finnegans Wake* as he did with me. It took me some years to get over that but I did. Time mellows everything, right?

So I took this idea of Anna Livia Plurabelle and I discovered that in order to create her in all aspects (you can't name a type of woman that she isn't) I needed to use James Joyce's language. And that meant I had to have actors and they had to be people who could deal with Shakespeare, at least, in order to do *Finnegans Wake*. We had a marvelous time making that happen. Joe came to my studio and gave two readings from *Finnegans Wake*. We had invited all the actors that had been recommended to me around New York to come and hear this, to see if they wanted to participate in this workshop.

That was back in 1961. The idea of story in dance hadn't

Jean Erdman in a performance from her off-Broadway show, The Coach with the Six Insides, *1962.*

been evolved and I didn't even know I was doing anything unusual. And then we had the good luck of opening off-Broadway in 1962, and being invited, after playing a whole season and winning a couple of awards, and going to Spoleto, to Ireland, to Japan, and various places around the United States and Canada.

It was in Italy, France, and Japan that we found out that because our theater was action theater, each country thought that we reminded them of their own action theater, their own total theater: the Kabuki in Japan, the Comedia in Italy, and the French mime, and so on. And the language was understandable to the same extent everywhere because of *Finnegans Wake*. That piece brought me into total theater, which had been a hope of mine that I'd almost forgotten: the idea that real theater, the theater I thought would be most exciting, would involve all the performing arts.

BROWN: How did the Theater of the Open Eye come about?

ERDMAN: The Theater of the Open Eye was a combination of Joe Campbell doing seminars and Jean Erdman creating total theater works. And that's where we have continued for about fourteen or fifteen years. I've made a piece about Paul Gauguin of Tahiti, which was developed using my Polynesian background, and another one based on Hawaiian myth, the legend of Pele, the great goddess of the volcano, which we call "The Shining House." Now I'm working on a piece of Greek mythology that might be performed in Greece, actually, at the Athens Festival.

ROBERT COCKRELL: Joe, would you say something about marriage as a mythological event?

CAMPBELL: My notion of marriage is that if marriage isn't a first priority in your life you're not married. It's an extremely important decision, that of marriage, because it does amount to and require a yielding and the yielding has to be total to now being a member of a dyad and acting in relation to that twoness. As I've said to people who are worried about it, when you make what you call a sacrifice to the other person, that's not what you're sacrificing to. You're sacrificing to the relationship. The relationship is the sacrificial field, where both of you are relating to the relationship and then you are, as it were, two together. Really like that yin-yang thing. (If you hang onto being the yin, or hang onto being the yang in this thing, as a separate unit, you don't have a marriage.) Then everything in your life from then on relates to that relationship. And when judgments of actions and decisions at various times have to be taken in that sense, then you're married.

The marriage has two stages. The first is what might be called the biological marriage—it yields the family. But then there comes what I would call the mystical marriage, or the alchemical marriage. You see so many families where that doesn't occur. I've been shocked by news from one or another of my friends, people who have already had their family, and you thought, What a lovely marriage. And then you hear, "Oh, we've gone apart."

But if you have been cooperating at all, that sense of identity really matures. It's there and it's a reality. It's a funny thing, people think that *this* is what marriage is about, and *this* is what marriage is about, and *that* is what marriage is about, and *that* is what marriage is about. What marriage is about is *marriage* and that means *marrying*.

ARRIEN: Is there such a thing as love or romance that isn't a projection? Or is it just a projection of this ideal image that we're uniting with?

CAMPBELL: I have really found when I look around that the romantic love I see is this ideal, the anima. The anima is the ideal that you carry within yourself that you put onto the different entities out there and you unite with that. Pretty soon you see through the projection. And then what happens?

ANDRESEN: Is there such a thing as a grand romance that lasts?

LAWRENCE FAVROT: It's a good question. Sometimes when you read Jung, for example, it's almost as if there is no room for true romance to exist because everything ultimately is a projection in his scheme of putting on the anima or animus. I wonder . . .

CAMPBELL: The ordeal of marriage is to let this projection dissolve and accept what comes through. When that's done, you can have a really very rich love relationship that goes on and on.

ARRIEN: Where does your "twinkle-twinkle" principle fit in?

CAMPBELL: [Laughs] I'm trying to think of a context . . .

Normally an individual grows up with a certain social circle, what I call the village compound. As long as you can acquiesce in the tasks and the ideals of the group that you are involved in, you can live very decently in a situation of that kind. If you find yourself not at home there, irritated, and your idea and ideals begin to shift around, then there takes place a total transformation in the psyche of relationships. The ego and its purpose begins to lose hold and unconscious ideals come up.

And there are two orders. One that is threatening, what Jung calls the shadow. This is what I call the "knock-knock" principle, when one is in fear of one's own self. I remember hearing a nice little gentleman say, "If I weren't a good Christian I would be a terrible person." This is the "knock-knock." Letting unconscious content come up is dangerous in that sense. Then there comes the allure of the exotic. Much more interesting. This I call the "twinkle-twinkle" principle.

Those are the two movements that come in when you begin to lose confidence in your moral stance. But the matter of falling in love—someone walks in the room and that's it! Bang! You think: This is it, this is my life. This is something that occurs in many, many romances, not only in Europe but in Asia, as well. I've had that experience myself.

So what is it you're in love with? You don't know who this is, and you don't know who that is; you don't know what the person is. If you marry someone onto whom this has been projected, it's bound to happen that the person begins to show through. Then you can face the problem. What are you going do? Are you going to say, Well, I'm disillusioned; I'm going to take my possession back and have it ready for repossession?

The other possibility is to say, Okay, I accept this. Then something else happens. The projection gradually either disappears or goes back; then around the age of thirty-five or forty (what my mother used to call the "dangerous forties"), it gets out there again. Then you have that problem, the Tristan and Iseult problem, you might say.

Sacred and Profane Love. *Titian, c. 1514.*

ARRIEN: Do you think that there's more loving out of need than loving out of love? Because if you're projecting, then how can you really be loving?

CAMPBELL: That's just what I'm saying. Yield the projection and accept what's there. That's why I call it an ordeal.

ARRIEN: Was that why you said that passion over the years changed to compassion?

CAMPBELL: Yes. That's the only way to get through—with compassion. Passion is different. With passion you want to possess. The conversion of passion into compassion is the whole problem of marriage.

ARRIEN: How do you define moral, in relationship to love?

CAMPBELL: Doing what the society tells us to do. That's what is moral. It's different from one society to another.

ARRIEN: Then should morals play a part in love?

CAMPBELL: Should they? If you say should, then of course they should. But do they? I would say no, all is fair in love and war outside the moral frame. The problem is to bring the two so that they don't collide. Each of us is but half of the entire original being and of the journey through to completion. If you're good you'll find the right other half; if you have the right purposes it'll be the right one.

Getting a perspective on our sexual relationships lets us know that they are not biologically grounded, they are culturally grounded. And our culture is not a fixed thing. Right now it's in a process of transformation. There's no reason why we should regard ourselves as committed to this system or that. This is a point that I think is very important: We don't have to wait for the society to wake up. The important thing is for the individual to find his or her own way in the field.

Society will come along to get it wrong another way in a few centuries; but meanwhile the individual can find within himself or herself these qualities that have been assigned to the female and what have been assigned to the male. They're unconditional. We can seek those things within ourselves.

COCKRELL: I read a paper by Kant on "The Beautiful and the Sublime." One of the things he talks about there is that women are beautiful and men are sublime. And he says that one of the functions of the male is to implant the sublime in women, so that it develops in her, and as her beauty fades she becomes sublime.

My feeling was that this went even further. I felt that if you associated man with the sun and woman is grounded in the earth, it was that dynamic in just fertilizing the female—not just in her womb but also in her mind, awakening the sublime in her.

CAMPBELL: I would say first that Kant wasn't married! A married philosopher is a contradiction in adjectives. I remember that particular essay of his, and there is one phrase that comes out in Dante's discussion of beauty and the sublime that has stayed with me and made me feel that Kant was a potential poet.

He said that blue eyes are beautiful, dark eyes are sublime. And this indicates the problem. The problem is beauty and the sublime. Beauty invokes; the sublime shatters. The sublime is experienced—I mean real sublimity, with enormous spaces or in areas of enormous power. For instance, if you were in a city with a saturation bombing taking place, you might experience the sublime. I mean that! As long as you were *there*. That's the sublime: The sublime shatters, overpowers.

You trick yourself into destroying the position that you're holding. Every time I take an extra drink, I know what I'm doing. I hardly ever get out of the room but—this is life [laughter]. In fact, you know, there's an Irish name for whiskey, *usquebaugh,* which, when translated into English is "water of life." And Nietzsche associates the Dionysian with drunkenness, where the principle is broken; and the Apollonian then with the retaining of form.

It's the experience of the *mysterium tremendum.* The beauty is the experience of the *mysterium fascinans:* that's the difference. Since woman is in herself fascinating, that's why Kant assigns beauty to woman, and the man is the destroyer and the killer; he always has been, and so his action is more on that level. That's why he said that.

You know, the point is that women are saying, We're not mysterious. The fact is, they are.

FAVROT: It's the kind of difference between Narcissus lost in the beauty of the reflection, and Job, at the end, faced with the *mysterium tremendum.*

CAMPBELL: Yes, he is.

FAVROT: Not as having power beyond good and evil; it's just beyond human comprehension.

CAMPBELL: That's right.

KENNARD: We sometimes hear a sort of basic love story like boy meets girl, boy loses girl, boy gets girl back again. Is this just a Western hang-up? That you always have to lose it and then rush around and do something tremendous to get it all back again as a prize for being very heroic and wonderful?

CAMPBELL: No, that's just a good story line [laughter]. Anyone who has studied writing stories knows you have to have a sort of black moment. They move toward disaster and then something that's been planted in the first paragraph or two comes up and rescues the hero . . .

KENNARD: How long has that story line been going on? Are Indian love stories like that?

CAMPBELL: No, although some of them are. But I think that's a sort of *Saturday Evening Post* story [laughter].

JOAN HALIFAX: Joseph, how have women inspired you in your life? Tell me about your experience with women, with pure anima, because I've worked with you for years.

CAMPBELL: Anima is never pure [laughter].

TARNAS: Touché.

HALIFAX: What is it? What is it?

CAMPBELL: It's all life contaminated, you might say, by a local example.

HALIFAX: For example?

CAMPBELL: Anima—as they say in the alchemical system, *anima mercuria*—keeps changing forms. The anima comes forth but one doesn't know anything about it until it finds residence in a certain person. I was just comparing these right around me now. They are very different from each other.

So what's pure anima? It always has a historical reference and a psychological ground. The real problem of life is relating these two. You have a psychological beginning and you have a historical initiation and then—what are you going to do with this goddamned thing? It shows itself to be very different from what you expected and you have to deal with this showing through of the historical fact. The problem of marriage is exactly that: You marry a projected anima, but what you really have married isn't only a projected anima but a fact. What you thought you had and what you actually got is the problem of, what shall we call it, the disillusionment. That is to say, you must take back the anima. You can go away and I'll project this over here! Then you'll have the same problem all over again.

I think the problem today is that we're taught, or rather, we're given to think, that marriage is going to be a long love affair and that you're going to have a lot of fun with the anima. The fact is you're not having fun after the first ten minutes. You're in confrontation with a problem and it turns into an ordeal. The ordeal is of acquiescing.

The pure anima is the thing that's got to go, to vanish. You've married this phenomenon and it's not quite what you thought you were going to get. Then the acquiescence in the characteristic of life as here exhibited is what we call maturation.

HALIFAX: You know, in my world I call men's inability to accept the anima in their own nature "anima sickness."

CAMPBELL: *No.* You've got to throw the anima out, dissolve the anima out. She'll occur about five years later, after the marriage, and then you have to deal with it. That's another problem. Particularly if the wife forgets that she is the incarnation of the anima.

HALIFAX: But I know that the anima has played an incredibly important part in your life, in your development.

CAMPBELL: Taught women for thirty-eight years! I've had it all over the place!

HALIFAX: As myth she has many historical names. She's been a character, a presence, which has formed your intellect.

CAMPBELL: Her name is Jean, Joan, and Jane—

HALIFAX: How has she inspired you? What has she given you?

CAMPBELL: This is biography and I just don't like biography.

HALIFAX: Not so much biography—

CAMPBELL: And my field is comparative mythology.

HALIFAX: Joseph, today I heard you say that teaching women at Sarah Lawrence taught you that you have to understand mythology not from just the point of your comparative mythology but in terms of reference.

CAMPBELL: Thank you. You have saved me the trouble of saying that. That was what I was about to say: that this subject is really a very large academic field of facts, facts, facts, all over the place. One can be interested in those in a purely academic way and you can write articles for the various journals. But in teaching women I found they were always asking to know the relationship of these materials to their own living. And this interest of women in *life* is something that is far more emphatic than the masculine interest in footnotes. Men can be too interested in the interesting mechanical details. Teaching women held me to this, and so—I've said it many times—it's my female students who taught me what the life value of these forms is.

Campbell and Rozanne Zucchet, Esalen, 1982.

ROZANNE ZUCCHET: Do you feel that women need to begin to feel better about themselves again or that society needs to change and reevaluate some of its values?

CAMPBELL: No. All they have to do is stop looking at the boys and wondering whether they are in competition with them. Just realize what effect they are having on the boys. It came to me at Sarah Lawrence. I was teaching these courses on mythology and at the end of my last year there this woman comes in and sits down and says, "Well, Mr. Campbell, you've been talking about the hero. But what about the woman?"

I said, "The woman's the mother of the hero; she's the goal of the hero's achieving; she's the protectress of the hero; she is this, she is that. What more do you want?"

She said, "I want to be the hero!"

So I was glad that I was retiring that year and not going to teach anymore [laughter].

AUDIENCE QUESTION: What do you think about the women who pick their careers out of love? Or are motivated into a career because of love?

CAMPBELL: Women have been doing this for ages in our culture. The ability of women to get the life sense of the career field that they are in is most remarkable. Is that what you were speaking about?

AUDIENCE QUESTION: No, I mean a woman who chooses a certain career because she feels the love in that work. Like a teacher who loves children or anybody who just happens to love to work with numbers or has a feeling for her work?

CAMPBELL: I think anyone who chooses a career for any other reason is a nut. I mean, that's the way to choose your life, to do something just to get a job; but if you don't love what you're doing, you're not in it at all.

AUDIENCE QUESTION: But in the state of being in love or appreciation or whatever it is, wouldn't the achievement level, the competitive level—wouldn't that sort of make it all right if the reason is for love?

CAMPBELL: I'm not against achievement. No. The problem is that in this woman's movement they started out in a perfectly legitimate way—a woman doing the same job as a man ought to get equivalent pay. That's the way it started. But now it comes that women are losing the appreciation for their own domestic life, their own domestic potentialities, to bring up children and so forth. They are turning it all over to the state and the schools.

ZUCCHET: What about women who go into the creative fields?

CAMPBELL: My wife is a dancer and those women have no problems. I know lots of them, women who go into the arts, a world in which one participates not in competition with somebody else but in her own development and own relationship.

ARRIEN: I think that's true of men too.

TARNAS: Love of the arts rather than love of achievement works for women, you mean?

CAMPBELL: An artist is not in the field to achieve, to realize, but to become fulfilled. It's a life-fulfilling, totally different structure.

ARRIEN: Remaining in touch with your intuitive sense?

CAMPBELL: Exactly. And it doesn't matter whether you're first-, second-, third-rate in the public eye. Each artist, as I know them, is in fulfillment in his or her own way. It's not a competitive field.

ARRIEN: Your art is your life then.

CAMPBELL: Right. Commercial art is something else. I mean direct, creative art.

BROWN: But maybe ordinary people who may not think of themselves as artists can indeed be artists.

CAMPBELL: The problem with being an artist is you have to practice a technique. This turned up when my wife Jean came here to Esalen one year. She's a professional dancer, and in her teaching she's teaching people who want to dance. And there's a lot of chores just moving your legs around, hanging onto a bar.

I was lecturing on mythology and Jean was going to do something with her dancers. In the evening, well, she was just terribly discouraged. I said, "Oh, Jeannie, what's the matter?"

She said, "They just want the 'Esalen' experience!"

So the next day or two I looked out the window and saw Jean with her pupils. She had them opening their arms to the sun and rolling downhill and skipping around.

It pointed out to me a very important matter with respect to the arts. There are two totally different aspects. The thing that irritated Jean was that these people were calling this thing creative—creative *art*. It's not. It's *therapeutic*. Here is a person who's off the rails trying to get back onto the rails by means of art: that's artist therapy. But the artist who is on the rails and works out of that sense—that's a totally different thing. Both are perfectly okay, but it's good to know the difference.

You don't ask a professional dancer to even know how to handle people who don't want to dance. Dancers are the most terrific artists. Dancing and singing, I think, are the most difficult arts because the body is an instrument; and since it has to be in perfect trim, that's what you're working for all the time.

AUDIENCE QUESTION: In my mind I often juxtapose the words *hero* and *artist*. They both are on this heroic path and then are finding themselves; that's a goal for both of them. So beyond just knowing the technique there is that inner spirit that's very important to an artist. Maybe you can say it is that feeling inside, even if it's running down a hill, that is what makes an artist, as much as technique.

CAMPBELL: You're bringing a heretical position here [laughter]. You get very sloppy art out of that sort of thing.

KENNARD: In so many societies in the past women don't seem to have been the artists; they don't seem to have run the societies. Every so often you get a society that is a matriarchy, perhaps where women appear to be in control for a hundred years or more. Now what happens there if women are for being and men are for acting?

CAMPBELL: There are certain fields in the arts, we think of them more as crafts, where women dominated. All of the arts, weaving and basketmaking, pottery, the certain arts having to do with sewing and embroidery; those are women's works.

KENNARD: But do you think men fall in love with women more if women are not doing, but just being?

CAMPBELL: Oh, that's just a statistical problem. The three ideals of women in traditional societies are the woman as mother and wife, the woman as courtesan, and woman as athletic warrior girl. Those are the three ideals.

The goddess represents nature. The god represents society. And when you have a mythology that accents a god over a goddess you have a religion that accents society over nature. Then with the Fall, nature itself is cursed.

Joseph Campbell

ARRIEN: What about Artemis?

CAMPBELL: There are two kinds of goddesses in mythologies. One is the primary goddess who's symbolic of the universe, of the earth and heavens and what not. She's the total, total being, total god.

The other kind is the goddess who's the consort of a god. When a god-oriented mythology comes in, the whole scene shifts. Whereas in the goddess-oriented mythology the male is subordinated to her, with the male mythologies the goddess is secondary.

Now Artemis, of whom you asked, is the goddess of the first kind. She comes from the Old Bronze Age period and Martin Nilsson, who's one of the major scholars in the whole field of classical religion mythology, regards her as the total goddess.

When a number of goddesses, each of whom is a total goddess, begin to come together—which happens when you have a culture that spreads over a large territory and takes in people of other kinds—the goddesses become departmentalized.

That is to say, each is given a certain portion of the goddesses' realm to run, to handle. And Artemis is the classical fifth-century goddess of the hunt. That's a sentimentalization of the goddess of the wild things, who is herself the goddess of the forest and all the beasts that are in it.

A statue of Artemis from the sculpture garden of the Statens Museum For Kunst, Copenhagen, Denmark.

In the very early periods the god and the animal are the same, and Artemis was associated with the deer. She was the deer: the deer was Artemis. And then later, as the human aspect becomes more and more accented, the deer becomes her companion.

Persephone and Demeter were pig goddesses. The pig was a tremendously important figure in the Bronze Age. Circe is the one who was transmuted to swine, and so forth, and she is the initiator. She initiates Odysseus into the wisdom of the underworld, and the wisdom of the realm of light of her father, the sun.

So these departmentalizations of goddesses are reductions, really.

HIGHWATER: When one looks at Eros and Logos—and let's remember what Socrates or Plato actually said: there are two forms of thinking. One is permanent and fixed and logical, masculine and good, and it's called Logos. The other, Eros, is intuitive and impermanent and not very good, and feminine. I think we've been stuck with that connotation.

ARRIEN: We're stuck with that duality: the Logos, the logical mind, and the intuitive. That's setting up a duality, and I think that what's really necessary is a bridge, that we start creating the new model.

ROBERT BLY: How do you deal with Joseph's idea, that the polarities of life are where the energies lie?

HIGHWATER: That's the problem. We're always talking about reuniting the psyche. But we always talk about the fact that it's essentially a process of making a duality into something else.

HALIFAX: So long as it's not pairs of opposites only.

HIGHWATER: Right.

ARRIEN: I think what's really involved here is the process that is associated with that beautiful myth about an individual who has black hair and he walks with a panther by his side as he is discovering who he is.

And as he begins to discover who he is, his hair turns from black to brown and the panther changes into a leopard. And as he fully realizes who he is, his hair turns fiery red. Then the person pinches the growth marks the leopard got from transforming into a beautiful lion, because he wants the memory of the dark places from where he's come.

I think that's the process that we're involved in. I think that there's an emerging process now where we're trying to get away from, or pinching, the dualities or polarities so that we can become something more.

CAMPBELL: I'd like to say I'm very much for duality [laughter]. But the problem is how duality gets to be interpreted. Now in the grandiose mythological systems of the Old World mythologies dating from Bronze Age times, we have two quite contrary systems. They appear, for example, in the yin-yang idea, and in the Hindu idea of male-female relationships. The woman is Shakti. In Europe and in the China/Japan area the yang, the masculine, is regarded as the part that is associated with heaven, with solar life, with warmth, with action. And the female principle, the yin, is associated with darkness and moisture and water. It actually is a term that comes from the two sides of a stream, the side that is lighted by solar light and the side that is in shadow. One is dry, the other is moist.

But in general the male is regarded as the active and the female as the receptive. This is something that I think dominates Northern thought in the Eurasian world, both in Europe and in China.

As one who grew up and was psychologically conditioned long before blue jeans came in, I have this observation to make. In the old days the male was dressed in black tie. He was recessive. And the women were beautiful, out in front. Now this was a characteristic of rather recent occidental civilizations. When you turn to the oriental or primitive societies, the women, like female birds, are quite recessive and the men have all the glory. The only place you get this in our society is in the military. But the women, nevertheless, are the ones who wear the feathers and are out in front.

Now this has interested me enormously. The traditional way—and it's the way of animals, as well as what might be called the traditional societies—is that the male is the flowering thing, the glorious thing, and the woman is quite subdued but is supportive, is the earth. And in those drums that are played in India, the deep sounding ones, that's the female drum. And the one that goes brilliantly on, that's the male drum.

What happened in Western society was that a good deal of the organization of thinking with respect to sex was based on putting the woman forward. You take your hat off (or you used to, at least) in the elevator. Or when a woman comes in to the room you give your seat to her. Now the woman begins to dress like a man and the man's dress hasn't changed; it's just deteriorated and receded into the background. And where the hell are we? We have unisex barbershops. It's ridiculous because the whole energy of life depends on polarity and when you give that up all you've got left is a blob [laughter].

Then you have a shock when you travel to India. You learn that the active aspect of the idea of energy is Shakti, female. And the male is inert. He is the one to be activated.

I thought, Where did the system come from? Why this complete contrast? They're both perfectly true. One is related to the physical relationship and the other is the psychological. The male, psychologically—he just wants to be left alone! I've seen it very, very strongly! I don't know how the females are, but God, the best times are when you're just *there,* kid, and you are where it counts.

And then this little twinkle bug goes by, and as Joyce says in *Finnegans Wake,* in Anna Livia Plurabelle, "the little rippling river stream."

And she says, "Oh, wouldn't it be nice to start the world again?"

And you think, Oh, goddamn, it really would. And the male then is activated.

Now I think this is perfectly correct. The female is the activating principle, and then she's amazed that you're activated and come at her like that! You know [laughter]!

HIGHWATER: Are you saying women never become aggressive?

CAMPBELL: They're aggressive; it's already there in the twinkle star. It's another kind of aggression. The power of women is psychological and magical, do you see, and their aggression is a magical one. They are perfectly innocent, and oh boy, something's going on, and they say, Oh, I'm not responsible, no, I just came in here *en décolleté,* and look what's happened!

AUDIENCE QUESTION: Joseph, you once said that modern man was kept in childhood for so long that there was a continent full of women in their mid-thirties who were unloved and unmatched because their men had not grown up to them. I think that is one of our crises in our civilization today.

CAMPBELL: Whenever one goes from one social world into another one gets a real culture shock with respect to the male-female relationship. I remember when I went to India. Now I had spent years studying Indian philosophy that had nothing to do with boys and girls together. When I found myself in India I began to think, What the devil does this remind me of? There was never a woman visible, except the street women, the women selling vegetables or whatnot in the street. The women who were the wives of the men whom you were consorting with were totally invisible. You'd see two policemen walking down the street holding hands, but you'd never see a man and a woman on the street together.

I began to think, My God, the last time I experienced this was when I was in prep school. There are no women around, just males together. And there's another world . . . And there's another world . . . A great shock came to me there in Orissa.

So India is a prep school. The women are somewhere else. In Orissa I was staying in a hotel when I was there with the Indians and being entertained by some young Hindu gentleman. One afternoon I found myself walking hand in hand on the beach with an Indian, and I thought, if Jean should see me now!

I said to him, "Well, I must thank you for the time that you have given to entertain me here." And he said, "Oh, no, it is so fortunate. It is my holiday." I said, "This is your holiday and you are spending it with me, walking on the beach? Why aren't you going somewhere for a pleasant time with your wife and family?" "Oh," he said, "we can't do a thing like that. It would be so complicated going anywhere with my family."

So I just knew, my God, there is a total discontinuity between the lives of the males here and the family. This was an amazing experience to me.

BLY: Joseph, can I ask you a question here? You said that you had learned a lot from your female students at Sarah Lawrence about relating to the obsessions of the male to life itself. If you were talking to a young male now, in the United States, would you suggest that he try to develop the feminine part of himself or the male part?

CAMPBELL: I'd say, Find what it is your life career's going to be and learn to do it well. That would be my information. Whether he's male or female, that's something else again. My whole attitude toward pedagogy is: Learn a job. And it's not going to be learned in a weekend. You've got to put yourself to it. What it takes to do that is what it takes to live your life. That's been my decision.

BLY: So you come away to what Yeats calls "passion." You're interested in finding out what a human being's passion is and then following that?

CAMPBELL: Yes. Let him go ahead and do it. It may or may not involve male or female relationships; those have to be handled in relation to the trajectory of what he has elected to be his career.

⧈

Eros and Psyche. *Antique sculpture. Rome.*

TARNAS: When you were talking about the difference in male and female roles in mythology I was thinking about how Psyche and Eros met, and how there are many male heroes in Greek mythology and relatively few females, Psyche being an example of the exception. Could you talk about how you see the difference between the two?

CAMPBELL: Mythologies always deal with traditional social situations. We are in a whole new phase right now. Women are released from the chores of domestic life, which absorbed everything they had. Now women are able to initiate careers for themselves. But typically in our Western civilization men have been able to say, I'm going to do this, that, and the other. The women now are released, you might say, for that kind of thing. It creates a lot of problems because the only models they have in their chosen careers are male models. A lot of them lose their sense of what it is to be a woman by thinking that their value is one of achievement, not one of being, and it makes for very important problems.

TARNAS: You're saying that achievement is more male—

CAMPBELL: —Absolutely. Right from the very beginning. Just look, for example, at the earliest art we have, the art of the Paleolithic. The female figures are simply standing female nudes; their power is in their body and their being and their presence. Many traditional societies regard magic as being originally the woman's possession and the men have stolen it or taken it from them because it's a woman's thing.

Then look at the images of the male. They are always *doing* something, they're always representing something: They are in *action*. Generally in a primitive culture context the woman is the one who brings forth the species, nature, and the man is the one who brings forth society. Those are the main polarities; and that comes right down the line.

⧈

FAVROT: Then is the problem in today's society that some women, in attempting to be more achievement oriented are actually creating a rivalry between two people trying to achieve at the same time? And that's why their union isn't lasting for any length of time?

CAMPBELL: The problem is not so much rivalry in achievement as the problem of the husband dealing with another person, on the other side of the tennis net, you might say. I have had this experience with my students. You see a student wake up to a whole new life possibility. That's a wonderful moment in teaching when that happens because you see a life career, a life trajectory, begin to show itself.

Then I meet her five years later, ten years later, twenty years later, thirty years later, at the alumni reunions, and you can tell the one whose husband let her develop as a human being.

The other possibility is that you see a man who marries and expects a wife. Well, we have the archetype of what a wife is. And it's a very helpful archetype. Both lines can develop, but it's in relationship to the man's career, principally, and the woman's with the children. But when you have two careers in the house and the individual developments are on two not always parallel courses, there's a lot of love required; I mean real pedagogical participation to help the other person to develop as a human being and still hang on to the relationship. The thing that holds them together is making the relationship the top thing. It's through the relationship that the development of each is taking place. And when you make a sacrifice, you are not sacrificing to the other person; you are sacrificing to the relationship. That relationship involves the progression of your own life.

So when people think of marriage as a continuous long love affair, then they are bound for trouble. Because it isn't. It is in a proper sense an ordeal [laughter]. And the ordeal is that of individual development. And if there isn't individual development taking place, well, what's the good of it?

When you have a woman identifying with the *animus,* you get the usual business of the executive female. She has identified herself with the masculine aspect of her own life and she has lost her femininity. She becomes interested only in achievement. The unfortunate thing about it is that she doesn't realize what her own effects are on her environment; her human relationship deteriorates all along the line. And then she begins to worry, What the hell's the matter here? I've watched it time and time again.

This is what you call an animus woman, a woman animated by her intent to be male. It destroys her life as a woman. And not only that, but all of her relationships.

KENNARD: Did Tristan and Iseult have individual development?

CAMPBELL: Now, Tristan and Iseult, this is a twelfth-century problem. All the societies of the world have had socially arranged marriages, not the individual one. Some of the early primitive people and some of the peasant societies will have that kind of thing. But in the structured society the family had made all the arrangements. Today in New Delhi, one of the major world cities, when you buy a newspaper there are columns of advertising for wives, and the advertisement has been put in either by a marriage broker or the family. And the young women don't know whom they are going to marry. I have heard the daughters ask their brother, "What is he like?" They don't see the person they are to marry until the wedding moment.

Well, this still goes on.

In the Middle Ages there was this same situation. Young women in the royal families and the aristocratic families were just political pawns. They would be sent here, there, or elsewhere, for all kinds of family relationships—

FAVROT: Which was politically more profitable.

CAMPBELL: Yes. And when the church sanctifies this, you hear about two bodies, one flesh, and all that. It was really two bank accounts in one. The aristocratic society there began to feel this was really degradation.

And then love came in, and the meeting of the eyes, as a much higher and more spiritual experience than marriage, and the idea of *l'amour*.

KENNARD: Love was a twelfth-century invention?

Morold Wounds Tristan. *Chertsey Abbey tiles, c. 1270.*

Tristan Teaches Iseult to Harp. *Chertsey Abbey tiles, c. 1270.*

CAMPBELL: No, but the *celebration* of love as superior to marriage in the troubadour tradition was. It's at that time in the southern part of France, in the Provençal poetry, that the whole problem of love comes up. And our psychological traditions begin right there, trying to analyze what love is.

There was one great poet, Guiraut de Borneilh, around the middle of the twelfth century. There were many, many discussions of what love was, but Guiraut de Borneilh's answer is the one that really epitomized the sense of it all. He wrote, "The eyes are the scouts for the heart and the eyes go forth to find an image to recommend to the heart." And when the image is found, if the heart is a *gentle* heart—that's the key word—a heart that's capable not simply of lust but of love (and those are totally different things), then love is born. As I've said, lust is simply the zeal of the loins for each other.

Now *Tristan* is the high work celebrating this mystery of love. King Mark had never seen Iseult. Iseult had never seen King Mark. It was Tristan, who when wounded in a battle by a poisoned sword, went to the place where the poison had been prepared and was cured by Iseult's mother, whose name was also Iseult. Then he fell in love with Iseult there; didn't even know he was in love with her, the silly fellow. He goes back and tells his Uncle Mark what a wonderful woman he met in Dublin.

The barons say, Well, it's good for the king to be married, so let's send for Iseult. So he goes back to get Iseult with a lot of crazy adventures.

Then Iseult's mother prepared a love potion so that the husband and wife would love each other. By chance, on the boat, the couple drinks the love potion and so they are in love—but this is a person-to-person love affair rather than a social situation. The whole tension of love versus marriage is developed there.

Of course there were other problems. Were they in sin? Now for a mortal sin you have to have a grievous matter, sufficient reflection, and full consent of the will. If you drink a love potion there is no full consent of the will!

A couple of the poets fixed it so the force of the potion would last only two or three years. By then, of course, they were in sin. From then on they had a mortal sin problem. That was something else.

Then came the problem of resolving this tension between marriage and love. *Amor* is the Provençal word for love. *Amor:* spell it backwards and you get *Roma*. So marriage and love are contrary.

In those days of Eleanor of Aquitaine and Mary de Champagne and Blanche de Castille, and her daughters and so forth, women had these affairs every year and we have the troubadour's reports of them. For example, some chap would come to the court with a case and say, "I have offered myself to this lady and she said no, she already had a lover. She said she would take me when she no longer had that lover."

So what happened was that the woman got married to her lover after her husband died. Then number two presents himself and he says, "Well, here I am." She says, "Oh, no, I love my husband." He says, "That's impossible, that's a contradiction of terms!" So he brought the case to the court and the court decided that she had to accept him!

The stories of the troubadours are just marvelous.

BROWN: Are you saying that most people have had a love experience like this?

CAMPBELL: I'm not going to say everybody, but plenty of people have had this experience. It's not always that falling in love happens to coincide with the most prudent form of accident in your life. It's that continuity between the run of your life and the pull off that life, which the love allure suggests, that interests people in a story like Tristan and Iseult. The solution to this tension in the Middle Ages came with Wolfram Von Eschenbach's *Parzival*. That was where love and marriage were brought together. It was an apple of a story. That's my favorite love story.

KENNARD: Will you tell us about it?

CAMPBELL: It's a long story, my dear friends . . .

This Grail romance of Wolfram Von Eschenbach (his date was 1215 for this), was really the finishing of this great, great romance. He faced this problem, the tension between Amor and Roma. And that's as it stood in the Middle Ages. Love was a calamity to come into your life because the punishment for it was death. I mean, there was punishment by death for love!

There's a wonderful scene in Gottfried von Strassburg's *Tristan*. After the couple has drunk the potion Brangien, the maid— who should have been watching the potion, not letting it loose like that into the sea—comes with shock and says to Tristan, "You have drunk your death!"

And Tristan says, "I don't know what you mean."

This anguish was the great thing that the Middle Ages was interested in, the pain of love, which is the pain of life. Your life is where your pain is; you might put it that way. And it was the experience of the anguish that held the essence of life.

So he said, "If by death you mean the punishment that will be ours if we are discovered, I accept that. If by death you mean eternal death in the fires of hell, I accept that, too."

That's a big, potent statement. Because those people did believe in hell.

The only answer I can think of to that is the wonderful saying of Meister Eckhardt that "Love knows no pain." So that even in hell, if your beloved is with you, it's going to be okay. That was the climate that Wolfram faced when he was working on *Parzival*. The medieval overcoming of the marriage/love polarity that is represented in Tristan and Iseult was achieved, really, by Wolfgang Von Esechenbach in his *Parzival*.

CAMPBELL: Now the problem of the Grail romance is what's known as the wasteland. What is the wasteland? You get a clue from T. S. Eliot in his poem "The Waste Land" [1922]. The question is: How is one to turn the wasteland into a land of flowers, with everything coming up roses? The wasteland is a land of people who are living inauthentic lives. They just get a job because they've got to live and that is rubbish. Where can life come out of this rubble? he asks somewhere.

The medieval situation was that people were required to profess beliefs they did not hold, to profess love for people whom they had married and had no love for. And they held positions that they had inherited and hadn't earned; and so it is a context of inauthentic lives. This is what Wolfram saw as the wasteland.

Now how does that get healed? It gets healed through the example of an authentic life.

Wolfram started the story with Parzival's father, Gahmuret, a knight adventurer, who began to serve the Caliph of Baghdad— Christian knight serving a Muslim monarch. Wolfram jumped the circle of the Christian tradition and recognized Islam as the sister religion of Christianity. So in the course of Gahmuret's service to the Caliph he came to a place called Zazamanc that was governed by a black princess. Her name was Belkarne. He became her champion and lifted a siege and then became her husband. He begot a son, but before the boy was born he took what we used to call "French leave."

He went back to Wales and there was the Queen whose name was Herzeloyde. He won the jousting festival and became her husband, and now he's the husband of two queens. He begets a child on her and then goes back to fight for the Caliph and is killed.

The child that was born in the Near East was Feirefiz because he was black and white. And the child in Wales was Parzival. So Parzival, the Christian knight, has a Muslim brother whom he does not know.

His mother decided she didn't want her son to know anything about knights, no more of this nonsense! So she went up to

The Grail romance is that of the God in your own heart. And the Christ becomes a metaphor. A symbol for that transcendent power which is the support and being of your own life.

Joseph Campbell

Connecticut or something like that and brought forth her little boy on a farm. And so he knew nothing about knighthood. But he had the spirit and heart, the noble heart of his father. He was a born knight, though he didn't know it.

So when he was about fifteen or sixteen years old, he is out in the fields and he sees three knights come by on horseback. He thinks they're angels; that's all his mother has told him about. So he gets down on his knees. They said, "Get up, you don't pray to us. We're knights. Of King Arthur's court."

He says, "What's a knight? How does one become a knight and get to Arthur's court?"

"Oh, it's just down there."

He goes back and tells his mother, "I want to be a knight." So she faints. Then she decides she's going to fix him. She makes a Fool's costume and he goes trotting off. She trots after him down the road and when he turns the corner she drops dead. That's the way his career begins—by killing his mother; it's not a good start.

And so, there he goes, riding all day. At night the horse pulls up at a little rural castle. The knight whose castle it is has lost three sons in jousting tourneys. But still he has his little daughter there with him, so you can see the situation.

In comes Parzival, whom they think is the great and famous Red Knight, and they greet him. Of course, when the time comes to take off the armor and give him a bath he's all covered with rust inside and when they remove it here's this Fool.

But this old boy, his name is Gurnemanz, recognizes good man flesh and sees a great boy here. So he takes him on and teaches him the rules of knightly combat, how to maneuver horses, the rules of combat. And one of the rules is: a knight doesn't ask unnecessary questions. That turns out to be a bad bit of news later on.

Gurnemanz recognizes that he'd like to have him as his son. So in a very pretty scene he offers his daughter as a wife to Parzival so that he would have another son and the girl would have a husband and all that.

Parzival thinks, I must not be given a wife. I must earn a wife. And that's the beginning of the new philosophy. You see? He breaks away from the idea of just accepting things that are given to you by society. In a very delicately handled scene, these two part. He rides away, now a changed knight. He lets the reins lie slack on the horse's neck. Now this is a major image in medieval mythology

In the Grail Castle, Parzival receives his sword from the king. Medieval manuscript, c. 1330.

and other mythologies as well. The horse represents the nature power and the rider represents the controlling mind. The reins slack means that he's riding Nature. His own nature. It's a noble horse who has the same heart as he.

The horse carries him all day and in the evening he comes to a castle that is in some distress. It's the castle of a little orphan queen. She's just his age and her name is Condwiramurs (from *conduire amour:* guide to love). When he arrives, of course, his armor's taken off, he's given a nice bath and soft robes and so forth, and presently it comes time to retire, and he's given a bed.

Well, in the middle of the night he wakes up and sees she is kneeling by the bed, weeping. And he says to her just what the knights had said to him, "You don't kneel to me, only to God. If you want this bed, I'll go over there." And here's what she said. "If you'll promise not to wrestle with me, I'll just get in and tell my story."

And Wolfram says, "But she was dressed for war. She was wearing a transparent nightgown."

So she gets into bed and she's crying and she tells him her story. "My castle is under siege. There's a knight, Clamide, the greatest knight in the world, who wants my property and me as his wife." Now there's the old medieval thing again. She also is resisting, do you see, as he resisted.

"But," she says, "you've seen how high the towers are in my castle. I would rather throw myself from the highest tower into the moat than to marry this man." The knight had sent an army with his great general to conduct the affair.

And Parzival says, "Well, I'll kill him in the morning."

And she says, "That'll be just fine."

So in the morning the drawbridge goes down and *brrrrmmm*—down comes the Red Knight, riding, and he collides with the seneschal, the leader of the king's army, and presently the enemy is on his back, and Parzival has his knee on his chest and rips his helmet off, and is about to cut his head off when the man says, "I yield!"

Parzival says, "Okay. You go to Arthur's court. Tell them you are my man and I sent you."

After a couple of affairs of this kind, King Arthur's court begins to think, Say, that was some chap that we let go! So they later decide that they're going to go out and try to find him.

Parzival comes back into the castle and Condwiramurs has put her hair up in the way of married woman. So there's a spiritual marriage. Each has chosen the other voluntarily. And he has chosen a wife indeed. And then they go to bed that night.

As Wolfram says, "Not many a lady nowadays would be pleased with that night's sleep." Because he didn't even touch her. He knew nothing about these things. Two days and two nights more they are happy in this way. And then on the third night he remembered how his mother had told him of embraces, and Gurnemanz, too, explained to him that husband and wife are one.

So then, as Wolfram says, "If you will pardon me, they interlaced arms and legs and felt that this is as it should have been going all the time."

Now the idea there is that the physical is the consummation of love and the sacramentalization of the physical is the love. There's no clergy involved here at all. Love is fulfilled here in marriage and marriage is the consummation of love. This just threw the whole thing into a new perspective. There were five virtues of the medieval knight: temperance, courage, loyalty, courtesy, and love. And this young man is endowed with them all.

FAVROT: What effect did the story you told have on Europe at the time it was written? Was it read by many people or was it just something that you feel had an effect, just through your study of mythology?

CAMPBELL: There was a great, great wave of Arthurian romance, first with the appearance of Geoffrey of Monmouth's *History of the Kings of Britain* in Latin. This was an account of the legends of the kings of Britain before the arrival of the Anglo-Saxons, starting with a hero named Brut, after whom Britain is named. King Arthur appears there as a fighter against the Anglo-Saxons when they're coming in.

This sprung a whole tide of stories having to do with the Celtic heroes and Celtic themes. Now the importance is not so much that this particular romance influenced people, but that it is symptomatic of a whole trend in thinking at that time. These romances parried an attempt on the part of Europe to assimilate Christianity. Christianity came from another part of the world; it came from the Near East, as an alien religion, and was forced on Europe. It's in the eleventh and twelfth and early thirteenth centuries that Europe begins to assimilate it. There was a bishop or an abbot, Joachim of Florence, who around the 1200s published a statement of what he called "The Three Ages of The Spirit."

The first age of the spirit is that of Islam and the Age of the Father. The preparation of a priestly race, worthy to become the vessel of the Incarnation. The Second Age of the Spirit was that of the Son and the church, bringing this message to the world. The Third Age of the Spirit, which is about to dawn in the fifteenth century, was to be that of the Holy Spirit, the Holy Ghost, where the Holy Spirit will speak directly to teach and the institution of the church will gradually disappear.

Now, of course, this was heresy and was condemned, but it caught on. The Grail Castle is a castle that participates in this new experience. The Grail Knight, whether his name is Galahad or Parzival, appears in flaming red armor, appears in Arthur's castle at the time of the Pentecost, the Descent of the Holy Spirit. So that the Grail Knight is the equivalent to Christ; that is to say, as the vehicle of the Holy Spirit.

This whole drift is what is marked in this book, and it's a drift away from the orthodox Christian pattern.

CAMPBELL: There's an interesting thing about the date of the Tristan story that comes at the end of the twelfth century, about 1160 to 1170. It's exactly the same period of the Krishna cult in India, where the god Krishna falls completely, totally, in love with a married woman, Radha.

Again, it's the rule-breaking, law-breaking thing, that the religious ecstasy represents, going past rational bounds into the irrational, complete giving of oneself. And here is the god himself who is involved in this.

The principle poem celebrating this is called the "Gita Kovinda" or the "Song of the Cowherd," and it was composed by a young brahmin who was in love with the daughter of his guru. He represents himself as Krishna, and his beloved as Radha. And that's exactly the same period.

A century before, or half-century before, in Japan, you have the Lady Murasaki's *The Tale of Genji,* which is a story of love and also the experiencing of the "sigh of things," the sensitive sigh of things, which is the "all life is sorrowful" teaching of the Buddha. Right across the aristocratic world, from Europe to the China Seas, you have this aristocratic love as a spiritual experience.

Now in Islam it comes along with the Sufis. In *The Arabian Nights* there are lots of stories of absolute love: the woman there is usually a 5,000-dinar girl over whom this chap goes nuts.

The whole world is full of this at this time.

And now the Sufis will tell you, yes, Europe got it from them, but they misunderstood it. But this is not what happened. They received it from them perhaps, but they didn't misunderstand it; they re-read it. In the Orient the woman is symbolic, really, of womanhood. And very often there's a woman of inferior caste; whereas in Europe it was a lady of equivalent dignity socially, and she remained that woman, addressed to a specific person, not as a goddess.

So there was a very important difference. And there's a difference also between the Provençal troubadour tradition, and the German *minnesinger,* which means the same thing—singers of love. In France the beloved is usually a lady of high degree. But in Germany there was this wonderful lyric poet, Walter von der

Krishna and Radha in the rapture of love. South India, eighteenth century. "Erotic mysticism was in the air in those days."

Vogelweider, the greatest lyric poet of the Middle Ages. His poems are full of just lovely, beautiful girls. He says somewhere the word *woman* is a nobler word than lady.

So this medieval idea of love can be inflected in various ways. But from one end of the earth to another, erotic mysticism was in the air in those days.

The full round, the norm of the mono-myth requires that the hero shall now begin the labor of bringing the runes of wisdom, the Golden Fleece, or his sleeping princess, back into the kingdom of humanity, where the boon may redound to the renewing of the community, the nation, the planet, or the ten thousand worlds.

Joseph Campbell,
The Hero with a
Thousand Faces

Campbell (left) and Henry Morton Robinson, coauthors of A Skeleton Key to Finnegans Wake, *1944. Robinson presented the photo to Campbell with this inscription on the back: "Dear Joe: This is your copy—suitable for framing. It shows you to be very handsome—and me, very bald. Rondo."*

5

The Boon

In 1943, on the suggestion of his friend and mentor, Heinrich Zimmer, the Bollingen Foundation invited Joseph Campbell to edit and write a commentary on its first publication, Maud Oakes's *Where the Two Came to Their Father: A Navaho War Ceremonial*. This, he said, brought him "full circle back to Buffalo Bill." The following year he published his first major work, a collaboration with author Henry Morton Robinson, *A Skeleton Key to Finnegans Wake*, as well as a folklore commentary to *The Complete Grimm's Fairy Tales*.

Zimmer died of pneumonia in 1943, and Campbell took on the painstaking task of editing Zimmer's American lectures, a twelve-year project that produced four volumes of Indian art and mythology. Campbell was also at work on the book that would earn him the devotion of students and artists and the scorn of many academics, *The Hero with a Thousand Faces*. Published in 1949, it won an award from the National Institute of Arts and Letters for Contribution to Creative Literature, and became the most popular book in the Bollingen Series after Richard Wilhelm's translation of the *I Ching*.

During the 1950s and 1960s, in addition to teaching at Sarah Lawrence, Campbell edited *The Portable Arabian Nights*, the *Myth and Man* series, and six volumes of the Eranos Papers from the Jung Conferences at Bollingen; served as president of the Creative Film Foundation; and wrote numerous academic articles and book reviews.

BROWN: Can you describe your early days as a writer?

CAMPBELL: I was learning so much, and experiencing so much in my reading, that although when I had been in prep school I had intended to keep on with writing, I had no ambition to write. I was just reading, reading, reading.

When *Finnegans Wake* came out in 1939 I had already found it when I had been in Paris; it had been appearing in Emile Jolas's *transition* magazine, in an earlier version under the title "Work in Progress." I had become fascinated in the material at that time because it meant something to me. So when the book came out I immediately bought a copy and spent the first weekend reading it through. And, oh, it was a grand, grand experience reading *Finnegans Wake* and being more or less ready for it.

In my days at Columbia, when I used to be running around, I got to know a young professor named Henry Morton Robinson, who used to come out and kick a football around the field. I had known him for many, many years, and when I went up to Woodstock in the middle of the Depression, there was my friend Rondo, as we called him, without a job and with a family, sweating it out. Finally he broke through and got a job with *Reader's Digest* ghostwriting three or four articles a month. And so he was a real pro in handling writing.

So one day this chap comes down from Woodstock for dinner with Jean and me and he and his wife. At dinner he says, "How's it going with *Finnegans Wake?* And I said, "Well, it's going just fine." He said, "Somebody's got to write a key to this thing and it might as well be you and I."

I said, "Oh, come off it."

And he said, "Come on! Let's do it ourselves."

We made an arrangement that we would write an introduction. I started really digging in and pulling it apart and I wrote, from the first page, about forty thousand words. When I brought it to Robinson he said, "For God's sake, what are you going to do, the *Encyclopedia Brittanica?*"

CAMPBELL: I want to tell you something, and anyone who is a scholar may enjoy this message. When you are going to collaborate with somebody, make a very strict line where your authority begins and ends and where your collaborator begins and ends. If you have that line good and clean then you will end up friends. Otherwise it won't happen.

We had it. Robinson was a good Joycean student, but if it came to a discussion as to what Joyce meant and we were in disagreement, I was right. And if it came to a question about how to write a book, he was right.

So I bring him my first statement. He said, "Joe, this is a funny thing to say but everything is upside down. You say at the end of your paper what should have been said at the beginning and this goes for every paragraph and practically for every sentence."

I went home that night and thought about that and I thought, This is why: I have been brought up as a scholar, writing for scholars, or wishing to write for scholars. The scholars always tell you what the other fellow had said about this thing and then they kick him off with one sentence, then they tell you what somebody else said and they kick him off with another sentence, then they tell you all the difficulties that they have had in finding their thing. Then they come out with this little "mouse" that comes out of the mouth!

And so that's one way of writing.

My friend Robinson said, "Listen, when you are writing for civilized people you are the authority. Tell them in the beginning what you are thinking. Then what you will say will be illustrative of that. They will get the idea first, then they will know why you are writing all the rest of it.

Well, that was illuminating. But it has deprived me of a good deal of, what can I say, academic prestige. That makes you a "popular" writer, you see, instead of the other kind.

CAMPBELL: Well, we worked on the *Skeleton Key* for, I guess, about five years. And, of course, when we had it done nobody wanted it. We were about to publish the thing ourselves somehow or other because we had sent it to Harcourt Brace, which was publishing his works, and they had returned it.

Then Thorton Wilder's *The Skin of Our Teeth* comes along. I went with Jean to see it one Saturday night, front seats balcony. Oh my God! What I was hearing was *Finnegans Wake*. One line after another. I was just full of the stuff. And so I said to Jean, "Do you have a pencil?" She had a woman's bag that had everything in it. So I had a pencil and I could just jot down the quotations as they came! I still have the program where I was copying down the quotes from *Finnegans* as they came.

I phoned my friend Robinson the next morning at Woodstock, and I said, "Hey, Rondo, I think we should write a letter to the *New York Times*. This is just outrageous. My God, *The Skin of Our Teeth* is *Finnegans Wake*. And he said, "I'll be down Monday and we'll talk about it."

When he heard what it was he phoned down to *The Saturday Review* to Norman Cousins. And we worked on the paper that day and in the evening brought it down to the *Review*. Cousins looked at it and says, "What should we call it?"

"Let's call it 'The Skin of Whose Teeth?' " So we published this. But it was just as the war had broken out, just after Pearl Harbor, and Wilder was in the army. He was a captain. The next thing you know he was a major and the next thing you know he was something more than that. So the newspaper boys came down on us from all angles just like a bunch of dive-bombers: "Who was this pair of Micks? This wasn't the civilization we were fighting for."

"Let's cool it," I said to Robinson, "Wilder's going to have to publish it in book form and we'll do the job on it then."

When the play did come out in book form I went through it with a fine tooth comb. There were at least four hundred quotations. Every character was right out of *Finnegans Wake,* and the problems were out of *Finnegans Wake*. And I located a four-line quote, verb for verb, noun for noun. And so we wrote "The Skin of Whose Teeth, Part I," and after that "The Skin of Whose Teeth, Part II," and that did it.

CAMPBELL: When I completed *A Skeleton Key to Finnegans Wake* I gave a copy to Mrs. Eugene Meyer and she sent a copy to

Thomas Mann. And he wrote her a letter, and that letter is published in the *Collected Letters of Thomas Mann,* of which I have a copy. Of course when I see a thing like that I look up my own name in the index and I find that there was a letter about me. This was the letter thanking her for *A Skeleton Key to Finnegans Wake.*

I had met him so I knew that he knew who it was. So I'm reading this letter to Mrs. Eugene Meyer, Agnes Meyer, about "thanking you for sending me Joseph Campbell's book. I appreciate it very much because I could not possibly, myself, read *Finnegans Wake.* But, reading this book, I am confirmed in my suspicion that I have had for some years, namely, that James Joyce was the greatest novelist of the twentieth century."

This from Thomas Mann! It's there in print. That's big on his part. That's real big.

BROWN: What was the genesis of *The Hero with a Thousand Faces?* It's my understanding that it was taking form all along, but the actual writing began while you were at Sarah Lawrence.

CAMPBELL: Robinson was publishing something of his own with Simon & Schuster at that time and they said, "Who's this guy, Campbell?" And Robinson said, "Oh, he's the greatest." So they said, "We'd like him to do a book on myth."

So we get a phone call from my friend Robinson, and he says, "Joe, Simon & Schuster's interested in a book on mythology and if you get up on your high horse and knock 'em down I'll never talk to you again." We arranged for a publisher's luncheon and they said, "Yes, we'd like a book on mythology."

"What kind of book do you want?"

"We want a sort of modern *Bullfinch.*"

I said, "I wouldn't touch it with a ten-foot pole."

They said, "What would you like to do?"

I said, "I'd like to write a book on how to read a myth."

"A sort of self-help book?"

"Yeah, okay."

"Write out a presentation and we'll talk about it."

So I went home, Jean was on tour at the time, and I spent one night just typing up a presentation, an idea for a book, and

Whether we listen with aloof amusement to the dreamlike mumbo jumbo of some red-eyed witch doctor of the Congo, or read with cultivated rapture thin translations from the sonnets of the mystic Lao-tse; now and again crack the hard shell of an argument of Aquinas, or catch suddenly the shining meaning of a bizarre Eskimo fairy tale: it will always be the one, shape-shifting yet marvelously constant story that we find, together with a challengingly persistent suggestion of more remaining to be experienced than will ever be known or told.

Joseph Campbell,
*The Hero with a
Thousand Faces*

My own first book,
The Hero with a
Thousand Faces, *I
wrote right after doing*
A Skeleton Key to
Finnegans Wake. *I
was just saturated
with Joyce in what he
calls the "mono-
myth," the one myth,
and the one cycle. I
took it from Joyce, I
took it from Mann,
took it from Ovid,
took it from Froben-
ius, and from Spen-
gler. There were a
whole group of influ-
ences, but Joyce was
certainly one of the
major ones.*

Joseph Campbell

brought it up to them, and by God I got a marvelous contract: $250 on signing the contract, $250 when the book's half finished, $250 on turning it in.

So I worked for four or five years.

What it was, was *The Hero with a Thousand Faces.* What it is, is my first lecture to my students at Sarah Lawrence College. And so I wrote the presentation, got the contract, started work on this thing. While I was writing the introduction I would read it to Jean, as I've read to Jean everything I do, and finally she said, "That's getting to be a pretty long introduction." I went back and checked it over and just divided it into chapters and I had the first half of *The Hero with a Thousand Faces.*

After five years or so I sent the manuscript up to Simon & Schuster. I didn't hear from them for months. I phoned up and they said, "Our staff has changed since we made the contract and we're not very much interested in the book. We will publish it, but if we publish a book that we don't care for it's not very good for the book."

I said, "Let me come up and talk about it and get the manu-script back." So I got the manuscript back and took it home.

I phoned my friend Robinson—you see, I was young and ignorant then and he was seasoned—and I said, "I've taken back the manuscript and I'm going to send them their money back."

He said, "You send them the money and I'll crucify you. You just—Those bunch of bastards! They have you work for five years and then they throw you out."

So then another publisher, Kurt Wolff of Pantheon, said he wanted to see the book. I gave it to him and he said, "Who'll read it?" He had the grace to tell me some years later he had also refused Spengler's *Decline of the West* when it was sent to him.

Then I sent it to the Bollingen Foundation and they said, "The Hero is a honey," and that's *The Hero with a Thousand Faces.* It's been out since 1949 and last year [1984], I'm pleased to say, it sold ten thousand copies. That's a pretty good record for a book that was rejected by two publishers. And that's how I got into writing.

AUDIENCE QUESTION: Is there a basic pattern, or list of tricks that you can talk about, since we have to at times be tricked to righteousness? It might be nice to know if there's some repeated patterns that you can identify.

CAMPBELL: There's a good list of them right here in the Jacob story, and if you want, the best thing that has been done on it is by Joseph Campbell [laughter] in *The Hero with a Thousand Faces*. That's the list. And I can tell you, when these things happen to you—and they happen every day—you can read them in terms of the myth, and you know where you are. That's the advantage of being mythologically indoctrinated. You know where you are when these stories take place. And they do. Read them not as something that happened out there but as something that is going to happen to you and is happening to you. That's translating this material into spiritual food.

COUSINEAU: When did you first encounter Heinrich Zimmer?

CAMPBELL: Oh, my marvelous friend, Heinrich Zimmer. I can't say enough about that man. His father was one of the major

---

I embarked on my next Bollingen assignment also at the proof stage, because the original editor had gone abroad. The book was Joseph Campbell's The Hero with a Thousand Faces, *whose galleys I eagerly began to read as I took them home on the subway. An encounter with psychoanalysis made me see significance in every image. (The encounter had been Freudian; some time passed before I realized that the Bollingen Foundation had something to do with C. G. Jung, not to mention Paul Mellon.) When I met Campbell over the Moorish coffee table, as we went through the index I had been commissioned to make, he seemed the easiest person* in the world to please, though the index, my first, ventured in directions far from index orthodoxy. The defection of the previous editor had thrown the publishing out and desolated Campbell, who would have welcomed almost any literate and willing substitute. My enthusiasm seemed to encourage him. When I commented on the aptness of the correspondences he traced between symbolic instances drawn from many mythologies and folklores on one hand, and individual dreams and fantasies on the other, he exclaimed, "Yes! You see, it all fits!"

William McGuire, *Bollingen*

Alchemical imagery is one way of telling this same story in terms of getting the gold out of the base matter. The gold is captured in base matter: prima-materia. And through the alchemical cooking and whatever else they're doing, pouring things in and so forth, the gold is brought out. And the gold is your own spiritual life that is clouded in the pure matter of your physical interests. The operation of the mythic meditation is to bring out, elicit, the gold of your spiritual character. You have to move into this slowly, and that's what ordeals are. The ordeal is a gradual clarification and purification of your life.

Joseph Campbell

Indologist Heinrich Zimmer (right) and Paul Mellon, cofounder (with his wife Mary) of the Bollingen Institute. Mary Mellon wrote of Zimmer, "When he is excited or has had a glass of Italian wine, he spouts vocabulary like a geyser or like James Joyce. To hear him is like watching Shankar dance. It is mythology orchestrated."

Celtic scholars of the generation before, and Heinrich was a *major* Indologist who left Germany when Hitler came in. He couldn't stand what it all stood for. He came over here with his family and then he couldn't get a job. There were very few oriental departments in the United States universities at that time. You know how the faculty who's there want to stay there and they don't want any competition. And so finally the ladies of the Jung Foundation got him a room in Columbia University up on the top of the library. And there he was giving his lectures.

I attended the first lecture and there were *four* people for Heinrich Zimmer's lecture. He lectured as though he were lecturing to an auditorium. He was a *magnificent* deliverer of a lecture. I remember him saying to me, "I'm glad you're getting this stuff." One of the other people present was the little librarian who was a person of the Jung Foundation who had arranged for him to be there. Another was a Polish female sculptor who, when she came into the room, emitted a perfume that would have sent all the gods to Amida's paradise.

That was it.

The next semester Zimmer had to have a larger room and the next semester after that he had an enormous room. And suddenly the man died. He caught a cold and was in pneumonia. Nobody diagnosed it correctly; it was absurd. Suddenly Zimmer was gone. I owe everything to Zimmer. His widow gave me his statue of a Bodhidharma from Japan when she asked me if I could edit his American lectures. So I spent, God, almost twelve years editing Zimmer's material and brought out four magnificent works out of his notes.

CAMPBELL: And in doing so I became associated with the Bollingen Foundation. The Bollingen people and that whole Jungian world. When I finally wrote my *Hero* it was refused by two

Zimmer continued quietly to bring promising Bollingen prospects to Mary's attention. One was Joseph Campbell, "a clever and intuitive Irishman, energetic, sound and full of life, who knows a lot about Indian stuff."

William McGuire, *Bollingen*

Joseph Campbell and Jean Erdman with R. F. C. Hull, the translator of Carl Jung's works, and his son Jeremy, on the Piazza, Ascona, Switzerland, 1954.

publishers and it was the Bollingen that picked it up. If they had not picked it up, I don't think anyone here would have heard of Joe Campbell. I'm sure of that. They kept me on course with grants while I edited Zimmer's work, and did work of my own editing the Eranos Lectures. It was that steadying along until somebody was interested in this kind of material until the day came when everybody was interested in it.

You know, it's a wonderful thing having been thrown out with no job, hunting my own way. I found things that other people were going to need when they lost their way too. The saying a friend of mine has given me for letting me know when you are in late middle age is: You've got to the top of the ladder and found it's against the wrong wall.

Well, I think I found what it is you need to break through that wall. This is one of the delights of my experience.

CAMPBELL: Zimmer, in relation to the Perilous Bed in the Sir Gawain story, asked what's the meaning of an adventure of this kind? He asked what is the masculine experience of the feminine temperament when it does not seem to have any rationale about it at all? Just be patient! Have patience, patience! And endure. And finally, he says, all the blessings of womanhood will be yours.

This is something I kept in mind on one occasion.

I was writing a great book on Indian art, a big two-volume work based on Zimmer's posthumous work *The Art of Indian Asia*. I had collected almost all the pictures necessary, but there were about four pictures that I couldn't find. But I knew they would be in the file of the Indian [art historian] Ananda K. Coomaraswamy, who had died a couple of years before.

So I phoned his widow and said, "I wonder if I can come up and look through the doctor's file and see if I can get a couple of pictures?"

"Come on up," she said. So up I went one hot summer day in Boston, in Cambridge. I was admitted to the library where the pictures were. There was a huge mass of pictures but I thought it wouldn't have taken more than an hour or so to go through them all and find the four that I knew were there. And they were there.

So I sit down and I start going through the pictures and she comes in about half an hour and she says, "Oh, it's kind of hot. Wouldn't you like a little orange juice or something like that?" I said, "Okay." So she sat down and a conversation developed that went on for about an hour and a half, and then she left me to go on with the pictures. I was just getting into it again when she came in and said, "You know I think it's about dinner time." So I said, "All right."

We had dinner and that brought us on into the evening and I'm going on, and she said, "Joe, it will be perfectly all right, you can spend the night here and just sleep on the couch there. It'll be perfectly okay." For three days this went on!

And I just said to myself the whole time, Here's the Perilous Bed and I'm going to stick it out! The superintendent thought we were having an affair and, well, anyhow, I got the pictures.

So this is a little example of how valuable mythological information is in life situations.

BROWN: Can you give us a picture of what it would have been like to be Joe Campbell working on all these manuscripts during those years?

CAMPBELL: I was teaching at the time, and the Sarah Lawrence teaching was a full day. It wasn't just a class and you're off. The full-time jobs were four full days a week.

When I began writing I took a three-quarter schedule and taught for three days a week, and then I had four days for my writing. That was the balance. Then of course in the summer holidays I had nothing but the writing. In the years from the time we'd published *A Skeleton Key to Finnegans Wake* in 1944 until I retired from Sarah Lawrence, I published fifteen mighty volumes, big volumes. You can get a lot of work done if you just stay with it and are excited and it's play instead of work. I'm rather pleased with that record, actually.

Just as anyone who listens to the muse will hear, you can write out of your own intention or out of inspiration. There is such a thing. It comes up and talks. And those who have heard deeply the rhythms and hymns of the gods, the words of the gods, can recite those hymns in such a way that the gods will be attracted.

Joseph Campbell, 1983

Maud Oakes in Guatemala, 1946.

The writing went on. I took the job of editing Zimmer and at the same time my Swami friend, Swami Nikhilananda, asked me to help him with the translation from Bengali of *The Gospel of Sri Ramakrishna.* A great big book here on my shelf somewhere. So I was working day and night.

I would write one book in the morning, one in the afternoon, and one in the evening. Actually there were three things going at a time there sometimes.

The first book that the Bollingen Foundation brought out was a study of a Navajo war ceremonial. Zimmer had recommended that I should write the introduction and commentary and edit the book. So that was another of my jobs. It was a real season of writing, and very, very exciting, and wonderful, wonderful material.

And whether it was *Finnegans Wake* or the Navajo material, or the Hindu material or Heinrich Zimmer's, it was all the same material. That was when I realized—and nobody can tell me anything differently—that there's one mythology in the world. It has been inflected in various cultures in terms of their historical and social circumstances and needs and particular local ethic systems, but it's *one mythology*.

CAMPBELL: Historians and ethnologists are interested in the differences of mythologies and religious systems of the world, and one can study the mythologies and philosophies of the world with an accent on these differences. On the other hand the problem emerges of Bastian's elementary ideas. Why are they everywhere? This is a psychological problem, and it's a problem that separates us in our discussion of the comparative forms from the whole research having to do with differences.

What happened in the West following the period of Aristotle particularly was a gradual attack on mythological ideas, so that criticism in the West tended to separate itself from the elementary ideas. However, there is also an undercurrent throughout Western thinking. It's associated with Gnosticism, alchemy, and many of the discredited manners of thought that carries on this interest in what might be called the *perennial*.

I'm thinking of the Perennial Philosophy as it has been expounded particularly by Ananda K. Coomaraswamy, and picked up, I think it was during the 1940s, by Aldous Huxley in that work of his, *The Perennial Philosophy*. I'm thinking of this as the translation into verbal discourse of the implications of the mythic images. And that's why the same ideas can be found in the mystical philosophies throughout the world. The continuities that we can recognize in myth come over into philosophy. And the basic idea of the philosophy is that deities are symbolic personifications of the very images that are of yourself. And these energies that are of yourself are the energies of the universe. And so the god is out there and the god is in here. The kingdom of heaven is within you, yes, but it's also everywhere.

The Book of Lindisfarne. Carpet Page with Scattered Panels, *late seventh century.*

Bhutan mandala wall painting, from the Drukpa Kagyupa Buddhist sect. Tashicho Dzong, legislative meeting hall of the Bhutanese government.

When you contemplate the mandala you are harmonized inside; the religious symbols are harmonizing powers. They help. That's the whole sense of mythology: to help you harmonize your individual life with the life of society.

Joseph Campbell

Now just as the idea of deity in these perennial traditions is greatly different from our idea of deity, so does the idea of consciousness differ. In speaking of deities in the terms that are proper to these mythologically grounded traditions, I say that the deity is a personification of the energy. It's a personification of an energy that informs life. All life, your life, the world's life. And the nature of the personification will be determined by historical circumstances. The personification is folk; the energy is human. And so deities proceed from the energies. And they are the messengers and vehicles, so to say, of the energies.

And there's that wonderful passage in the *Chandogya Upanishad.* "Worship this god, worship that god, one god after another, those who follow this law do not know." Because the source of the gods is in your own heart. Follow the footsteps to that center and know that you are that which the gods are born on.

Dream, vision, god. The gods of heaven and hell are what might be called the cosmic aspect of the dream. And the dream is the personal aspect of the myth. Dream and myth are of the same order. And you and your god are one. This is you and your dream god. And your god isn't my god. So don't try to push it on me. Everyone has his own deity and consciousness.

And this is what is known as the Perennial Philosophy.

Now myth comes in the same zone as dream, and this is the zone of what I would call the Wisdom Body. When you go to sleep, it's the body that's talking. And what it is moved by are energies that it does not control. These are the energies that control the body. They come in from the great biological ground, whatever it may be, protoplasm. They are there. They are energies and they are matters of consciousness. But we also have in this body, this affair up here, the head, and it has a system of thinking of its own. And that's a whole manner of consciousness that stems from the head-set, and it is different in its knowledge from that of the body.

When a baby is born it knows just what to do with its mother's body. It is ready for the environment into which it is put. It doesn't have to be instructed. These things happen, and this is the work of the Wisdom Body. That same wisdom brought the little thing into form in its mother's body. It was shaped by these energies that lie in us, and of which we are the carnal manifestation.

This wisdom of the dream, wisdom of the vision, is the wisdom then of the Perennial Philosophy.

So that's what came of that. I'm writing all the time now. The real sorrow is that it's cut down on my reading time. There's still a lot to learn.

BROWN: Over the course of your long career, Joe, what has been the most satisfying aspect of your work?

CAMPBELL: For me one of the most exciting and really moving things about mythology is this universality of certain things. It becomes particularly striking when you turn, let's say, from some very simple people like pygmies of the Congo and then go to another very simple people, like the Yagan or Ono or Tierra del Fuego, and find the same motifs coming along there. It's not so surprising when you are in the field, for example, of any of the great high culture systems, where we know that there has been great trade and diffusion of techniques and everything else from one place to another.

But this other matter—you just wonder whether people have carried from primordial times, you know from the very beginning, motifs of this kind.

One that I find most recurrent is of the men's secret society, men's secret rites, which usually involve some kind of bull-roarer, a noise-making machine, a horn of some kind. There's a *whoo-hoo-hoo!* And this is kept hidden in the woods. Women aren't supposed to know anything about it. Then the men bring it out and they're going to have some ceremony, and the women are supposed to run away and hide and not see it. In some of the cases the men become very brutal to any woman who does see it. This we find among the pygmies of the Congo, and we find it again down in the rain forests of Brazil. The same kinds of themes occur in Tierra del Fuego.

One explanation that I've recently heard from some people that have been working in the Brazilian rain forest is that the idea of magic power which adheres in the horns is originally associated with women. We see that with the goddess Circe in the *Odyssey*, who had the magic power, and the man just had the physical power. The little legend that one finds in three or four of these places, or perhaps all of them, is of the men having stolen from the women the knowledge of the power of magic and they are now keeping it from the women. Now we don't often hear from the women's side because the male anthropologists don't get in touch with their actual women's thinking. But there is a couple who were studying the Barasana people in Brazil, a man and his wife, and she studied with the women. What I got from her learning was that the women are actually protecting their power against contamination by the men's power when they go and hide. The idea is that of women having power, the power in their body, the magic of their body, and men having to gain power.

Now the sign of the women's power is menstruation. It is there that the woman is taken over by a power, namely the power of nature, biology. And the men are treated in their initiations brutally so that they too will open up. The men's instruments are equivalent to the women's menstruation. That is to say, something transcendent of the intentions of the individual is moving in. It's at that field of the overtaking of the individual by mythic energy— or a biological energy, any kind of energy—but at the overtaking is the point where ritual comes in and mythic forms.

KENNARD: How do you explain the similarity of image and ritual in so many cultures? Are we all one humankind, really?

HIGHWATER: The world is full of biological inequities, but I do think that there are things that make for a kind of spiritual unity. But I think the notion has overtaken us to such a degree that we are beginning to confuse conformity and equality. That's a dreadful mistake, I think, another form of Western imperialism. I certainly agree with Campbell that we all have a touch of that *orenda,* that flame, within us, that is all the same fire. But what interests me is the ways in which that fire, those different images, is cast upon the world in which we live.

GUILLEMEN: With all we know of the structure of the brain, regardless of where the neurophysiologist cuts, there is no evidence that the fundamental wiring of the brain is different, whether you were born as a Hottentot, Melanesian, or Caucasian from one place or another. The wiring of the brain is absolutely the same.

HIGHWATER: I think there's no question that the murals of the Dreamtime people of Australia and those of Altamira have absolutely nothing in common. The appearance is superficial not fundamental. When we're looking at early art we're looking at it superficially not fundamentally. Because I think the differences begin to occur at a very early time between cultures.

CAMPBELL: Well, there *are* certain basic biological expe- riences that people have to undergo. For instance, in most culture circumstances, the first object, first subject, after an individual is born, is the mother's body. And the whole system of references of the female body is pretty consistent throughout the mythologies of the world.

And you have culture transformations. For instance, you have a people who are hunting and gathering people and then come people who are planting. The position of the female in relation to the productivity of the earth will change and the mythology will change and the imaging will change, but there is that basic thing.

Particularly in the initiation of young boys, one of the problems is to disengage the boy's libido from the mother's body. This is undertaken in the boy's initiation rites by various means in various cultures, but it's the same problem that all are facing. In the first twelve years of a human being's life he or she is in a position of dependency on authority. Then the whole psychology is that of respect for authority, expectation of approval, disapproval, all that kind of thing. One of the functions of the rituals again is to kill that infantile ego. Then you have a death-rebirth motif. So the individual falls into the ground of his own being and comes out an adult, a responsible adult, who's undergone certain transformations.

The way the body is mutilated will change from one people to another, but the mutilation of the body goes on. Then you have another situation where the person is being disengaged from the society and moving into old age. There is another constant situation that the human being has to face. These represent constants. It's not always easy to recognize that these constants are modified in their manifestation, what I called, when I was quoting Adolf Bastian, the difference between the elementary idea—the universal motif or form—and its local manifestation.

The local manifestation will change enormously when you move, let's say, from an Arctic people to a people in the jungle, or from a very simple gathering tribe to the Persian Empire. The imagery is going to change a lot. And much of the conflict that you recognize between two tribes in the Andes that are very close together is the result of background experiences they brought in from elsewhere. They're living close together, but the same culture form meets them and then they transform it in their own utilization.

AUDIENCE QUESTION: I'm curious about the title of your book *Myths to Live By*. What myths can we live by today, and what realm of life can myth really apply to us on a workable, everyday level? And how can myths be used to manipulate other people's lives—or your own life—for better or for worse? I think I've missed the point somewhere.

CAMPBELL: Learning how to manipulate people by myth is something I am not very much interested in.

But the person in most recent times who was most successful in this was Hitler. He also knew how to handle a ritual. I have a couple of Dutch friends who were in concentration camps, and when Hitler was to give a speech in the neighborhood where their place was, they were brought out and had to stand at attention while he gave his speech. And one of them told me that he had all he could do to keep his right hand from going up and saying, "Heil!"

The power of a well-constructed ritual to move you from some centers that are beyond those of your personal, intentional control is terrific. We've lost all sense of that. We just don't know anything about that. But here comes a man with a genius for that kind of thing and look what happens.

With respect to yourself, *Myths to Live By* was based on a series of twenty-five or so lectures I gave over the course of twenty-five years [1958–1971] at the Cooper Union Forum in New York City. They were dealing with subjects that had been proposed to me by Johnson Fairchild, the man directing that series. They were all subjects that did have relevance to people's lives at that time. That was a long time ago. I have forgotten even what the chapters of the book are. But I can remember that there was the problem of mythology in relation to love, mythology in relation to war, mythology in relation to the transformations of puberty, and all that kind of thing. There is plenty of mythological material round about.

We're living in a period that I regard as a kind of period of the terminal moraine of mythology. It's as though a lot of mythological rubbish is all around. Mythologies that built civilizations and are no longer working in that way are just in rubble all around us.

So an individual who puts himself to the task of activating his imaginative life— the life that springs from inside, not from response to outside information and commands—that person can find stimulation in this wonderful literature that is pouring into the libraries. Now the world is full of these wonderful things again.

So there is no rule. An individual has to find what electrifies and enlivens his own heart, and wakes him.

AUDIENCE QUESTION: Then you should actually try and follow the poetic or spiritual feelings that you feel welling up within yourself?

CAMPBELL: I think that the world of the arts and literature, what we call the liberal arts, is the world in which to find all this. One has to pursue something like that.

Now what a religion does, in an orthodox church for one hour or so a week, is that one goes and puts oneself in an environment that is supposed to awake that system again. Then you go out and do the chores, and you go back to church again, or you're supposed to say your prayers in the morning and evening, which means putting yourself in touching with those centers. But if the religion hasn't put you in touch with those centers, it's somebody else's religion, really, and well, then you're cut off, and that's one of our problems.

BROWN: Recently on the talk show circuit you had an ordeal while you were launching *The Way of Animal Powers*.

CAMPBELL: You mean the metaphor story.

BROWN: Yes, that was a fascinating vignette that sounded as if it helped to inspire subsequent work.

CAMPBELL: Sure, I'd love to tell that story. A simple realization came to me last year with respect to this whole problem of the function and relevance of myth to life.

When *The Way of Animal Powers* was published the publisher sent me on a publicity tour. It's the worst kind of tour to go on because you're talking with people who don't know anything about the subject that you've devoted the book to. And the first question they would ask, normally, is "What is a myth?"

Finally I had thought of the definition that I thought would hold them. Of course, I knew that nobody knew what it was anyhow, but it would *sound* like a definition.

And so toward the end of this tour I came to—I won't say what city it was in or who it was—but it was a talk show, one-half hour, live, on radio. And I walked into the room, and the red light is not on, so I can have a little conversation. And the first thing this young man sitting across the table says to me is, "I'm tough," he says. "I'll put it right to you, no fooling." He says, "I've studied law."

So, all right, that's okay with me. Then the red light goes on and he starts out with this popular idea. He says, "Myth is a lie. A myth is a lie, isn't it?"

I said, "No, you must talk about a mythology, a whole mythology by which people live. A mythology is an organization of symbolic narratives and images that are metaphorical of the possibilities of human experience and fulfillment in a given society at a given time."

Of course, that was out the window already.

"It's a lie."

"It's a metaphor."

"It's a lie."

About five minutes to go, I realized, this young man does not know what a metaphor is. So I felt I could be tough too, you know. I've got him in a hammerlock, you might say, and he's not going to get out.

I said, "No, I'm telling you that myths are metaphors. Give me an example of a metaphor."

"You give *me* an example of a metaphor," he says.

I taught school for thirty-eight years so I said, "No, I'm asking the questions this time. Give me an example of a metaphor."

Well, the poor man fell apart. I mean, I felt ashamed. You don't do things like this to people.

Nietzsche has a saying in, I think it's *Thus Spake Zarathustra,* or *The Will to Power,* about the pale criminal, the one who has the courage of the knife but not of the blood. And now I had no courage to face what I had done to this young man on his show, live to his public. The show was in his name.

He fell apart and he said, "I don't know what to do. Wait a minute." Then he comes up from the floor (we now have about a minute and a half or two minutes to go) and says, "I'll try."

He says, "So and so runs very fast. People say he runs like a deer."

I said, "That's not the metaphor." Tick, tick, tick goes the clock. The metaphor is: So and so *is* a deer."

"That's a lie!" he said.

"That's a metaphor!" I said.

That's the end of the show.

And that got into me. It is *so* simple.

People say they believe in God. God is a metaphor for a mystery that absolutely transcends all human categories of thought. Even the categories of being and nonbeing. Those are categories of thought. I mean it's as simple as that. It depends on how much you want to think about it. Whether it's putting you in touch with the mystery that is the ground of your own being. If it isn't, well, it's a lie.

So half the people in the world are religious people who think that their metaphors are facts. Those are what we call theists. The other half are people who know that the metaphors are not facts and so they're lies. Those are the atheists.

CAMPBELL: I had a fantastic experience with Martin Buber. He was lecturing in New York to a group of about this size, a series of three Wednesday evenings. He was an eloquent man. The first evening he was talking about God and it dawned on me I didn't know what he was talking about. Was he talking about the mystery that now lies behind the galaxies and the subatomic particles? Or was he talking about one or another period in the development of Yahweh in the Old Testament? Or was he talking about someone with whom he was having a personal conversation?

He stopped at one moment and said, "It pains me to speak of God in the third person." (When I told this to Gershom Scholem he said, "Sometimes he goes too far.")

So I'm sitting there and I raised my hand and he very politely said, "What is it?" And I said, "There's a word being used here this evening that I'm not understanding."

And he said, "What is that word?" And I said, "God."

"You don't understand what God means?"

"I don't understand what *you* mean by God. You tell us God

has hidden his face. I've just come from India where people are experiencing God's face all the time."

It was as though I'd hit him with a brick.

He said, "Do you mean to compare?" That's monotheism. We've got it. No one else has it.

And then the next week, this wonderful little man, he's marvelous, he's saying very nasty things about the Phoenicians because they're killing their eldest sons for Moloch. Sacrificing their eldest sons to Moloch: terrible thing to do. Fifteen minutes later he gets around to Abraham about to sacrifice Isaac—and now this is the greatest act anybody in the world had ever given himself to. This is the key act indicating what a wonderful man Abraham was.

And so I couldn't help it. I raised my hand again and I said, "Dr. Buber, how does one distinguish between the divine and a diabolical invitation?"

He said, "What do you mean by that?"

I said, "Fifteen minutes ago you were excoriating the Phoenicians for sacrificing their eldest sons to a deity. Now you're praising Abraham above all living for having to do the same thing."

Now comes the answer.

"We"—capital W—"believe that God"—capital G—"spoke to Abraham." That's his answer. So where are you? This is the problem in dealing with mythology in a monotheistic community. It's not myth; it's fact. This is the concretization of a symbol and it's losing the message in the symbol. You've lost the message. All you've got is a symbol.

And so everybody who says, "I and the Father are one," or as the Moslem mystic Hallaj said, "I and my beloved are one," gets crucified. I think it was Hallaj who said the function in the orthodox community is to give the mystic his desire: namely union with his God. Kill him, he's joined then. *Liebestod,* the love death. You're united with the beloved.

This is a tremendous subject and it's played a loud tune through the centuries. There are a number of people who have burned to death for celebrating their identity with the divine.

Then you cross Suez into the Orient and the whole goal of religion is to realize that you are one with that which you seek to know. You are it. So there you have the difference between religions of identification and religions of relationship. Identification with the divine. Relationship with the divine.

Our highest god is our highest obstruction. It represents the consummation of the highest thoughts and feelings that you can have. Go past that. Meister Eckhardt says, "The ultimate leave-taking is the leave-taking of god for God." That is to say, the folk-god, for God, that is to say, the elementary idea.

Joseph Campbell

CAMPBELL: A man spoke to me the other day, a very intelligent man, a man who was a man of considerable dignity in our literary world, an agnostic. He asked, "Are you possibly an agnostic?"

I said, "I *know* too much to be an agnostic."

What I know is that all of these images are metaphors. And they're metaphors for what? A metaphor has a connotation and the mythic metaphors have connotations of the spiritual powers within the individual. And when one is preaching religion, if you're not preaching the connotation of the metaphor, you're preaching pseudo-history or sociology or something of that kind. So there's very little true religion in the world.

Well, what could I do? I could only write another book. So I interrupted the work on my big *Historical Atlas of World Mythology* to write another book which should come out some day, hopefully soon.

BROWN: Is that how *The Inner Reaches of Outer Space* came about?

CAMPBELL: You know when you write a book you get it off your chest and you somehow forget what's in it. I'm not sure I can tell you. Very well, what it is that I have put into that book has to do with describing how the metaphors are used. I have found, or had known, a Navajo sand painting that in its symbology duplicated almost point for point the symbology of the Hindu Kundalini yoga.

Now these come from two totally different parts of the world; there cannot have been any diffusion or any influence whatsoever. They represent a symbology of the psychology of the human system in symbolic terms. The Navajo understand it symbolically and they tell you how to participate in it and how the symbols actually work upon you.

The first big chapter deals with the inner reaches of outer space. I use the moon shots and all that as my key. You get a picture of the cosmos as we now have it with hundreds of thousands of galaxies and each galaxy as big as the Milky Way. Hundreds of light years of distances. Then you come to the myth of the Ascension of Jesus to heaven, and of the Assumption of the Virgin. Now either you throw it out and say it's a lie or you say it's symbolic of something. And what it is symbolic of is this flight to inner space. And it's rendered as outward but you're going to the place from where life came, your own deep ground of being. So I deal with the interpretation of mythic images in that sense.

The introduction of the book, which I call "Myth and the Body," picks up and makes fundamental my basic feeling that myth is a function of biology. It speaks of the energies that move the consciousness. They're all determined by the organs of the body. They do not all have the same intentions so there are conflicts and dissonances. But myth has to do with the harmonization of one's consciousness in relation to the ground of being in nature, in the body, which is itself a manifestation of a *mystery*.

It's a big subject. As you turn to it and touch any aspect of it, it just opens out and offers new mysteries—provided you follow it in terms of connotations instead of simply denotations. The denotations just don't work, that's all. And I think religious people know that they don't work and that's why they're so damned deliberate and dogmatic about you having to believe what I believe because if you don't then perhaps I'm wrong. They just don't know how to read the symbols.

This is the whole thing in my own life in relating to the Catholic religion, which I've been brought up in. All the meditations have to do with something that happened two thousand years ago somewhere else to somebody else. Unless those can be read as metaphorical of what ought to happen to me, that I ought to die and resurrect, die to my ego and resurrect to my divinity, it doesn't work.

Then the last chapter, the one I regard as the culminating one in the book was inspired by a remark from my wife, Jean. One day when we were talking about things like this she said, "The way of the mystic and the way of the artist are very much alike, except that the mystic doesn't have the craft." I use that as the key here for paralleling the two ways of the mystical life and the artist's life. The artist with a craft remains in touch with the world; the mystic can spin off and lose touch and frequently does. And so it seems to be that the art is the higher form. I thought Jean put her finger right on it.

Mythology is an organization of symbolic images and narratives metaphorical of the possibilities and fulfillment in a given culture in a given time. Mythology is a metaphor. God, angels, purgatory, these are metaphors.

Joseph Campbell, interviewed in the *New York Times*, February 1985

If the hero in his triumph wins the blessing of the goddess or the god and is then explicitly commissioned to return to the world with some elixir for the restoration of society, the final stage of his adventure is supported by all the powers of his supernatural patron. On the other hand, if the trophy has been attained against the opposition of its guardian, or if the hero's wish to return to the world has been resented by the gods or demons, then the last stage of the mythological round becomes a lively often comical pursuit. This flight may be complicated by marvels of magical obstruction and evasion.

Joseph Campbell,
*The Hero with a
Thousand Faces*

Campbell enjoying a meal at Ten Ri Kyo, Japan, in the summer of 1956.

6

The Magic Flight

For two years in the mid-1950s Joseph Campbell taught courses in Oriental philosophy at the State Department in Washington, D.C. The strong reception he received from the diplomats he was helping prepare for overseas assignments gave him his first clue that he had something vital to teach people other than students and scholars.

His next clue came in 1968 when Michael Murphy invited him to teach at Esalen Institute in Big Sur, California. Over the next nineteen years Campbell co-taught classes there with writer Sam Keen, Tai Chi master Chungliang Al Huang, psychologist John Weir Perry, and many others, constantly widening the scope of his approach to mythology.

Campbell resumed his travels after retiring from Sarah Lawrence as Professor Emeritus in 1972. Over the next years he journeyed to Iceland and Turkey, Egypt and Greece, and made a long tour through Southeast Asia.

The fourth and final volume of his twenty-year project, the four-volume *The Masks of God,* was published in 1968. It was a study of the historical development of mythology and the religious differences of humankind, designed to complement *The Hero with a Thousand Faces'* portrait of the intriguing correspondences. It was followed four years later by *Myths to Live By,* a collection of his lectures at the Cooper Union Forum in New York; and in the same year he published *The Portable Jung.* In 1974, he published *The Mythic Image,* the capstone book of the Bollingen series.

BROWN: You know, Joe, I've driven up and down this Northern California coast with you and had a tremendous time reminiscing as we came down to Carmel, to the nooks and crannies that you had been in as a young man. But I've no idea how you got here to Esalen originally.

CAMPBELL: I guess it was about sixteen or seventeen years ago (1968). Alan Watts suggested to Mike Murphy that he ask me to come down here. I think that was about the time that Esalen was beginning.

I was flying to Milwaukee and there was an hour break in San Francisco between my flights. Mike came up there at that time, together with Richard Price, and asked me if I would come down here. All I did was lecture on mythology—right here in this room. This was about all there was at that time. Apparently people liked what I was doing so I kept coming back.

But a big advance, a big change came along when Sam Keen came to visit me one time in New York and we decided we'd do something here together. We had a theory. Sam was very good at finding out where people are when they're stuck, when they're in trouble. I don't think you have to go through a deep psycho-analysis for that. There's just some kind of idea that's blocking you. Remove the idea—the person is released.

That's a good mythological principle. In India demons are simply obstructors of consciousness, those things that block con-sciousness. We had an idea that Sam would be able, by interviewing people and in dialogue with them, to find where they were stuck. And that I would be able to find and recognize the mythological analogue to their problem.

It was a nice theory and nobody was going to get hurt and it actually worked. We had three or four events that were really spectacular. And that was the first time that I really came to under-stand the relationship of my scholarship, which was simply about mythology, to actual psychological problems.

And it's been going fine ever since.

BROWN: It sure has.

BROWN: As a psychiatrist I'm particularly curious about your work with John Perry. How did you first meet him?

CAMPBELL: That was a marvelous meeting. Mike wrote to me one time and said he'd like me to come out and talk with John Perry, a psychiatrist in San Francisco, about schizophrenia. I said, I don't know anything about schizophrenia. He said, Well, he'd like to have me give a lecture anyhow. I said, Well, how would James Joyce be? And he said, That would be just fine.

So I agreed to come out and talk with John Perry. And Perry sent me some of his monographs, his articles, on the symbolism of schizophrenia. The sequence with which these images emerge in a patient's mind, who's in a deep schizoid crack-up. And it matched *The Hero with a Thousand Faces,* just like that, step by step.

And so there again I came to understand the relationship with something that had been simply a scholarly interest of mine in mythology to actual life problems.

And it's been pretty exciting ever since.

BROWN: That's really how I got acquainted with you. In the middle of the 1970s I read a book of yours, *Primitive Mythology* from *The Masks of God,* and it sounded like what my patients in psychoanalysis were telling me.

CAMPBELL: Yes. That's marvelous. Actually I guess the big crisis in my popular career came in the 1960s when people were taking LSD and my book *The Hero with a Thousand Faces* became a kind of triptych or mythological map for the hippies.

For more than twenty years, Joseph breathed new life into Esalen. Seminar participants, staff, and work scholars alike came away from his seminars like people from revival meetings, inspired by Galahad, Kali, or Hermes, rather than visions of hellfire. No one brought their audiences to their feet like he did. No one in Esalen's history joined enthusiasm, scholarship, and wisdom so fully.

Michael Murphy

Campbell lecturing animatedly to an audience of diplomats at the Foreign Service Institute in Washington, D.C., 1957.

KENNARD: Do you remember any people who came up after your lectures and asked you something which made you say to yourself, "Oh, my God, I have thirty seconds to tell them the true meaning of life?"

CAMPBELL: [Laughing] No, no, I haven't had that problem.

KENNARD: Do you remember ever going up to somebody and actually asking them?

CAMPBELL: No, I don't ask questions like that. I'm usually asked [laughter]. One of the worst things, though, is after having given a lecture and taking questions from the audience, somebody comes up to you afterwards with his whole soul in this thing. That's the hardest thing to handle. Then others are writing PhD theses and they want specific book references; things like that. Those are the only real annoyances on this job.

TARNAS: So, PhDs and soul searchers! What are some of the PhDs that people are writing? Serious or straight stuff?

CAMPBELL: Well, you'd be amazed at what people are getting PhDs for writing! [laughter] I knew a chap who was doing a thesis on the use of semicolons by Milton in his sonnets.

KENNARD: And he asked you about that?

CAMPBELL: No, he told me about that. It's a funny business, actually.

KENNARD: Joe, what are some of the more interesting questions that you've heard after your lectures? Did any of the questions people asked you just out of the blue at the end of your lectures ever introduce you to something new?

CAMPBELL: The most interesting question I ever got was when I was lecturing here at Esalen in the [Abraham] Maslow Room in 1967. Somebody asked, "What about the symbolism of the Waite deck of Tarot cards?"

Well, I hadn't thought about it. I'd seen Tarot packs and I can remember my old master, Heinrich Zimmer, giving lectures on cards, and I remembered a couple of things he'd said. So I said, "Well, give me a Tarot pack and let me take it back to my room and I'll say in the morning what I found."

That was a very exciting thing. I had the luck to recognize a couple of sequences there. There is one for the Four Ages of Man, Youth, Maturity, Age, and what Dante calls Senility. He also calls it decrepitude. Dante discusses this at length in his *Convivio*.

Then above that I saw another sequence where there was a woman pouring water or something from a blue vessel into a red one and this was called Temperance. And the next one was The Devil, Hell. And the next was a thunderbolt hitting a tower, the Tower of Destruction, which is the traditional sign for purgatory, you know, the tower of evil being smashed by the thunderbolt of God's destruction of all of your tight ego system relationships.

And the fourth one was the beginning of life, Paradise, the two red vessels being poured out to the world below. Dante's *La Vita Nuova,* the New Life pouring from the physical into the spiritual vessel.

Put those four here, put the other four here, and the whole thing fell out into a beautiful system, interpreting the transformation of the psychological relationships through not only the four stages of a lifetime, but also in the shift of accent from purely earthly to high spiritual ideas.

The four suits are interesting because this is a medieval pack. The first evidence of the Tarot we have is from about 1392,

The Marseilles Tarot deck. After his examination of the Waite deck at Esalen Institute, Campbell's imagination was seized by the Marseilles deck, with its rich vein of medieval imagery. Reprinted from Joseph Campbell and Richard Roberts, *Tarot Revelations,* Vernal Equinox Press © 1979, 1987, Richard Roberts.

a pack that was made for King Charles I of France. This was shortly after Dante's death, but we are in the same field as Dante. It's also medieval. The four suits are swords, which are the aristocrats, the nobility; cups, which are the clergy of the Catholic mass; coins, which are the moneyed estate; and batons or staves, which are of the peasants. Those were the four castes of medieval tradition.

Now there are two stages in a lifetime. One is the stage of entering life, which reaches a climax around thirty-five or forty, and the second is a stage of leaving life. And the four suits have to do with entering life in one or another of your occupations, whatever your task might be. And then the big set at the end, the Honors Suit, the Major Arcana, has to do with the mystical path. It worked out just like that; it was right in front of my face. It was a fascinating experience, the most interesting I have had here.

KENNARD: What interests me here is that somebody came up to you and first turned you on to the Tarot just by a question. You explained the Honors Suit and you explained that it told you where you were in life and so on. So what? Why was that such a turn-on when somebody turned you on to this and you saw where you were in life? Does that affect us now? Why did you get a sudden flash and say to yourself, Oh, yes?

CAMPBELL: It's a pack of cards that's used in fortune telling, you know, in reading character and so forth. And as it straightened itself out as I saw it there, what it represented was a program for life that derived from European medieval consciousness. And actually carried into symbolic form many of the implications of Dante's philosophy. That was the one that really hit me.

Dante died in 1321, and the earliest evidence we have of cards of this kind come from sermons around that date, against the cards, and you wonder, Why against cards? You find out why when you look this thing over. It's basically agnostic philosophy that's there. To make the point, there's a notion in orthodox Christianity that the end of the world is coming. This is a mythological symbol, the end of the world, interpreted in terms of the historical event; for the orthodox Christian, it's got to be a historical event. But mythological symbols do not talk about historical events; they talk about spiritual events. The end of the world is a spiritual event, not a historical one.

Now there's a gospel that's known now as the Fifth Gospel, the Gospel According to Thomas. It was dug up in the Egyptian desert about 1945. Toward the close of that gospel the disciples asked, "Master, when will the Kingdom come?" And the answer Jesus gives there is in great contrast to what you get in Mark 13, where the King was going to come with clouds and all this kind of thing, and wars and everything else. Here Jesus says, "The Kingdom will not come by expectation. They will not say, See here, see there. The Kingdom of the Father is spread upon the earth and men do not see it."

That's what's known as the Hermetic Gnosticism—*bodhi*, in Sanskrit. Change the perspective of your eyes, and you see the whole world before you now is radiant. Do you see?

In this Tarot that's the doctrine that comes out. The last figure, called the World, is the dancing female figure of the alchemists in a mandorla. In the four corners of the cards are the Apostles, the signs of the Apostles, Matthew, Mark, Luke, and John. In other words the coming is right here, now, in the world, and not at all something to wait for, not for a historical experience.

That's what hit me.

ARRIEN: Do you believe in the Tarot? You can read the cards. But do you believe what you read when you use them?

CAMPBELL: No, I don't do anything like that. I just see. I can show you how it works and what a beautiful thing it is.

ARRIEN: But you don't believe that it could tell you anything?

CAMPBELL: It gives you a program for life, what the concerns are in the different stages of life and what the spiritually lower and spiritually higher attitudes are toward the experiences of life at different stages. It's a wonderful thing.

ARRIEN: Do you feel that you can see the Kingdom here?

CAMPBELL: Sure you can. There was an old preacher back in the Depression, the deep Depression, Father Divine. He used to give wonderful sermons, you know, and then he'd say, "Can't you see the mystery, ain't you glad?" And everybody would say, "Yes, Lord!"

Well, *can't* you?

ARRIEN: Yes! Yes! Marvelous . . .

CAMPBELL: Yes. It's just that you're not taught that this is it. That's the big problem. I don't think there's malice behind it; it's just that this is not an idea that is in our culture history. It's been screened out for one reason or another and unless you get it, you don't, of yourself, come to the realization. But just get a little clue, and this Tarot is one . . . and then there's nothing difficult about it.

ARRIEN: You've also said that the Tarot was accessible. Was that a threat to the church?

CAMPBELL: I don't know about that. I don't know what the actual situation was. There are just these few clues, as far as I know, from the fourteenth century to let you know that something was coming in. Another thing about this is that a lot of people have the idea it comes from Egypt. It's sheerly medieval, the symbolism is medieval; it's the European idea.

BROWN: Does this inability to see the Kingdom here and now have something to do with our disastrous relationship to nature?

CAMPBELL: Let's see. There's a trend in our whole religious tradition toward ethical rather than metaphysical insights, you know, good and evil and all that kind of thing. In our tradition one doesn't trust nature, because nature has *fallen*. There is the god of creation and then a fall so that life is mixed of good and evil. You can't lean on nature; you're always correcting it; you're always making an ethical standpoint, good against evil, you know?

Think of the contrast with Taoism, where you yield to nature and give yourself to nature. Or primitive cultures where people rest well in nature.

And it makes for a total transformation of consciousness to realize nature is good. And this is what I felt and learned in Japan. There is a saying in the Shinto religion, "The processes of nature cannot be evil."

And then you turn to Heraclitus and Heraclitus says to God, "All things are good and right and just, but for some men some things are right and some are not right." And so: metaphysics.

ARRIEN: How did you learn this? What happened that showed you?

CAMPBELL: I was in Japan studying Buddhism and Shinto [1954 to 1955], and these things come out in the text. I remember

Campbell at the Giza pyramids, 1976.

Worship, worship, worship. People coming from all over India, a great pilgrimage place. The whole idea of pilgrimage here is translated into a literal, physical act, the pilgrimage of moving into the center of your own heart. It's good to make a pilgrimage if while you're doing so you meditate on what you are doing, and know that it's into your inward life that you are moving.

Joseph Campbell

the feeling I had there. What a pleasure it is to be in a place that never heard of the Fall. I used to say to my friends, If you are thinking of psychoanalysis, save the money and go to Japan. It clears away an awful lot of rubbish. I just totally fell in love with it. And when you're in love like that you have no pain.

FAVROT: But isn't their society so structured that individually you have a hard time breaking out and being independent?

CAMPBELL: I don't know the answer to that. I was just there for about seven months. And I thought it does one no harm to have a structure. At least you keep your agonies to yourself! People smile whether they're happy or not, and that's very nice. Perhaps a certain amount of individual freedom is not quite desirable.

Another wonderful thing is the railroad train. If the train is two minutes late there's a public apology over the public address for being two minutes late. When you get on that bullet train and you're going at, what is it, 150 or 200 miles an hour, something like this, and it's as steady as *that,* you know?

When you get on one of our trains, my God! There's one I took from New York City north to Stamford, and there you are, rattling along, sitting there in the dining car, and when it comes into Stamford the train tips and everything goes on to the floor. And the wonderful old porter comes in and says, "Every time we come to Stamford this happens."

FAVROT: Do you think there is too much freedom in our particular culture?

CAMPBELL: No, I'm not saying those things. I'm just saying how nice it is to be in Japan. What I learned there is about this trust for nature. You can't tell where art begins in nature and nature leaves off.

In Japan things just overide from one to the other and the temples and shrines, they are always in accord with the local nature. The gardens of Japan are arranged, like the ones in Kyoto [Sanzen-in, Kôzan-ji, Ryôan-ji, among others], so that as you go in the garden you are climbing up and suddenly a whole new vista opens.

Daisetz Suzuki at Matsugaoka Library, Kamakura, 1959.

Joseph Campbell and a Japanese friend on the castle grounds of Fukuoka. In the foreground is fellow religious historian and mythologist Mircea Eliade and his wife, Christine, 1958.

Flagstones. Katsura Palace Grounds, Kyoto, Japan. "In Japanese gardens you don't know where art begins and nature ends."

Living in Japan is such a pleasure because these are people with very strong aesthetic accents. And everywhere you look you experience the radiance, at least I do, and that is really the earthly paradise . . . I think that the Japanese artists are the ones living out Buddhism even more than the monks nowadays. The world of art is the earthly path. . . .

Joseph Campbell

151

It's arranged so that you get an amplification of consciousness just by experiencing that garden.

This union of the spiritual and physical intensity is so great. Now I was in athletics when I was in college and a couple of years afterward, too; but it was just athletics. When you go in for karate or something like this, and you realize their spiritual psychological attitudes, placements, all that, they're so important. Everything works that way in that part of the world. They realize the reference of religion is psychological, what happens to you.

We have the question of what happened in Jerusalem in 30 A.D. And did it really happen? What's that got to do with anything?

There's a marvelous little story that Daisetz Suzuki, the Zen philosopher, brought up in one of his talks on Zen. He tells of a young man who asks his guru, "Am I in possession of Buddha consciousness?" And the guru said, "No." And the young man said, "Well, I heard that all things are in possession of Buddha consciousness. The stones, the trees, the flowers, the birds, the animals, and all beings."

"Yes," said the Master, "you are correct. All things are in possession of Buddha consciousness. The stones, the flowers, the bees, the birds, but not you."

"Why not me?"

"Because you're asking the question."

That is to say, instead of living in the knowledge of himself from that transcendent source, he's living in the knowledge of himself as a separate unit. And that throws him off. So he isn't living out of his Buddha consciousness.

Now that's the trick for the artist: to present his material so that it doesn't put a ring around itself and stand there as separate from you, the observer. And that *Aha!* that you get when you see an artwork that really hits you is, "I am that." I am the very radiance and energy that is talking to me through this thing. In purely empirical terms it's called participation. But it's more than that: it's *identification*.

You know the Hindus ask, Who am I? Asking this is a big discipline. Am I this body? I was once giving a lecture to a group of prep-school boys on Buddhism, and I wondered, How could I render this idea to them? Because what is called the Buddha consciousness is the one consciousness of which we are all manifestations. We are all Buddha things. We are all separate manifestations of this great consciousness that informs the whole universe. The plants are conscious. The stones are conscious. All things are conscious.

So I said to the boys, "Look at the ceiling. You can say the lights, plural, are on, or you can say the light is on. These are two ways of saying exactly the same thing. The *lights* are on is accenting the individual vehicle, the bulb, and the *light* is on is accenting the general light. But they are two ways of saying exactly the same thing."

Now in Japan the accent on the individual thing is called the *ji hokai,* or the individual realm, and the accent on the general is called the *ri hokai,* the general realm. And there's a little saying, *ji-ri-mu-ge—individual, general, no obstruction. No difference.*

So, when one light breaks, the superintendent of buildings and grounds doesn't come in and say, "Oh, I was particularly fond of that bulb. That was the important one. This is a calamity." He takes it out, puts another bulb in.

What is important? Is it the light or the vehicle? They are the vehicles of consciousness. So which are you? Are you the head or are you the consciousness? With what do you identify yourself? With the vehicle or with what is carried? And if you can identify yourself with what is carried, namely consciousness, that's the consciousness that's in all the bulbs. And so you are identifying yourself with that which is the unifying principle and that's what the person identifies himself with who goes to save another person spontaneously. These are two approaches to the realization that the separateness is secondary and the separateness is a function of the experience within time and space.

When I was a kid walking through the woods, I'd come every now and then, as everyone will, to a barbed wire fence and the barbed wire that runs alongside it and leans right up against a tree so that the tree will have enclosed it. The tree took the barbed wire into account.

Or you cut yourself and the white corpuscles come. You can interpret these things mechanically or you can interpret them in terms of actual will.

TARNAS: The Christian tradition compared to the Buddhist tradition seems to lack a certain understanding of mythic symbols. Now I'm wondering whether that would be true only of orthodox institutional Christianity, and whether there's in Christianity itself some sort of core of mythic understanding that is just as valid as in Hinduism or Buddhism.

CAMPBELL: The problem here is that in Hinduism or Buddhism the historical interpretation of the symbols, the reference to the life of the Buddha, is quite secondary. The accent in Hinduism and Buddhism is the relevance of the symbolic forms to your own life. You understand these references inward to yourself. For instance, most of the Buddhas had no historical existence at all; nobody thinks they ever had. To the Chinese, Kwan Yin, or to the Japanese, Kwannon, the great Bodhisattva of inexhaustible compassion, is a purely mythic figure but represents something.

Whereas in the Christian traditions the accent is on the historical understanding of the terms, of the images. If you say to a Christian, Jesus did not resurrect from the dead physically, did not ascend to Heaven, that's a challenge to what he regards as important in his faith.

With the Jews, if you begin to question the whole thing of the Exodus and Moses going on the mountain, coming back with the law, and then breaking it, and going back for a second edition; if you express doubts about all this, this is a direct hit.

The importance for the Hindu would be not what happened two thousand or three thousand years ago somewhere else, but what's happening to you now. What is the symbol doing to you now?

Now since both Judaism and Christianity are mythologically structured orders of symbol, they are susceptible to the other kind of reading. And that comes breaking through every now and then with a prophet or mystic, when he suddenly sees the symbol as saying something totally different. And it's something that has to do with an immediate attitude of you to *life*.

For instance with the Crucifixion, if you think of this as a calamity that is the result of your sins and Adam's sin and all that, that Jesus had to come down, the Son of the Father, give himself up on the Cross for death, and look sad there—That's one reading.

But you can read it another way: as the zeal of eternity for incarnation in time, which involves the breaking up of the one into the many and the acceptance of the sufferings of the will as part of the organic delights, the Wisdom Sheath and rapture, the bliss—he is in *bliss*. St. Augustine says this somewhere, where he says, "Jesus went to the Cross as the bridegroom to the bride." That's a total transformation of the idea.

Another one: the idea of the end of time. The end of time as a historical event. That's nonsense. And what does it matter? The importance of the end of time is as a psychological event. Then you have to render it and experience it that way.

When you have seen the radiance of eternity through all the forms of time, and it's a function of art to make that visible to you, then you have really ended life in the world as it is lived by those who think only in the historical terms. This is the function

Vierge Ouvrante, *France, fifteenth century.*

Entrance to Jerusalem. *Giotto do Bondone, ca. 1305.*

of mythology; that's a mythological reading of what was otherwise a theological statement.

TARNAS: So in some ways the Christian institutional religion has erred on the side of historical concretism?

CAMPBELL: Radically.

TARNAS: And it's just built into the side of the religion.

CAMPBELL: Well, right now, in competition with all the gurus and rinpoches and rishis who are coming over here, the Christians are beginning to think, yeah, perhaps not sociology and just helping the poor, but: Find the divine within yourself. And living not you but Christ in you. We need the Orient to teach us about the aspect of personal experience in religion.

The Christ idea and the Buddha idea are perfectly equivalent mythological symbols. Two ways of saying the same thing:

Shakra Reappearing from the Golden Coffin. *"The Christ idea and the Buddha idea are perfectly equivalent mythological symbols. Two ways of saying the same thing: that a transcendent energy consciousness informs the whole world and informs you."*

that a transcendent energy consciousness informs the whole world and informs you.

To become aware of that, and to live out of that center instead of out of this mind center, is the salvation of your life. That means putting yourself in accord with Nature. That means also that you must understand nature to be harmonious; whereas in our biblical tradition with the Fall, a good God created a good world, then a diabolical intruder broke it up so that nature is corrupt. Then you have to distinguish this and distinguish that. You can't *yield* to nature that way and say this is where I'm going to have to yield. All of their codes of right and wrong, sin and atonement, that whole—

I don't know what lies behind the institutional insistence upon that. I think of it very often as, well, remember the old

Listerine ad where it would say, "Even your best friend won't tell you but you have bad breath"? And the way to rescue yourself is to buy Listerine.

What the church tells you even your best friend won't tell you. But you are in sin. And we've got the medicine for you right here.

And when you've got an invisible cure for an invisible disease, you've got something you can sell.

BROWN: Why have we in the West lost this sense of what you are calling "accord with nature"?

CAMPBELL: We're getting back to a kind of Lamarckian view—Lamarck was earlier than Darwin—and of Goethe. Goethe had a theory of evolution. And Schopenhauer has a wonderful paper called "The Will in Nature," where he speaks about these things.

FAVROT: So you think at the protoplasmic level there is some intention—

CAMPBELL: There has to be! I saw a film of my friend, Stanley Keleman, made at the University of Pennsylvania, I think, of just raw protoplasm under a microscope. And you see this acts as a flow, and then there's a flow this way, and pretty soon the flow is building a little channel for itself; it's building a house for itself.

When I drove down here to Esalen from San Francisco after that film, all I could see as I drove was protoplasm! Protoplasm in the form of cows eating, protoplasm in the form of grass, and protoplasm overhead. It was a kind of satori, a kind of revelation, the whole world as intentional protoplasm, with consciousness and energy.

From then I come to the feeling of energy and consciousness being two aspects of the same thing.

FAVROT: The physicists are saying that nowadays.

CAMPBELL: I know they are. I got a wonderful letter from a biologist from Harvard, a professor emeritus, an old, old man. He sent me a paper that he had read at one of the international congresses, and he said, "It shocks my scientific consciousness but I have to conclude that there is an intention in nature."

BROWN: But doesn't that run against his grain? He just comes spiritually to that sense because the physical theories don't allow that kind of thinking.

CAMPBELL: One of the great things about a good scientist is, whether it runs against his grain or not, he speaks out what he finds as evidence. That's a thing that most religious people don't do. They stick with their religious thoughts and no amount of evidence will dislodge them.

But the scientific attitude is: We haven't found truth. We have found a working hypotheses that explains a new fact. We may have to change the whole thing. It's in. People don't understand this about science.

Now I'm interested in the biological thing because I think of mythology as a function of biology. Let's say that every organ of the body has its energy impulse, an impulse to action, and the experience of the conflicts of these different energies inside, is what constitutes the psyche.

It's nature talking. And mythology is the expression in personified images of these energies.

BROWN: How can we channel these energies into our daily lives?

CAMPBELL: That's what we're talking about, the relationship of mythology and mythological studies to contemporary lives. My point is that I'd actually seen it work in inspiring art careers. Mythology puts you down in that level out of which the imagination functions, and it comes out of the imagination. A mythological image that has to be explained to the brain is not working. When you move through a culture field that is so alien to your own that the images don't click off any response, any recognition, then you're out of sync.

This is one of the problems with our tradition, with our inherited mythology, let's say the Judeo–Christian tradition that

Mythologies are in fact the public dreams that move and shape societies, and conversely one's own dreams are the little myths of the private gods, antigods, and guardian powers that are moving and shaping oneself: revelations of the actual fears, desires, aims, and values by which one's life is subliminally ordered.

Joseph Campbell,
The Mythic Image

relates to the Near East in the very first millenium B.C. It has nothing to do with life here. Everything has to be explained.

"Washed in the blood of the lamb"—so what does that mean if you've never even seen a lamb?

GUILLEMEN: In cultural distinctions I can just envision that when we think of the mythology of Medea and Jason and her brewing this soup to rejuvenate the old man, and her searching for the nepenthe in her witch's soup. Eventually, when I isolated the first of the endorphins, you may say that this was the ultimate crystallization of such an idea.

CAMPBELL: Witches' brew!

GUILLEMEN: Yes. Even though I honestly cannot say that it was the story of Medea and Jason that led me to look for the endorphin in the brain.

KENNARD: When you were researching, did you think these mythological thoughts?

GUILLEMEN: When you are involved in isolating, characterizing one of these molecules from the brain, you don't have much time to think of Medea and Jason.

CAMPBELL: I should think not!

KENNARD: My tradition is Judeo–Christian and I'm so far from the Near East. Your tradition, Jamake, is much closer to you. What difference does that make?

HIGHWATER: It makes a great deal of difference. When Joseph Campbell was talking about the washing of the blood of the lamb, I was thinking of the funny fact that to the Inuit, the Eskimo people, it's inconceivable that this terrible place that bad people apparently go from our culture is *hot* [laughter].

Their afterworld is generally very cold and dismal. Now is that just a matter of setting the thermostat differently? I don't think so. I think it has a basic kind of human poetry. And I don't think poetry is limited to artists. As I understand it Einstein was not a great scientist; he was a great poet. He was capable. The scientists or technologists later proved what he intuited. But largely what he did was not anything remotely like nineteenth-century science. And that is why I think he's such a master of twentieth-century science.

KENNARD: Aren't scientists always telling art what to do? Aren't scientists always accused of having no mythology?

CAMPBELL: Well, these are two totally different perspectives. The problem of science is to give you an image of the uni-

The Masks of God

Every mythic image points past itself.
Every deity opens to mystery.

Joseph Campbell

The Bodhisattva, Kuan Yin, Chinese sculpture,
eleventh to early twelfth century.

The Light of the World, Holman Hunt, 1853.

Cretan snake goddess, discovered near the Palace of Knossos, 1600–1500 B.C.

Mithras Slaying the Great Bull, Roman relief, third century A.D.

Kwakiutl sun mask, featuring the head of an eagle at its center, from the Northwest Coast Indians.

The Zapotec maize god represented on a clay urn, Monte Alban, Oaxaca, Mexico, fifth to eighth century.

Amaterasu, the Japanese goddess of the sun, colored woodcut by Utagawa Kunisada, Japan, 1857.

Cernunnos, Celtic stag-antlered god, detail from the Gundestrup Cauldron, second century B.C., discovered in Denmark.

Robert Bly, Stanislav Grof, and Roger Guillemen discuss the relevance of the work of their friend Joseph Campbell in the gardens of Esalen Institute, 1982.

Angeles Arrien, Jamake Highwater, and Bette Andresen relax on the cliffs of Esalen Institute after a day of filming with Joseph Campbell, 1982.

verse, what it's like, what it actually is like. And this changes from decade to decade. No scientist says, "I've found truth." There's a working hypothesis, and the next season we have another structure.

GUILLEMEN: Mmmmmm. I would qualify that. Enormously. *Enormously* [laugher].

CAMPBELL: Okay, they think they've found truth! So, the problem of mythology is to relate that found truth to the actual living of a life. Mythology has to do with how you live your life.

CAMPBELL: There's a famous line at the close of Goethe's *Faust:* "Everything phenomenal or temporal is but a reference, but a metaphor." And then Nietzsche topped that a few years later by saying, "Everything eternal is but a reference, but a metaphor."

Now the function of mythology is to help us to experience everything temporal as a reference. And also to experience the so-called eternal verities as merely references. Mythology opens the world so that it becomes transparent to something that is beyond speech, beyond words—in short, what we call transcendence.

Without that you don't have a mythology. Any system of thinking, ideologies of one kind or another, that does not open to transcendence cannot be classified or understood mythologically.

The first function of mythology then is to function by showing everything as a metaphor to transcendence. The first field that has to be transcendentalized this way is the field of the environment that we're in, the world that we live in. So that we can see the whole world as opening to a dimension of wonder and mystery. Every object in the world speaks of this mystery, the mystery of life, and consciousness pours in through the various bodies and beings round about. It must then show you yourself that you are similarly transparent to transcendence.

And finally, in a mythologically organized society, all of the rituals are organized in such a way that they help you to experience yourself, the world, and the social order of which you are a part, in this mystical way.

And of what I regard as four major functions that mythology serves, the first one is the *mystical* function. The second is the *cosmological,* relating to the cosmos. The third is the *sociological,* and the fourth is the *pedagogical,* carrying the individual through the stages of his life.

The myth guides you through the rituals, initiation rites, fertility rites, puberty rites, funeral rites. These are for guiding the individual through the inevitable course of a lifetime, and the human lifetime in this matter has not changed since the time of the Auragnacian caves.

The *mystical* function is opening the transcendence, opening the heart and mind, pointing out that the ultimate mystery that we all try to solve lies beyond the range of human thought or naming. When you have given it a name and a thought you have fallen short. You're no longer in the mystical tradition. For instance, in Judaism where God is named and he tells you what's good and what's right, these are the fire words and reduces mythology to ethics. There are moments of reverence, of what I call worship, where one gets an experience that seems to correspond to something named in the scriptures; but this isn't mysticism. Mysticism actually goes beyond this whole field of separation, I and Thou; and when a deity says, "I am It" he becomes a roadblock. As they used to say in the second and third centuries, the problem with Yahweh is that he thinks he's God! The final reference has to go past the god. The god has to be transparent and transcendent. And the word *transcendent* is the key word to mythology. All of these figures are flickering, just as we are ourselves in the field. In a mythology such as the American Indian tribes the whole world is understood that way. The animals give themselves, the body animal gives himself as a willing victim to participate in this game of, Now you eat me.

And with the knowledge that the life energy survives death, is transcendent of the temporal experience, the belief is that the animal will come back and you can relate to it properly next year.

Am I not right here?

HIGHWATER: Even to a further extent, which I think is the hardest thing for a Western people to understand, in that in most tribes there is not an individuated goal. The Iroquois word for it is *orenda,* the tribal soul. From the native American standpoint it is an energy, it is a power and it exists in rock, it exists in dogs and cats, and it exists in you and me. It flickers in us for a moment but we do have a classic way of making it burn bright or hardly burn at all.

CAMPBELL: Yes, yes. Well, that's the first of four. There's a second function I call *cosmological*. And that is in the world as the science of the day presents it or as the knowledge of the day presents itself, radiant of this transcendent energy. Turn the whole world into an icon so that it's radiant. And that's the function of art: to take the world so it is radiant. That's the *Aha!* in art; that's the aesthetic arrest when the object is presented in such a way you don't ask the artist, What does this mean? If he wants to insult you he'll tell you. The thing has to come through and hit you with an *Aha!*

HIGHWATER: Or the painting will ask you, What do you mean?

GUILLEMEN: What you've described in terms of a community soul where there is no specific individuality is in some ways exactly the description of what modern science is. Science belongs to everybody. And no subject, no discovery is really the work of a single individual. That's saying in other words what you're saying about the individuality of the soul: that it is more the tribal soul, or community, or people, which is exactly what science says. The contribution with my name is infinitesimal. Add to that more contribution in the name of other people and eventually you have the movement of modern science.

HIGHWATER: Art, which seems so transient, so unimportant, seems to be the most transcendent of human creative activity. Whereas science seems to be the most revisional, seems to need to criticize itself in order to move forward, and in fact reverses itself. I can't think of any scientist in the last ten or twenty years who hasn't actually said just that.

GUILLEMEN: That's how science progresses, in contradistinction to philosophy, which appears to want to remain or to keep what it had at one time. Science gives us an image of the world. But that's the second step. I would like to get a difference between believing and looking at an image and knowing that the structure of a molecule in two thousand years will still be the same. That truth is a truth, which by the way existed years ago, but we did not uncover it. Molecules existed long before the observer was born. This is the uncovering rather than the discovering of science.

AUDIENCE: You can't separate the observer from the observed. That's what modern science seems to be getting into. That's the way you make mythology and you make science. By saying that the process is all ultimately the same.

HIGHWATER: When I hear you use the word "mythology" it's a little bit like hearing someone use the word "wilderness" when they look at nature. And I try to say there's nothing wild about it. And I think you think of mythology as a kind of "faction" and science as a kind of a fact.

CAMPBELL: What I'm trying to say is that the structuring of a mythology is conditioned by the science at that time. There's no use in constructing a mythology based on an archaic science. I wouldn't know what to do with an atom, but I do recognize that when we had a Ptolemaic cosmology there was a whole interpretation of the relationship of the earth to the different planes of the universe that was mythologized. What happened to that was it was given an ethical and moral value, the stages of a ladder of the heavens represented the stages of the psyche.

Well, anyhow, the myth has to deal with the cosmology of today and it's no good when it's based on a mythology or on a cosmology that's out of date. And that's one of our problems. I don't see any conflict between science and religion. Religion has to accept the science of the day and penetrate it—to the *mystery*. The conflict is between the science of 2000 B.C. and the science of 2000 A.D.

HIGHWATER: Isn't it possible that the very pursuit of the scientist is a mythological form itself?

CAMPBELL: The quest is a vision quest. It is the scientist's enactment of the vision quest that everybody's engaged in. How

164

do you find the truth of your own being and relate to it? Isn't that true?

HIGHWATER: What is fundamental to all this apparent diversity.

CAMPBELL: Exactly so.

HIGHWATER: That's a mythological process, isn't it? Yet I think that the word "myth" is so completely confused with the word "falsehood" that we come to it with a very inadequate emotional response.

CAMPBELL: Now we've come to the *sociological* function of mythology. All mythologies have had among other functions that of validating and maintaining a certain specific social system. The moral system is culturally established and it will be very different when you move from here to there. And we find in all basic mythologies that the whole world is a manifestation, an emanation, as the god itself comes into being, as a personification of certain of those energies. He's not an external thing at all.

Then the fourth function of mythology—and this is the one where you suddenly feel the lack of myth today—is the *pedagogical,* the guiding of individuals in a harmonious way through the inevitable crises of a lifetime. That's the main one. Linking the individual to his society so he feels an organic part of it. The individual is carried by the myth in a very deep participatory way into the society and then the society disengages him.

And so what happens to all his energy? It has to go down deep into himself, and that is the mystical part, the interrelation to the life cause. First induction of the individual into the society; then disengagement of him and the carriage of him through mystical meditations and the understanding of the symbols to the seat of his own life within himself.

Now what is the seat of life? I remember a very pretty little book by [Edwin] Schroedinger, where I believe he uses the ultimate terms *brahman* or *atman*. Here's a fundamental modern scientist, who, ultimately, when he comes to speak about the relationship of the individual to it all, has to use these words that are not of our crystallized tradition where God is there and man is here, and this is the good society and all the others are junk. And when you look at the cosmos, is the mystery behind that cosmos interested in just these people being in that place or in getting them there to the other side somehow?

It's a fantastic story we have.

I find that the main result for me [in my endeavors] has been the confirmation of a thought that I have long and faithfully entertained: of the unity of the race of man, not only in biology but also in its spiritual history, which has everywhere unfolded in the manner of a single symphony, with its themes announced, developed, amplified and turned about, distorted, reasserted, and, today, in a grand fortissimo of all sections sounding together, irresistibly advancing to some kind of mighty climax out of which the next great movement will emerge. And I can see no reason why anyone should suppose that in the future the same motifs already heard will not be sounding still—in new relationships indeed, but ever the same motifs.

Joseph Campbell
The Masks of God

BROWN: How do you explain the severe fundamentalist religious movements around the world these days?

CAMPBELL: What you have there is the result of the concretization of the symbols. To think that this symbolic statement refers to a historical fact. And the two prime ones that are troubling our world are the image of the Virgin Birth, which has nothing to do with a biological problem, and the image of the Promised Land, which has nothing to do with real estate.

These are symbols of the birth in the heart of the spiritual life, in contrast to a biological one where all the values of the biological life suddenly move into a secondary position, and one is moving then along a spiritual trajectory. And the goal of that spiritual trajectory is the relationship of the individual to the land and the world of harmony. And *that* is the Promised Land. It has to do with what you're doing inside yourself, not whom you've got your weapons pointed at to kill. The shift is dramatic.

And so you can say that history is simply a function of misunderstood mythology.

COCKRELL: What system of images *would be* the best window to an experience of the transcendent?

CAMPBELL: I find that when I read either an Upanashadic text or one or another of the Buddhist sutras, that does it. Those traditions were—and still are—traditions that are really centered in transcendence. They realize that all phenomenology of life is a shadow display of powers that are not fully given in the display.

There are energies that move in our body. No one knows whence. They come from something transcending our consciousness. We can't even conceive them. And those energies that come in the subatomic particle displays—you know, they come and go, come and go. Life is throwing up these forms, these forms, these

166

forms, then our consciousness becomes interested in something else there or gets some ethical idea that is contrary to nature.

Mythological images are transparent to transcendence. Every mythic image points past itself; every deity opens to mystery. You know: The Kingdom of the Father is spread upon the earth and men do not see it.

Well, you have to open up to that seeing.

COCKRELL: What is unique about those traditions that they've been able to continue to be translucent, while our traditions have become opaque?

CAMPBELL: Our traditions haven't *become* opaque, they started by *being* opaque. And it comes from the fact that the mythic figures are read not as poetically inspired but as prose. And when you read mythology as prose, and apply it to the aggrandizement of your particular group or society, you're off the trail. This is what I would call pathological mythology. The whole idea of a chosen people, for example, is pathology. *Every* people is a chosen people. The realization that you're being chosen does not distinguish you from anybody else, but tells you what it is about everybody else that is wonderful—that, like yourself, they are of a mysterious, transcending ground.

All beings are Buddha beings. Now, we don't know more than one or two or three names associated with the sages. The hearers who delivered the Upanishads. But this starts already back in the ninth and tenth centuries B.C. They realized that the whole phenomenology of the world is a projection of a mystery ground. And that mystery ground in the ground of your own being.

You are that mystery which you are seeking to know. But it's not the you that you fancy. It's not the aspect that your friends are enjoying, that thing in the phenomenal world that is moving around. It is that ground of being that was there, will be there, is what you are to refer to.

One might say that the function of a ritual, and of a mythology, is to put the conscious mind—which is in touch only with the phenomenology of the world—in touch with the ground of those phenomena, particularly of your own action. So that you act not as an ego, but as a carrier of a process that is transcendent in its course. When a myth links you, for example, to your society, it's linking you to something bigger than yourself. But it's not big enough. The society itself must be seen as linked to something bigger than that, which is the world of the environment. If you get stuck with that, that's not big enough either. That has to become transparent. Karlfreid Graf Dürkheim's word. Become "transparent to transcendence" is the key to the whole thing; that's a key word. And as soon as a myth is read as a fact, you lose the transparency and it becomes an aberration and a deluding guide.

One of the problems that's going on now is with the enormous accent on sociology rather than biology. It hit me when I read of [the Russian biologist] Vaviloff, whose biology differed from Lysenko, who was standing for the idea that society can shape nature.

It can't. That man was sent out to Siberia; nobody even knows when he died. One of the great biologists of the century. But his point of view differed from Stalin's.

And I find also in our colleges that the accent that has gone into sociology, sociology, sociology, sociology in interpreting how one should live is distracting because *our* sociology is far away from the biological ground. Economics is what controls us. Economics and politics are the governing powers of life today and that's why everything is screwy. You have to get back in accord with nature; and that's what these myths are all about. Now in the nineteenth century sociological anthropologists had the idea that myths and rites were an attempt to control nature. Totally wrong. They are not to control nature, they are to control the society and put it in accord with nature. The festival that has to do with the seasonal realm, with the stages of human development, with the stages of the preparation for war and the return from war, getting in touch with the biological ground with these movements, so one is always in accord. And the economic motive just destroys it all.

COCKRELL: I wonder if you could speak a little bit of the tree in the Garden, the tree of the Cross, the tree of the Buddha's illumination, and how they can be read in a way that opens to an experience of the transcendent?

CAMPBELL: A few years ago I saw a tree that was growing on a ravine where the roots, instead of continuing to grow outward, just turned back and went the other way, inward into the side of the ravine. You can't explain that in sheer mechanistic terms.

Tree of Death and Life. *Miniature by Berthold Furtmeyer, from Archbishop of Salzburg's missal, 1481.* "To get back to the garden you have to realize that all is one, you see?"

Woman Embracing a Tree. *Miniature, Guler, Punjab Hills, early nineteenth century.*

And what's happening now with the imagery of the evolution of man? The four great stages in the human evolution, *homo faber, homo erectus, homo sapiens, homo sapiens sapiens.* Each of those transformations take place following a maximum movement of the brachial ice, where a whole new environment comes along and there's a sudden adaptation. It happens too fast for the earlier kind of theory to work, you know, the thousands and thousands of years and all that kind of thing.

And then there was the time at the end of the Myocene when Africa and Arabia, which had been separated from Europe and Asia by a great sea, moved up, and then the Himalayas rose—whole new environments. Within a few hundred years there were whole new animal species taking advantage of those environments, and other animals to eat the animals that evolved.

"The Tree of the Soul."
Figure by William Law in
The Works of Jacob
Behmen.

It all happens too fast for just the Darwinian thing to work. That doesn't mean that evolution is refuted; it means that the mechanistic way of interpreting it is refuted. And so we're getting back to a kind of Lamarckian view. Lamarck was earlier than Darwin.

Then Goethe, in *The Metamorphosis of Plants* (I think that's where I read it), speaks of the evolution of life. Of course Goethe was half a century before Darwin came along and his interpretation was not the Darwinian one of mechanistic interaction, the dynamics from inside the organism that brings about evolution. It's inherent in protoplasm that it should differentiate, evolve. And he speaks of the two great lines of evolution, of the animal and the plant. And the culmination of the animal evolution is the human being. And the culmination of the plant is the tree.

And so the tree and the vegetable world represent the undestroyed simplicity and directness of the natural production of a form. A tree is symbolic, you might say, of home. One returns to the nature world that is explicit in the tree. So the Garden is the natural realm of the vegetable world and man is put there as a nature being. His problem is to remain natural while moving into this next stage of high consciousness and differentiated consciousness. He can lose himself in consciousness but the tree pulls him back.

The problem in the biblical Tree is that there are two trees there; you're in the garden of timeless being, see, and you're going to move into the realm of time. In the realm of time everything is dual, is, was, and is to be, past and future. There's you, and there is I, so when you move into the realm of opposites the Tree of the Garden is of good and evil, is the gate going out. So they didn't have to be kicked out of the Garden by God; they had already kicked themselves out. Their shame and wearing of clothes comes from recognizing male and female are differentiated. To get back to the Garden you have to realize that all is one, you see?

So the second tree, the Tree of Immortal Life, is the tree of the return. But the thing about the Book of Genesis is that God doesn't want man to return; I mean, this is a peculiar God, a unique God. He does not want you to realize that you are immortal. He says, "Lest man should now eat of the Tree of Immortal Life and become as we are, therefore, let's put him out." The guardians at the gate are the pair of opposites, and the flaming sword in between is the fear of going past that and losing your separateness. And so we're held out.

Kongo Rikishi. *At the Todaiji Temple, Nara, Japan.*

The gate guardian is a symbol of your own fear and holding to your ego, which is what is keeping you out of the garden, where the Buddha sits under the tree, and his right hand says, "Don't be afraid of those guys. Come through."

Joseph Campbell

CAMPBELL: There was a very interesting moment in my understanding of these things during the Second World War when we were at war with Japan. One of the New York newspapers published a photograph of one of the door guardians, the gate guardians in Nara, in Japan, right outside Tokyo.

And here was this gate guardian: This was the cherub put at the gate of the Garden of Eden. And that guardian stands at the gate to the Buddha sitting under the tree of immortal life. But what it said under there was, "The Japanese worship gods like this!"

Well, they *don't!* That is a symbol of your own fear and holding to your ego, which is what's keeping you out of the Garden,

I remember hearing a marvelous talk by Daisetz Suzuki in Ascona, Switzerland. It was, I think, his first talk there at the Eranos Foundation, and here was this group of Europeans in the audience and there was a Japanese man (he was about ninety-one years old at the time), a Zen philosopher. He stood with his hands on his side, and he looked at the audience and said, "Nature against God. God against nature. Nature against man. Man against nature. Man against God. God against man. Very funny religion."

Joseph Campbell

where the Buddha sits under the tree, and his right hand says, "Don't be afraid of those guys. Come through."

It suddenly dawned on me *our* God was apparently that guardian at the gate because he has put the guardians at the gate and told us that they're emphatically there and we mustn't go through. That shifts the whole thing.

So our religion is basically a religion of exile.

In the Christian tradition Jesus has, as it were, gone through the gate and eaten of the fruit of the tree and become the tree, which is the Crucifixion. That's the sense of the crucifix. *Yield.* Let it go. Join into your mentality not this but the divine immortality, which is in you and in all things.

And so Jesus hanging on the cross, which is the second tree in the Garden, is equivalent to the Buddha seated under the Tree of Immortal Life, the Bo tree. Bodhi means "the one who has waked up to the fact that he is that which he seeks to know." Namely the eternal being. The two religions are interesting in that we are told that we are not one with Jesus, but he is to be our model and we're to follow him. But in the Thomas Gospel Jesus says, "He who drinks from my mouth becomes as I am, and I am he."

That's the difference between the Buddhist and the Christian thing. So we are, again, in exile. You cannot be Jesus. But in the Buddhist religion you *are* the Buddha already, and just don't know it.

Now I was lecturing on this point in saying that for the Christian one should live in terms of the Christ *in* you, and a woman came up to me some weeks later and said that she was sitting next to a priest and he said, "That's blasphemy."

Well, if that's blasphemy, what in heaven's name are we talking about?

CAMPBELL: I remember when I was a kid in school, when I was reciting catechism.

"Why did God make you?"

"God made me to love him, to serve him, and to honor him in this world and be happy with him forever in heaven."

That has to do with a *relationship* to God. God did not make me to realize *my godhood*.

There was a lovely young woman who was a nun and is now no longer a nun because she heard me lecture once. After one of my talks she came up to me and said, *"Do you believe that Jesus Christ was the Son of God?"*

And I said, *"Not unless all of us are."*

That's the difference. Do you see what I mean? If you specialize the revelation then you've removed the humanity from it. And insofar as that specialization takes place, you have removed yourself from the human race. This is a terrible thing, I would personally think, to insist on these special revelations. This is a reactionary system. And it's antithetical to the dynamics of time. It's bad stuff.

Particularly at the present moment when all the special traditions of the world are coming into *collision* and are transforming. The *globe* is our homeland.

CAMPBELL: The divine lives of saviors are symbolic of the meaning of the savior's teaching. It is not like Carl Sandburg's life of Lincoln, where you get documentation of the actual details of the life. It has nothing to do with what happened in life. It has to do with the implications of the life.

The Buddha lived from 563 to 483 B.C. The first life of the Buddha is 80 B.C. in Ceylon. We don't know anything about the Buddha. We don't know anything about Christ. We don't know anything about Zoroaster. All we know are the legends which tell you what the meaning of their lives is. You see?

And what the Buddha said—and what Christ said—I mean, read the four gospels and then read the fifth. Read the Gospel According to St. Thomas. And what was he saying?

Who wants to be remembered by the notes of his students?

The idea of the Bodhisattva is the one who out of his realization of transcendence participates in the world.
The imitation of Christ is joyful participation in the sorrows of the world.

Joseph Campbell

*How teach again . . .
what has been taught
correctly and incor-
rectly a thousand
thousand times,
throughout the millen-
niums of mankind's
prudent folly? That is
the hero's ultimate
difficult task. How
render back into light-
world language the
speech-defying pro-
nouncements of the
dark? Many failures
attest to the difficulties
of this life-affirmative
threshold.*

Joseph Campbell,
*The Hero with a
Thousand Faces*

Joseph Campbell after receiving the Medal of Honor from the National Arts Club for Literature, 1985. "It's one grandiose song I've found."

7

The Return Threshold

Joseph Campbell became a much-sought-after lecturer on college campuses and human potential institutes around the United States in the 1970s and 1980s. Many accomplished artists and scholars publicly expressed their admiration of his work. At symposiums in New York and San Francisco to celebrate his eightieth birthday and the theme of the hero's journey, sculptor Isamu Noguchi, choreographer Martha Graham, author Richard Adams, poet Robert Bly, anthropologists Barbara Myerhoff and Marija Gimbutas, and many others expressed their gratitude for his awakening of the mythological dimension in their lives and work. But it was in the movies that Campbell's cultural impact gained its greatest notoriety.

"No book has come close to influencing contemporary movies as pervasively as Joseph Campbell's *The Hero with a Thousand Faces*," wrote film critic Michael Ventura. Filmmakers such as Steven Spielberg, George Miller, and George Lucas all credited Campbell with inspiration for the mythic underpinnings in their stories. In February 1985, Lucas joined Adams, writer Nancy Willard, and psychologist James Hillman at the National Arts Club in New York when Campbell was awarded its Medal of Honor for Literature. The following year, at the age of eighty-two, Campbell was invited by the Grateful Dead to attend his first rock and roll concert. "To think that my work has been influential to people like George Lucas and the Grateful Dead," he told reporters in 1986. "I'm absolutely delighted!"

CAMPBELL: I guess this is the big moment of my life [winning the Medal of Honor for Literature]. I knew that I had found something when I started writing *The Hero*. It came up very slowly. I worked about five or six years on it. It came out of my course that I was giving in comparative mythology to my students at Sarah Lawrence College.

Now it was Euripides who said, "The myth is not my own; I have it from my mother." And I think I can say, The myth is not my own, I got it from my students. Because they were all young women and they were not interested at all in just who wrote the myth and what the date was. They wanted to know what it meant to them, what it could mean to the children they were going to have.

And then to hear, as I have heard tonight from these really majestic artists that we have had the wonderful privilege of hearing speak, and to hear my name in relation to their work, makes it difficult to stand up and talk. It has been a large, large experience, because that's what I was hoping for when I was writing, namely that I was giving people the key to the realm of the muses, which is where myth is.

It delights me particularly to receive the award from the Arts Club and to receive it for literature and not from some scientific society or scholarly community because to think that my contribution has been in the way of literature instead of scholarship is a marvelous promotion . . .

I remember Alan Watts asked me one day, "Joe, what kind of meditation do you do?"

I said, "I underline sentences."

Now there is a beautiful phrase that I ran into in Novalis: "The seat of the soul is there where the inner and the outer worlds meet." The outer world is what you get in scholarship, the inner world is your response to it. And it is there where these come together that we have the myths. The outer world changes with

Joseph Campbell at the National Arts Club. Beside him (from left to right) are Jean Erdman, filmmaker George Lucas, and singer Linda Ronstadt, 1985.

historical time; the inner world is the world of anthropos. The mythological systems are a constant, and what you are recognizing is your own inward life, and at the same time the inflection to history. The problem of making the inner meet the outer of today is, of course, the function of the artist. To think that my work has had some influence on people who are doing this is why I feel so proud, so proud of this moment . . .

The other experience, of course, was being married to an artist, Jean, a dancer, and to see an artist manipulating these wonderful things, turning them into dances, and then into that wonderful play, *The Coach with the Six Insides.* In 1962 it first appeared based on *Finnegans Wake,* and we had three or four years of quite vivid experiences in Italy and Paris and so forth and so on. And then her later plays. This participation is from a distance. I'm the one who sees it for the first time and I say, "Oh, they're just talking too fast and I can't hear." That's about the extent of my criticism and contribution to these things. But that's also helped me to stay with this mythological world in relation to creative life.

I can't tell you how grateful I am for this event. It lets me know in spite of my nonacademic career, you might say, I must have been doing something right to have influenced the people such as I have been meeting and hearing tonight. I can't tell you how deeply moved I've been by what I've heard from these beautiful people who have spoken in my name. It is a culminating moment in my life.

COCKRELL: What I would like to do is have a Upanishadic conversation, a "sitting close in." Artists have always, as in the Renaissance, had a great deal to do with establishing the strength and the interpretation of Christianity. Do you think that contemporary artists could, through their powers, reinterpret our current symbols?

CAMPBELL: What happened in the Renaissance is fascinating. Cosimo de Medici received a manuscript from Macedonia that was brought by a Greek monk. It was a manuscript of the *Corpus Hermeticum*, which was a body of late classical text about the *sense* of the symbology of the classical world, which was *exactly* contemporary with the formative period of Christianity, the first two centuries.

This text was translated by Marselio Ficino, and immediately it was realized that the symbology of the Christian faith, and the symbology of the late classical myths, were saying the same thing. That's what inspired Renaissance art. Botticelli is full of it, and Michelangelo, and the whole lot of them. This gave a new

Ladies, and gentlemen, we are here this evening in honor of Joseph Campbell. And I say in honor and not to honor him, for that has been accomplished by his work, its massive and sufficient scholarship, its conviction and its delightful fascination, and by what his life of dedication has given to our culture: the deepening of its soul into myth. And this gift to our culture and its soul continues to honor him throughout America, in bookstores and classrooms, in movie theaters and in therapists' offices, in the imaginations of writers and dreamers. No one in our century, not Freud, not Thomas Mann, or Lévi-Strauss, has so brought the mythical sense of the world and its eternal figures back into our everyday consciousness. In his own words, "[to see] the continued romance of Beauty and the Beast, stand this afternoon on the corner of 42nd Street and 5th Avenue waiting for the light to change." The myths are in our daily life.

What is not on your program is the passion *which underlies the accomplishment. This passion as desire, together with the painstaking care desire always imposes, can be condensed into Joseph Campbell's maxim for how to be, how to live on this earth. The maxim can be traced to a life involving the gods, the goddesses, the heroes, the animals, the little people, and the daimones that aid you in you following your bliss forever.*

James Hillman, National Arts Club, 1985

A kind of chain reaction comes from his discoveries that have reverberated out into writing novels, into psychiatry, into anthropology, into mythology, into filmmaking, into creative work, and apart from all that, he's a damn nice guy. . . It's hard to believe that Shakespeare didn't read Joseph Campbell.

Richard Adams, National Arts Club, 1985

vitality to the Christian imagery itself. Because they understood its spiritual sense, not its historical reference. Do you see? The reference is not to something that happened which has released us from sin. *It* didn't release us from sin. What the Crucifixion did was give a model so you could release *yourself* from it. And that's the whole difference. This is the big inspiration of Renaissance art.

Now the problem of the contemporary artists would be to recognize in the conditions of contemporary life the possibility of transparency to transcendence through those conditions. The artist's function is to *render* the forms of the world in which we live, and the social actions that we engage in, render them transparent to the transcendant: turn them into transparencies.

COCKRELL: As Joyce says, "Any object properly regarded can be the gateway to the gods." So when you look at Cézanne's apple—I'll put it your way—you don't want to eat Cézanne's apple because they hold you in what Joyce called "aesthetic arrest."

CAMPBELL: That's right. That's in *Ulysses*, in the maternity hospital chapter.

CAMPBELL: If you had the opportunity to speak to the artists of the world and point them in the right direction about what to do with the bodies of mythology that we have, what would you say to them?

CAMPBELL: I'd say [laughs], "Buy a copy of *The Hero with a Thousand Faces!*" And I'd say, Look at things not as them being the things in themselves, but as manifestations of a *mystery*: the idea of a mystery is what it's all about. And that mystery of these things is *your* mystery.

Somebody once said to me, Just think of a thing as a "Thou" instead of an "It" and then our experience changes.

In one of those cockeyed theaters that are in New York, on 42nd and Broadway, I saw advertised Fire Women from Outer Space. *That was a mythological idea. In Tibetan Buddhism these are called* docheles—*or fire women from outer space! And in their spiritual powers they can excite you a little bit. And so I thought, Well, we're getting back to the old days in a very funny way.*

Whenever the human imagination gets going, it has to work in the field that myths have already covered. And it renders them in new ways, that's all.

Joseph Campbell,
Esalen, 1982

BROWN: One of the areas that's been of interest to those of us who know you and have watched things happen in the last couple of years has been your involvement with George Lucas and the themes of man versus machine.

CAMPBELL: One of the big delights and surprising delights has been to find how my books have helped other people. In the arts, in the dance, for instance, Martha Graham's work, in Jean's work, and in Merce Cunningham's early work, and so forth. These mythic themes are the realm of the muses.

It's not that I tell people what to do, but my work points out where the inspiration is. And you move in, yourself, as an artist, and pull it out. So lately I've learned that Richard Adams with his *Watership Down* came over to see me, to thank me for what I had given him in the way of *The Hero with a Thousand Faces.* Then suddenly, George Lucas with *Star Wars.*

Now of course I hadn't seen a movie in years—I mean, when you're reading and reading you can't have time to do all the things you'd like to do. Movies dropped out of my life a long, long time ago. Besides, when I was in Europe a terrible change

---

About ten years ago I set out to write a children's film, and I had an idea of doing a modern fairy tale. My friends all around said, "What are you doing? You're crazy. You have to do something important. You have to do something that is socially relevant. You have to do something that is art with a capital A. You have to do what we're doing." I had been working on a project about Vietnam [Apocalypse Now] and I had abandoned it—gave it to a friend of mine [Francis Coppola] and said I've got to do this children's film.

I didn't know what I was doing at the time. I started working, started doing research, started writing, and a year went by. I wrote many drafts of this work and then I stumbled across The Hero with a Thousand Faces. *It was the first time that I really began to focus. Once I read that book I said to myself, This is what I've been doing. This is it. I had been reading other doctors—Freudians, and also dealing with an ample supply of Donald Duck and Uncle Scrooge, and all the other mythical heroes of our times. But* The Hero with a Thousand Faces *was the first time a book began to focus what I had already been doing intuitively. I began to see a lot of parallels and began to become very fascinated with this whole process and as a result I picked up several other books,* The Flight of the Wild Gander, The Masks of God, *as I continued to write.*

This whole process went on over a period of years. Then, as I say, I went around in circles for a long time trying to come up with stories, and the script rambled all over and I ended up with hundreds of pages. It was The Hero with a Thousand Faces *that just took what was about 500 pages and said, Here is the story. Here's the end; here's the focus; here's the way it's all laid out. It was all right there and had been there for thousands and thousands of years, as Dr. Campbell pointed out. And I said, "This is it." After reading more of Joe's books I began to understand how I could do this. When that happened to me I realized how important the contribution that Joe had made to me was. I had read these books and said, Here is a lifetime of scholarship, a life of work that is distilled down into a few books that I can read in a few months that enable me to move forward with what I am trying to do and give me focus to my work. It was a great feat and very important. It's possible that if I had not run across him I would still be writing* Star Wars *today.*

I think you can say about some authors that their work is more important than them. But with Joe, as great as his works are, there is no doubt in my mind that the body of his work is not as great as the man. He is a really wonderful man and he has become my Yoda.

George Lucas, National Arts Club, 1985

had taken place. When I left this country we had only black and white, silent movies. There was a wonderful art developing then of mime and all of that. I come back and you have talkies. I never really caught onto the talkie as an interesting art. Too naturalistic, you know? Naturalism is the death of the art. And that's one of the big problems in our American arts, I think, they don't understand the metaphor. It's all naturalism.

So the whole business of the movies was unknown to me when George Lucas came over to me to talk to me and let me know how much my work meant to him. He invited me and Jean to his place outside of San Francisco for a couple of days to see what he had done.

Well, my God, we had *Star Wars* in the morning, and we had *The Empire Strikes Back* in the afternoon, and we had *Return of the Jedi* in the evening. I tell you, I was really . . . *thrilled.*

Here the man understands the metaphor. What I saw was things that had been in my books but rendered in terms of the

C-3PO (Anthony Daniels), Luke Skywalker (Mark Hamill), and Obi-Wan Kenobi (Sir Alec Guinness), in a scene from George Lucas's Star Wars, *1977.*

modern problem, which is man and machine. Is the machine going to be the servant of human life? Or is it going to be master and dictate? And the machine includes the totalitarian state, whether it's Fascist or Communist it's still the same state. And it includes things happening in this country too; the bureaucrat, the machine-man.

What a wonderful power the machine gives you—but is it going to dominate you? That's the problem of Goethe's *Faust*. It's in the last two acts of *Faust,* Part Two. His pact is with Mephistopheles, the man who can furnish you the means to do anything you want. He's the machine manufacturer. He can manufacture the bombs, but can he give you what the human spirit wants and needs? He can't.

This statement of what the need and want is must come from you, not from the machine, and not from the government that's teaching you, or not even from the clergy. It has to come from one's own inside, and the minute you let that drop and take what the dictation of the time is instead of the dictation of your own eternity, you have capitulated to the devil. And you're in hell.

That's what I think George Lucas brought forward. I admire what he's done immensely, immensely. That young man opened a vista and knew how to follow it and it was totally fresh. It seems to me that he carried that thing through very, very well.

COUSINEAU: There seems to be an uncanny parallel between myth, dream, and the movies: magical transformations, dream time, the hero's journey, vision quests, and so on. Do you see the filmmakers in what they've called the "dream factory" of Hollywood as modern myth-makers?

CAMPBELL: They could be if they'd make myths. All they do is put people into bed and take them out again. This naturalism in our art world is . . . all flat-footed prose. And in flat-footed prose there are only two things that are interesting: violence and sex. That's what it's come down to. Everything leads up to it and out of it.

Campbell in the library of his Greenwich Village apartment, about 1960.

"Working out of your own discovery, out of your own realization, who's going to want it? Well, you may be surprised. It's a very difficult decision to make, to do this thing that is an experiment, the creation, bringing forth of a form that was never brought forth before. Now I found it in writing sentences. You can write that sentence in a way that you would have written it last year. Or you can write it in the way of an exquisite nuance that is writing in your mind now. But that takes a lot of waiting for the right word to come."

Joseph Campbell

COUSINEAU: Because of books like yours, especially *The Hero*, there seems to be a movement with writers, including screen-writers, to go back to classical structure, to use myths and fairy tales to try and impose some structure in a medium that's been very free-formed for years. Do you think this could cause some movement between movies as just entertainment into myths?

CAMPBELL: There's no better medium in the world than film; I mean, my God, you can do anything with it. The only thing is to find out what it is that's worth doing.

But there's so much money in a popular show that the temptation to do the popular thing—and that means corny, obvious work—is very difficult to overcome. One of the problems in American art, and it's a problem that's particularly conspicuous in the novel, is the temptation of money. Years ago, when I was a student, I was interested in the American novel in that period of my lifetime, the 1920s. And one after another—you can name any of them, Dreiser, Sinclair Lewis, Hemingway—one after another had been working in their early years to *find* something. The works would get to be more and more exciting as they went on.

Then they'd hit it and suddenly the money would begin to come in. And then the next work has to do the same thing the last one did—and down it all goes.

Now, working out of your own discovery, out of your own realization, who's going to want it?

Well, you may be surprised. It's a very difficult decision to make, to do this thing that is an experiment, the creation, bringing forth of a form that never was brought forth before.

Now *I* found it in writing sentences. You can write that sentence in a way that you would have written it last year. Or you can write it in the way of the exquisite nuance that is writing in your mind now. But that takes a lot of . . . waiting for the right word to come.

Then you send it to the publisher and the copy editor corrects it.

We have to have artists who will be courageous that way. I have mentioned George Lucas. I think that young man opened a vista and knew how to follow it. It was totally fresh, totally fresh.

COUSINEAU: Once you mentioned that the reason that the Japanese are forging ahead of the West is because they know "form." I feel that one of the real delights in reading your work is the thrill of recognition. Your books seem to help people to look at the icons of popular culture, a Superman, a Michael Jackson, or Darth Vader in *Star Wars,* and see the archetypes coming through. Did you plan on this when you were writing early on? Were you trying to resurrect the old stories so that we could resurrect them in our lives?

CAMPBELL: No. I was getting out of the old stories the information as to where the archetypes were. All I have done has been to try to show through the traditions that have come to us where this realm of the muses really is, and what happens when a real artist gets hold of it. I've seen it in the dance, as I say, with Jean's work and in others like Martha Graham and Merce Cunningham or in the work of sculptors or painters. They don't try to copy something that has been given to them; they see an experience of their own life in these terms and that takes knowing what the archetype is and *forgetting* it, then reading out of that something that kicks back all the way. I remember back in the 1940s and 1950s how there were a couple of very important artists who were just doing clichés. This whole thing of the archetypes came up and they were *copying* archetypes. That's not what it's all about; it's to see and experience the archetypology of a *living* moment. What the artist must render is a living moment somehow, a living moment actually in action or an inward experience.

COUSINEAU: With that in mind, isn't there a combustible

power in these archetypes? For an audience to see one, like the witch flying across the sky in *The Wizard of Oz,* there is a visceral feeling like electricity that runs through them. That suggests artists have a responsibility for the archetypes that they use.

CAMPBELL: Oh, no doubt about it. The power of these things is very deep, very deep. And the more one understands them the deeper they get. I mean it goes right down to the ground of biology. The energies that we're living with is what this is all about. No doubt about it.

COUSINEAU: Seeing the influence that your work has had in the arts, I wonder if you have seen transition periods in its influence? First it influenced the students, then the artists, then the society as a whole?

CAMPBELL: What's happened in my own work is that it has influenced largely *people*. And among these people, artists. I don't see how it could influence, let's say, an insurance agent, or somebody like that, in his work, but it might. There are directions I don't know about. But certainly in the arts there's a primary relationship because for me mythology is the homeland of the muses. That's what it's all about. When you touch in there the muse talks to you in your own language. Not *my* language, but your own. In the arts I've seen it work, as I've said already, and I know what it does to people.

COUSINEAU: Of all these myths are there any that stand out over the years that seemed to have influenced people more than others?

CAMPBELL: The main thing is to get into this marvelous literature. It's just a glorious field. All I can say is *go in there* and enjoy it. A big range of reading. If you're not going to go in there and enjoy it and read, you're not going to find the myths. If somebody just reads the newspaper every morning—if that's his only reading, and then he gets *Newsweek* or something else at the end of the week—he's not getting it. You've got to *read*. Or find some other medium to get in touch with them. And then the individual can find the one that talks to him, all by himself, and knows that this one excites him. And if it doesn't excite you, well, phooey. It's not yours.

So I would just say the main thing is to get into this marvelous literature. It is enormous. And if you can read a couple of other languages besides English, you've got a still greater range. It's a glorious field.

BLY: Something happened to me when I heard Joe giving a talk in a conference on beauty in San Francisco. He started to describe Joyce's description in *A Portrait of the Artist as a Young Man,* that there is a difference between proper and improper art. And that improper art is art that when you finish it makes you want to desire something, or loathe it, either way.

And Joe would say, if you have advertising where a woman is saying, "Buy this refrigerator," you say to yourself, I'd like to have that refrigerator. This is art that's pornographic. Because it wants you, it desires you, it leaves you with a desire to have that object. Political art is didactic because the art is still moving, but it makes you want to flee from the politicians.

So then Joseph says all of the novels of the last hundred years, the novelists, have been didactic pornographers. And I was the only person in the audience that clapped! And he looked at me and he smiled. The rest of them were shocked at the immense generalization.

COCKRELL: He told me that the last novel he read was *Finnegans Wake;* since then he has not read a novel.

BLY: Yes, well, this difference between proper and improper art is that proper art has a center, a thread of silence going down the middle of it. So then when you are finished you're at the center of yourself. And you do not move either way.

The funniest thing was that while he was saying this, and I was agreeing with him about proper/improper art, a woman stood up and said, "There will be an antinuclear reading tonight given by Robert Bly at the Women's Center!"

COCKRELL: So *you* were fulfilling a political purpose.

BLY: I was! A lot of my art during the Vietnam war was improper art—

COCKRELL: Yeah, but which is appropriate sometimes.

BLY: No. I would say that during the war improper art is appropriate, but, nevertheless, nobody had ever made that distinction to me. And so what is important to me about Campbell is that this concept is extremely important. It was handed down from poet to poet, indeed from Aquinas originally. It went from

Old friends Joseph Campbell and poet Robert Bly share a private moment during the filming of The Hero's Journey, *Big Sur, California, 1982.*

Aquinas, and then Joyce picked it up from him. But it was not handed down to *my* generation. Joseph is the one who is carrying that knowledge. When I got it from him I immediately realized how important it would be to younger poets.

So I am going to carry it from Joseph, to me, for some of the younger poets.

COCKRELL: The knowledge of how to achieve an aesthetic stasis?

BLY: Yes, yes, there is a difference between proper and improper art. It isn't all the same. Political art can be in some extent improper. You can still respect it but you can see it more clearly. I have done both kinds; I have done proper and improper art but I didn't understand the difference. Joseph's explanation of these functions of myth is really important. Therefore there is something

Creativity consists in going out to find the thing that society hasn't found yet.

Joseph Campbell

wonderful in him because he is like the classic older man who takes the highest ideas of the civilization and carries them and allows them to appear.

COCKRELL: A wise old man embodying wisdom. He is the archetype. That's his archetype.

BLY: That's right.

COCKRELL: He's the guardian.

BLY: And to some extent Eliot and Pound didn't really have a respect for culture, even though Pound is described as the great hero of culture.

COCKRELL: I recall him saying that Aquinas's definition of art required wholeness, harmony, and radiance.

BLY: Yeah, that's right. That's terrific. That's unbelievable. That's right.

COCKRELL: Wholeness, harmony, and radiance, and that when a work had that then you could achieve the status of art.

BLY: Joseph, what is ritual in art, that is to say, inside the poem? I haven't written free verse for many years and I'm getting suspicious.

CAMPBELL: Just looking at it from a purely academic point of view, a ritual is an action that puts the individual not only in touch with, but in the place of, being the agent of a power that is not out of his intention at all. He has to submit to a power that's greater than his own individual life form. Animal rituals, for instance, occur in relation principally to sex games, and also to confrontations between males.

BLY: Which is a greater power.

CAMPBELL: Which is a larger power that's operating in terms of the impulse of the species, you may say, and then the whole thing becomes marvelously ritualized. And who composed the dances of birds? Who composed those dances? They are not individually invented. They are suddenly in the species relationship.

The formality in art releases the individual into a species relationship, and the formality in art releases the individual from his individual system of desires and intentions and links into something else so that he becomes a unique expression of something that is not of himself, of nature. And when this drops out in poetry you get all this art that comes from—well, you must be getting it too, with people sending you their poems.

BLY: What you're saying is that if ritual was understood, confessional poetry would not happen. Because confessional poetry—

CAMPBELL: Wouldn't be confessional! Who wants a confession except some minister who's trying to get you to pay dues to his church?

BLY: That's very interesting. Therefore (and here's another question): Why is it—as I have noticed in reading Pasternak, Makatova, in certain Russians who keep tradition of form very strongly—that there is such respect for sound? The quality you're talking about is in the poem that touches on a force greater than the individual writer, of the Russian person, even no matter.

Also, don't you think one advantage of the city over a more natural environment is that it can fertilize something powerful in the human being, in the artist?

CAMPBELL: Well, I feel that New York's a good place to work, but I think one addresses the city as though it were an *It*, not a *Thou*. And then you're in a situation of combat and relationships to something that's quite other. I've just come out of New York, you know, and a place like this on the Big Sur coast just wakes another whole consciousness. It's further down. And the body feels, Yes, this is my world; I've been missing this. And it seems to me it's out of the body and its relationship to experiences of this kind that the mythic imagination comes. This other experience of the city is far more rational, ethical—

BLY: Well, are you saying that in the city, for example, you don't have as many living beings, so there's not enough things to have an *I-Thou* relationship, and here in the country you have more of them? Is that what you mean?

CAMPBELL: The *I-Thou* relationship in the city is to people.

BLY: Hmmmm.

CAMPBELL: The environment in the city is geometrical and rectangular, and there are no curves; it's contrived by man. The whole environment is also manmade. And here you find that there is a primal being experience of which man and nature are themselves manifestations; whereas in the city you just don't get it.

BLY: You see, it's been a shock to me because I was brought up in poetry to have the *I-Thou* relationship with human beings. And yet, when you look at archaic poetry, ancient poetry, Homer and so on, you have a tremendous amount of awe in relationship to the rocks, to the—

CAMPBELL: To the wine dark sea and the rosy-fingered dawn. We're right in that environment here.

BLY: But you know how it is for me, I'm from Minnesota. I have an *I-Thou* relationship with plant things. What do I do?

CAMPBELL: I don't know. This is the same environment you have in Japan and the East Coast of Asia. There's a long tradition of relationship to the sea. You know, the Chinese idea that art and poetry require water and mountains. The water is the source. In the beginning all was water. One after another of the myths give us that. And it's out of that, then, that the forms come, where life generates.

Years ago, with Ed Ricketts, I went from Carmel, California, right up to Sitka, Alaska, along the coast doing intertidal collecting, and you just felt this was the place of generation. This was the germ bed of our life.

BLY: Mythically, when you look at this, what do you see?

CAMPBELL: Mythically I immediately see the world when the whales swim by. The world is a mystery of the dark depths of the unconscious and the dark out of which all has come. And here I see the security of the enduring, which is what the rock world represents, then the beautiful life of the trees.

Goethe has a wonderful line when he's speaking about the principles of evolution, how along the two lines of the vegetable and the animal world, the culminating mysteries are of the human being and the tree. One finds the nobility of nature here and the power, the *tremendum,* the *fascinans,* of the *mysterium.*

BLY: Can I go back a second? I'm trying to learn from you and what you've done in relation to poetry. I was taught to believe that poems have in them the importance of good sound, the importance of good broken rhythm, the importance of some form. But one of the things that wasn't mentioned to me is the myth, the story, in poetry.

And yet, in ancient poetry, always the poem leads on into a story, which in turn takes the mind of the human being far out into this world, far out into the transcendental world and far out into this.

So the surprise to me is that not only in the form should there be something human, but there should also be this mythic world. Strangely enough, a myth takes a human being and brings some of this incredible material into an apparently domestic or ordinary human being.

CAMPBELL: What the myth does is open the human being and at the same time the natural environment to what Dürkheim calls the transcendence. And the sense of myth is that we all ride on a mystery, and we are manifestations of it, whether it's the nature world or the human world. They are not apart.

BLY: But how does a myth do that? Specifically.

CAMPBELL: It does it always by giving reference *past* the individual. Now what happens in that theological situation is that God becomes concretized; he closes, he's a roadblock. When he becomes mythologized—as in Goethe's words, when "everything transitory is just a reference"—he opens, becomes a reference to something which is the ultimate mystery transcendent, which is the mystery imminent in you and in all things. So there's a participation, a deep realization of participation, and that's the radiance of art.

BLY: Then Jehovah actually in some way prevents us feeling this?

CAMPBELL: Absolutely. It puts you in a relationship-to-him, which has to do with sin and atonement.

BLY: Does this mean that if you start to worship Jehovah for a long period that your sense of myth would disintegrate?

CAMPBELL: It *has* disintegrated. There is no sense of myth in the Judeo-Christian tradition. It's all historical. Fact stuff. Because of this we want to disengage from nature and make our ritual to do with participation in society. The Jewish tradition and a good deal of the Christian leads you to the society. We are one in Christ, not in nature.

Whereas you turn to the Tao and look at this, here is the revelation. And it's a revelation of what? Of a *mysterium*. A mystery. And there are two aspects to it: one is the *tremendum,* the horrific, and the other is the *fascinans,* the charm.

And the function of art is to show these things so that, as Joyce says, they become epiphanies of a radiance.

BLY: I'm a Protestant, and of course, in the Protestant churches we've gone even farther in removing the *tremendum*. We don't have any statues of the Virgin. I was in church in California the other day and there was nothing living in the entire church, and yet we were reading texts that talked about the holiness of the meaning.

CAMPBELL: When I was in Japan for a congress for the study of religion we were at Ise—you know, the beautiful shrines of the royal families, the tradition of the goddess Amaterasu, and so forth. They were beautiful. They're in a wooded environment so that you get the participation with the whole nature world. The goddess is herself the sun goddess.

And beside me was a big Swedish scholar, a very tall fellow. I was looking at this and was trying to feel the way I feel right here, one with all this thing, and he said to me, "Isn't it too bad? I'm a Protestant; I can't appreciate this."

To get removed in that way from participation in this wonderful world you see here! In our tradition there has been a Fall and Nature is not good, Nature is to be criticized, and there is this idea of standing for the good against the evil. Why would a good God create a world of this kind? What a question!

BLY: Hmmm. Shall I recite that little Goethe poem to you?

CAMPBELL: Do that. I would love it.

BLY: Goethe's on a hilltop: "On the tops of all the hills, there is silence. In the tops of the trees, you feel hardly a breath. The little bird falls silent in the trees. Simply wait. Soon, you too will be silent."

There you feel that he's brought the other world of nature into the poem.

CAMPBELL: He's quoted the mythic organic experience.

BLY: How did he get ahold of it?

CAMPBELL: In the first place he's German. They live close to nature. Jung brings this out, you know, from his having been brought up in the country where all these things are taken for granted. There's a continuity from old mythic times in that German world. Somehow the city never took over in Germany. I also saw it when I was a student in Paris. Paris, Paris, Paris. That's a wonderful city.

BLY: Joseph, I wanted to tell you how important I think your teaching is for American poetry. Because poets have what they have from generations past. And when poetry was carried down to us, it came through Eliot and Pound, and there were two things that they did not carry down to us.

One was the difference between proper and improper art, that Joyce got from Aquinas, and which you are the only one who is saying is a distinction. I've been very grateful to receive that from you, that distinction.

CAMPBELL: Thank you, Robert.

BLY: And the second thing is this. The power of myth and story in poetry. You are the only one who is carrying that. Eliot brings it into "The Waste Land," and yet it is so broken, and so used for symbolic means. In some way he did not respect the actual story that he used in "The Waste Land." And Pound did not respect those stories that he broke into fragments in the "Cantos."

You are the only one who has carried down the ancient view that a myth and a story is a holy thing; it's a natural part of art and is not to be fragmented or symbolized or rationalized.

And I am very grateful to you for the work you've done your whole life on this.

CAMPBELL: That's a beautiful thing to hear, Robert, and from you it means something. I really do appreciate it.

BLY: The last three or four years in my association with you, your teaching of the second thing has changed my poetry tremendously.

CAMPBELL: That was my thought in the beginning, that this material was material for poets and artists. Jean, my wife, is a dancer; she has fed on it. I know how it works. But, gosh, the chance to hear it from you is a big experience, and I thank you.

The modern hero, the modern individual who dares to heed the call and seek the mansion of that presence with whom is our whole destiny to be atoned, cannot, indeed must not, wait for his community to cast off its slough of pride, fear, rationalized avarice, and sanctified misunderstanding. "Live," Nietzsche says, "as although the day were here." It is not society that is to guide and save the creative hero, but precisely the reverse. And so every one of us shares the supreme ordeal—carries the cross of the redeemer—not in the bright moments of his tribe's great victories, but in the silences of his personal despair.

Joseph Campbell,
*The Hero with a
Thousand Faces*

Joseph Campbell, age eighty, next to a Kwakiutl totem pole in the room he visited as a young boy enchanted with American Indians. The Museum of Natural History, New York, 1984.

8

The Master of
Two Worlds

In the twilight years of his career Joseph Campbell basked in his status as maverick scholar. He lectured to overflow crowds, made frequent radio appearances, and worked relentlessly on his final project, the ambitious four-volume *The Historical Atlas of World Mythology,* a rhapsody on a theme of an unfinished book of his, *An Outline of Everything,* which he wrote in graduate school.

After a particularly grueling book tour in 1983, Campbell was prompted to articulate his deepening perceptions on the meaning and roots of myth. The result was *The Inner Reaches of Outer Space: Myth as Metaphor and as Religion,* published in 1986. The book was a fusion of his ideas that the laws of outer space and inner space—the human imagination within the body—are one and the same. The authentic source of a new, global mythology is in the psyche of today's creative artists, a synthesis of science and spirit.

In February 1987 *The Hero's Journey: The World of Joseph Campbell* premiered at the New Directors/New Films Festival at the Museum of Modern Art in New York City. Four months later, in May 1987, at the West Coast premiere of the documentary at the Director's Guild in Hollywood, Joseph Campbell and his wife Jean Erdman saw the film in public for the first time. The panel discussion that followed proved to be Campbell's next-to-last public appearance.

BROWN: If you had had a computer to accelerate the time spent in retrieving information, what kind of difference do you think it would have made in your life?

CAMPBELL: If I had a computer when I started my writing, my reading, my note taking. . . . I had files: one, two, three, four, five, six, seven, eight, nine, ten, eleven, twelve, thirteen regular business files, cabinet files, packed tight with notes taken by hand. If that had been done on a computer I could have retrieved my own information immediately. I can't now. I have to remember where it is and go futzing around getting it. It's all sunk into the files, you might say, and that's the only loss I feel with a computer.

The important thing about information and the way that I got it is not the information but the *experience* of the information. It's a love affair, really, of getting in touch with a world of thinking and experiencing that you can't get from just the supplying of information. In writing, of course, I need the information that I already know, and yet I want to know exactly what the page is and the book I got it from.

Up to five weeks ago I did all my writing with a pen or pencil, and I look at this thing, and you know what this kind of thing costs, and I think, my God, what a substitute for a pencil. That's all it is, really. But, what it can do! I'm becoming enchanted. It's a world of magical action, this funny little thing with all its little people in there who would do these things for you.

BROWN: I remember you telling me once a great story about Eisenhower and the computer during the 1950s.

CAMPBELL: Oh, yes. There's a story about Eisenhower. It was in his time that we began to realize what an important thing the computer was. He's said to have gone into a room full of computers and put the question, "Is there a God?"

The computers worked around and lights flashed and wheels turned and all that kind of thing. Finally a voice came out and said, "Now there is."

196

Campbell writing at home in Honolulu. The statue of the Bodhidharma that Heinrich Zimmer's widow gave him sits atop the desk, 1985.

So I've got a god in the room here. I know a lot about gods and I have found what god this is by the way it behaves. This is the God of the Old Testament: a lot of rules and no mercy. And if he catches you picking up sticks on Saturday you're finished.

COUSINEAU: Have you named your computer?

CAMPBELL: Ha! The young woman from IBM who prepared my software took some of my books that I'd written and she saw what she thought I would require and made a beautiful program for me. Then she surprised me while she was putting it all together by saying, "Well, what's the *name* of your computer?"

Suddenly I had to figure the name and I named it Parzival, who is my idea of the great occidental hero. The Grail romance, the whole business of transcending the ego system with the experience of opening of the heart with compassion: That's what Parzival is all about.

Well, *he* doesn't have compassion [pointing to his computer].

COUSINEAU: And what's the story behind this Parzival?

CAMPBELL: It works this way. Parzival, seeking the Grail Castle, went back and forth over the place where the Grail Castle was and it wasn't there. Then one time it was there—and the next time it wasn't there.

That's the way it is with this darned thing; I try to get it to do something for me and I do the things that I think I'm supposed to do and the wrong thing happens. Then I do what I think's the same thing and the right thing happens. So, I'm in the magic territory, part of the Grail mystery, and getting to know exactly the rules. Another thing I think of here is those Arabian knights and the jinn in the bottle. They come out and work and work and work for you, but they are very tricky. They can kill you.

COCKRELL: How do you feel about your personal life at this point in what you want to accomplish?

CAMPBELL: What I want is to enjoy it. It's like a boat having come into harbor. I remember when we used to be on boats; it's a lovely thing to come into a harbor and see the environment . . . and dwell there. That's where I am.

I'm finding more and more that the Indian idea of renunciation for old age is a very good idea. You give up any system of

Joseph Campbell proudly accepts an honorary PhD from the Pratt Institute in Brooklyn, New York, 1976.

commitment and just live out of this moment and the necessity of this moment, because, God, you've already given everything that's necessary, and your life has made its statement by that time. Anything you put on top of it now is just a footnote.

And so this isn't the time for footnotes. This is the time for enjoying the experience of fulfillment; it's a moment of fulfillment. And it's a rich and beautiful moment.

Somebody asked me, "Would you like to be younger?"

I said, "Yeah, I'd like to be seventy-one!"

I wouldn't want to go back of that.

COCKRELL: When you look back over your life to see who the great inspirations were, who do you think of? I know Spengler was very influential on you—

CAMPBELL: Oh, well, the reading of Spengler was, I think, the great intellectual crisis of my life.

COCKRELL: And what was it that Spengler opened for you? What was that impact?

CAMPBELL: The realization that the growth, flowering, and aging of societies is an organic process and inevitable. And that at certain stages in the social development you are in a period, as it were, of youth. Then comes a period of maturity, and then comes a period of aging and disintegration and a shift of accent. There is a change in what might be called spiritual energy.

Now at my age I'm able to experience something that otherwise I could only have talked about. And that is this problem in life of the proportion of energy to mass. You see kids running around with all this energy, and since I'm living now with much older people here in Honolulu, there's this *mass,* and the energy just isn't there. This has happened in society, too. The *massiveness* of our life conditions and the energy to enliven them is what we lack.

The other thing about Spengler was that he was a man of great intuitive power. He foresaw *date by date* what was going to happen to us in our spiritual and cultural life. I read Spengler in 1932, and so we have fifty years since then, and I would say, date by date, he puts his name on it.

COCKRELL: Age does have its compensations—

CAMPBELL: Oh, the compensations are *enormous.*

COCKRELL: The experience of the present where the future is no longer so important and the present comes through with the vitality it doesn't have in youth.

CAMPBELL: Every decision made by a young person is life-decisive. It really is. What seems to be a small problem is really a large one—whether the water falls six inches this way or six inches that way, down the other side—and so it is in life. Two people looking at each other in youth and their life destiny waiting there. So everything that is done early in life is functionally related to a life trajectory. And then comes the time when there is no future, nothing to live *for;* it's been lived. And the mind is then dwelling in the richness and wealth of something already lived and the moment that one is in, a moment of plastic presence, not just something serving something else, but *it* is *it.*

That's a grand experience.

I think it's important that one should be careful early in life to live with integrity because I find, for example, in my own thinking, that those things that I did that were a little off, which are the ones that sit in my mind, are really reprehensible acts. They may not have been regarded so, but in your terms of your own sense of integrity this comes back as a challenge. And it's not nice to live with. I think that's what purgatory and hell are for: remembering what you should not have done.

COCKRELL: What role could mythology serve in helping this troubled world today—

CAMPBELL: You asked about newspapers before, well, let me tell you, a little bit of honesty would be what we need there. Not just the sensationalism that's going to sell the newspaper.

Today you read of our interest in clearing up apartheid in South Africa and we don't think about our own Native Americans, what we have done to them, what we are doing to them. We're taking the mote out of our neighbor's eye with a beam in our own that isn't matched in the history of civilization. And those people, our own native people, are still living in a subcivilized condition that's been put upon them. I don't see any of our ambitious youth picket-lining to give Indians their due.

COCKRELL: What did Joyce mean when he said, "History is a nightmare from which I am trying to awake?"

CAMPBELL: He meant exactly that. Nightmares are moved by powers out of rational control, and they represent terror and fear, and that's what history is. Judging history in terms of the chakra system, history is chakra number three: the chakra of aggression—beating up the guy next door. That's where it starts. That's the way it is.

COCKRELL: For you, personally, where are the real nuggets of mythology for the people of the world, the individuals in their quest for self-fulfillment?

CAMPBELL: The way mythology is integrated in life is by way of ritual. What has to be ritualized is what is essential to the life of the day. If one is to try to bring a mythological perspective into *action* in the modern world one has to understand the relationship of what is being done to the essentials of life, not to the superficialities of life. The essentials of life remain the same; they've been the same since the Paleolithic caves. Eating, reproduction, being a child, being mature, growing old. To realize that these things one is doing are not personally initiated acts but are functions of a biologically present world within yourself is to live in a very different way from the way one lives if one feels that one is the volitional initiator of everything going on.

Just, for instance, the business of growing old. Trying to hang onto youth, trying to hang onto what was really great twenty

Joseph Campbell and Jean Erdman during a break in a seminar at the Featherpipe Ranch, Montana, 1978.

years ago, throws you totally off. You've got to go with it and seek the *abundance* that's in this new thing. If you hang onto the old thing, you will not experience the new. In traditional society, like that of India, which really had ritualized everything, the different stages of life are clearly marked off. The individual actually will sometimes change his name. His name becomes changed as he moves from one stage to another.

Another thing is that when you initiate someone into a role in government, or to play the function of supervising a field, the person must know that he's not acting as himself. He's acting as a functionary. When the judge walks into the courtroom people stand. Not because it's the guy, but because he represents a function. One is not standing out of respect to him; we're standing out of respect to his role. To act as though and live as though your role is what is significant about you in a social way is what a mythologically grounded life will enable you to do.

Individualism is perfectly fine if the individual realizes that the grandeur of his being is that of representing something. Even representing a system of ideals and images that the rest of the world and the environment doesn't have; he still is the agent of something and he is a presence. But when the individual is acting only for himself or for his family or for his team, then you have nothing but chaos.

The myths, when they are translated into rites, organize the field. Now you can see why the world today is in trouble. What is the social field today? The social field is the planet, and there isn't a single system of action that has to do with the planet. They all have to do with one interest group or another interest group. And to bring out in newspapers, or one or another of the media, the sense of humanity as being the totality of which you are a member—into your tribe, not your social class. I think that it's an absolute necessity.

I know what the power of education is because I was brought up in one era with the ideas of democracy. And I saw those democratic ideals disintegrated and eliminated in teaching in schools when a lot of people with an idea of society as being the shaper of everything came in. What came out very clearly at Sarah Lawrence when I went to teach there was, as I've said, the great joy in finding what the student wanted and needed and then trying to furnish the information that would render it.

Then I found that more than 50 percent of the faculty were

not doing what I would call educating, drawing out, they were *indoctrinating*. Giving a discipline of a certain sociological perspective that became dogma on campus. And that was happening on every campus in the United States. And as a result there was total destruction of a whole point of view that was taken for granted when I was a kid.

Formerly, on our campuses, we never read modern novels, we did not read daily newspapers, we were hermetically sealed from the journalism of the day, from what was happening today. And instead of always responding to, "Oh, no, what about this and what about that and the other thing? There's picket lines over here and there . . ." you are in touch with eternal concerns.

And it can be done. I know what the power of education is . . . and an education will do it . . . has done it.

COUSINEAU: You've spoken in depth about what the study of myth can do for an individual. And we've spoken about the influence that reading myths has had on artists, scholars, and scientists. What about children and young students? I understand that you and Robert Bly went to North Dakota a few years ago for a conference on education in the year 2000 and that you suggested that mythology be a required subject. Just what effect do you think it would have on society if kids were raised thinking mythically? What effect on society as a whole?

CAMPBELL: It would certainly have an influence on the kids. It would change their lives. It would also change their attitude toward life. And, of course, the society is constituted of kids, so that in a sense it would be a society of people who were living not only for the superficialities which the mind and the appetite indicate as being worth living for, but would be living for something that they had found that was of deeper, more inward value than those things.

Something like this is coming up now in this anti-war movement that we have, which has become actually a sociological fact. I've had a century of wars. And after each one all you realize is disappointment, that what they said it was all about wasn't what

Once in Eugene, Oregon, after a lecture in which I had dealt with the age stages as described by Dante, this young woman comes up to me later and says, "Well, Dr. Campbell, you don't understand. Today we go directly from infancy to wisdom." I said, "That's marvelous. All you've missed is life."

Joseph Campbell

it was about. And that the chap on the other side had as much right for his impulse as we had for ours. People are beginning to think there are deeper values than those which are achieved through these sociological, pathological madnesses.

And it's also coming out now in the ecological movement. We have to live in relation to nature; we mustn't conquer it, as the Bible tells us to do. We must live with it.

COUSINEAU: What kind of curriculum would you suggest?

CAMPBELL: When I was teaching at Sarah Lawrence I gave a course in mythology, and that course related to every other course on the campus. It had a relationship because it was a core course. This was the most popular course on campus. I could see how it enriched all of their understanding of the work they were doing.

And so everybody thinks his own subject's the great one. I think this is the one subject there is! And it could be introduced in the freshman year. A course in the archetypes of myth: It would be a wonderful course.

COUSINEAU: If one of the divisive forces of our culture is that we don't have common stories any more, the common myth, can that be changed for the good by the power of the modern media? When *Star Wars* can be shown in the jungles of Thailand or the villages of the Philippines, will that change how knowledge and tradition are passed down because of the immediacy of our storytelling?

CAMPBELL: My thought about the present moment is really a sociological one. Every mythology is scheduled or composed in the service of a certain society. Everyone has developed within a certain horizon. The experiences of that society in that horizon are what are the living element in the myth, what grabs people and holds them to the society in which they're dwelling.

You cannot export myth. Either through space or through time. And this is one of the problems of our whole biblical tradition. Here is a mythology that grew out of a social context that is so far away from what we have now that it is not servicing our psyches. It always has to be interpreted to us. And artwork that you have to have someone tell about is not working on you. But it's the *Aha!*, which tells you it is you, that is necessary in myth.

And so the myth that we think we are living by is not operating on us. Hence confusion; hence a sense of tension; hence a sense of anxiety; everything that you're doing, the very nature of your life is denied by the myth that we have. Every natural act is a sinful act, as I say, unless it's been baptized or circumcized. This denigration of life is one of the terrible things about our ideals because they're not out of our life. Nietzsche has a saying in *The Will to Power* that all ideals of this kind must be rejected, that they denigrate the life which is. You see? Ideals have to grow out of experience.

Now that's the artist's function: to take the experience. With respect to the sociology, to what society do you belong? The society of the planet is the only valid one now. It is the only one that's valid. And yet what we see is everybody pulling back into in-group loyalty, class loyalty, even, you might say, of school loyalties. No one is courageous enough in the major field to think in terms of a planetary commitment. The themes of myths will be the same a hundred years from now as they were four thousand years ago, the basic themes. But the *evolving* situation is *one* community to which the myth is in service, and the other is the natural and scientific field of experience that one is having. There's no use having a mythology that's talking about something that was true in 4000 B.C. but is no longer true.

A couple of years ago Joseph and I were invited by the colleges of North Dakota to give them advice on what the curriculum should be in the year 2000. Joseph said that he thought that mythology should be at the center of it because it is the only thing that could unite science and humanity, as mythology did in ancient times.

And then we developed this idea that when people came into the university they would read thirty or forty myths, each of them. They would choose then one myth. Because the idea is that we are probably being related to by a myth and we are being lived by it unconsciously because we are too stupid to study the myth. And there's a very big difference between living something consciously and being lived by it.

Then the student would choose the one myth that attracted him and then spend time in college seeing how far he lived it and how far the myth lived him. And that would be valuable for the scientist as well. He could be living a myth unconsciously and not know it.

Robert Bly,
Esalen, 1982

FAVROT: Do you not think that a single individual can create a group mythology? That someone like the Buddha could possibly, through his own powers and inner sense, depict a mythology for an entire group?

CAMPBELL: This whole problem of the origins of mythology and how they relate to prophecies and teachings is a very delicate one. I don't think anything that I would say should be taken as a final statement. But my feeling is that on the primitive level the mythology comes out of very small groups, which have the whole genus experience. They are all having essentially the same experiences, they all have the same inward life, and so the spontaneity of that is indicated in its behavior.

The question finally involves the problem of: What is the group? The early mythologies come out of very small groups. Every mythology has grown up within a bounded horizon and the people within that horizon are having equivalent experiences, more or less. So that a signal like this will strike the same responses in everybody in the group. If you can't do that you don't have an operating mythology. The people who become the teachers and spokesmen are those who go into trance states, and they experience the unconscious system of the others in the group. They all have about the same psychological situation. He becomes the mouthpiece, and unless you have the type of people who are in touch with that kind of group need, you're not going to have real group mythologies.

FAVROT: What you're saying then is that the myth has to be projected on to fertile soil so that it can develop in the group?

CAMPBELL: It *comes out* of the fertile soil by means of a visionary, a shaman, a person who has gone out and come back. It then falls on the same fertile soil and you have a group situation.

Just think of the origin myths of any mythology whatsoever. Take the Hebrew thing of Moses going up on the mountain and coming back and giving it to the people who all are in the same fix! You see what I mean? They are! And it's a new fix! It's a different fix from the one that was there before. And poor Aaron with his Golden Calf represented the other situation out of which the people had come that was typical worship of the divine lunar power through the symbol of the moon bull.

Now Moses comes down from the mountain with his horns of light on his head and he has this little message. He had to enforce it actually; that sometimes happens, too, that people come in with what you might call an elite, a special doctrine, which they force on a people. This is how Christianity was brought to Europe.

Even before the Buddha comes along (563 to 483 B.C. are his dates) there had been a development in India, the development of the Upanishads. The whole theme of the Upanishads is really that the ultimate mystery is right within you: *Tat tvat svi.* You are it. You are yourself the mystery.

How to find it? There are techniques for the search. And the Buddhists' way was one of five or six other ways working in the same field, concern, consciousness. So what the Buddha is talking to is the result of an elite group of people now moving into positions that make it possible for them to understand and to take on the Buddhist doctrine. From there it spreads.

It's quite a different kind of missionizing from that of Christianity and Islam. The Muslim and Christian way has been by violence, going in and converting people. Now in Buddhism and Hinduism one waits. It's already there.

BROWN: But what if you don't know what myth you're living by? How can you ever know?

CAMPBELL: You can ask yourself, if you're wondering about your own mythology, What is your group? With what group do you identify? The requirement of today is becoming more and more obvious. It is the recognition that the world is so small and so tightly interlocked, that the community, the actual community, is a world community. There's no mythology to take that in. And in reaction to this need for a total society, you have a lot of in groups, people pulling back into their own Chosen People group, or Black Power group, or capitalist group, or this blue-collar group, and you get mythological groups oriented to parts of the totality. So it can't last.

FAVROT: Do you recognize any modern myths being developed, or do you see that we are living on myths of the olden days?

Professor Campbell and students, late 1960s.

CAMPBELL: You've got to live on myths of the olden days! The elementary ideas are constant, they remain, they remain, they remain.

The problem is the inflection. How are the myths represented? And the function of the artist is to present these eternal mysteries in terms of a contemporary context of life. Obviously not many of them have been doing it. There have been some, artists and literary people. I take Joyce; I take Thomas Mann; I take Proust; I take Eliot; I take Yeats. These are visionaries, poets, for modern man. I think, for instance, of Joyce's work as a kind of *purana,* a kind of sacred text, for contemporary man. It's all right there.

But as for popular mythology you have to deal not only with the intellectuals but also down to the very roots, and a good mythology works right up and down the line. Christianity in its best period did, and the Buddhist tradition still does. You can pass from a very simple naturalistic interpretation of the deities and powers to a highly sophisticated one without a break. You don't have to lose your childhood mythology to achieve things. But in our tradition that continuity has been lost.

ARRIEN: Where do you think we are now in the history of civilization?

CAMPBELL: It's interesting when you think of the history of civilizations, the early civilizations or Gothic civilizations in Europe. When you approached a town the first thing you would see was the religious center, the high cathedral.

In the later centuries, the sixteenth or seventeenth centuries, the most important building you would see would be the palace.

And now when approaching a city what do you see? You see economic privilege, office buildings and dwellings. The whole thing is illustrated in a magnificent way in Salt Lake City. Brigham Young built it with the idea of the religious center. The temple was in the center and so you had the structured city, a beautifully structured city. Very soon the capital would be erected, on a hill a little higher than that where the temple was.

When you approach now the tallest building is the office building that executes all the prisoners of the temple. So the whole of civilization is there, and of course, that's the end, the end.

So the question is whether a civilization that has run its course can be reactivated. Goethe has a wonderful paper, which is called, "The Ages of the Spirit." It starts with the poetic Mythic Period, then there is the Religious Period, and then the Philosophical Period, and then the period simply of "naturalistic prose," as he says at the end of the paper, "out of which God himself could not generate another world."

Now that's a pretty pessimistic view but I do think that we are at the end of a civilization. And I do think we're at the beginning of a global age. That is to say, it's now once more a globe. No longer do you have different cultures within their bounded horizons, ignorant of each other and indifferent to each other. All horizons are broken.

That's another thing Black Elk brought out. Do you know the passage? "I stood on the highest mountain of the world and I knew more than I saw, I understood more than I knew, because I was seeing in a sacred manner. And what I saw were the hoops of all the nations interlocking in one great cycle." So he saw it.

And so that's a new age.

DREESSEN: One that regenerates the heart.

CAMPBELL: It does, I think, to get that thought across.

Well, who knows what the sea is going to produce next, this milky ocean from which all our lives come, with the whales going by, always the whales going by.

∞

CAMPBELL: When life becomes only problems, as in marriage, or with this silly chap, Hamlet, "to be or not to be," then you're in a late stage of civilization and you're on the way down.

Life has to be spontaneous. It has to come from what's called in India the *anandamaya* culture, the Sheaf of Bliss. Life is an expression of bliss.

COCKRELL: I've always wondered where you were first inspired with this idea of following your bliss.

CAMPBELL: There is this wonderful theme of the Five Sheaths in the *anandamaya* culture in India, that life is an expression of bliss. The Five Sheaths are sheaths that enclose the mystery of the life germs. The outermost sheath is called the Food Sheath, *anamayakosha*. A body is made of food and it becomes food for the worms or vultures or the flames. That's just the outer matter.

The second sheath is called the Sheath of Breath. *Pranamayakosha.* Here you draw in the oxygen that oxygizes and turns this simple food sheath into something alive.

The third sheath is called *monamayakosha,* the Sheath of the Mind. This mind that I'm talking about, this one up here, is in touch with what's going on out here. It feels pain, it feels pleasure, it relates to all of that. Then there's a great gap and the next sheath is inwards, the fourth sheath, this is called *vigyanamayakosha,* the Sheath of Wisdom. This is the sheath that built the body in the mother womb, that is keeping us alive here and in form, that moves the grasses and the trees. It's deeper than the *monamayakosha,* which is in touch with pain and pleasure.

This other is a Sheath of Spontaneous Wisdom. When we're digesting our breakfast or we have digested it, not one of us here could furnish the chemical formulae for digesting a meal and turning it into a body. Yet each of us has done it. That's this inward sheath.

The disparity between the way of thinking between the Sheath of the Mind, *monamayakosha,* and the way of experiencing of the Wisdom Sheath is the disparity that is bridged by mythic symbols. The myth is the voice of the Wisdom Sheath speaking to the Sheath of the Mind which can get way off center, bringing it back to fit the nature order.

Deeper than the Wisdom Sheath, and this is the ultimate sheath within, is the Sheath of Bliss. *Anandamayakosha.* All life is driven by bliss. The mind up here thinks it's in pain and in trouble and the body's saying, No, sir, you're in bliss, only you just don't know it.

The function then of mythology is to connect you to your bliss and find where it truly is. When you get yourself off course or you accept some moral principle that is altogether cockeyed and related to something that isn't natural at all, dismiss it and follow the bliss.

CAMPBELL: I don't know whether you know those forms in Cambodia. There's a great temple there with a lot of heads, four great heads, and they're all in bliss. There's a smile in bliss. On the top of each there is a lotus. That is the lotus of the known world. Our *monamayakosha,* the Mental Sheath, is up here on top. The goal of meditation is to get you down below the lotus petal into the root and you will find bliss there. Even when one is in the greatest pain, it's a great salvation in the course of the crises of life to realize that no matter what happens up here or down here, you are in bliss. You can accept these events in terms of accidents and ambitions. But, no, you rest well in bliss all the time.

For example, some of the puberty initiations of the American Indian tribes were terribly painful ordeals. The young men were battered around and actually made to pass out in pain. And they'd pass out into bliss. This relationship of the two is a fundamentally logical theme. In our culture we're always thinking about ethics and morality and pain and the greatest good of the greatest number and all that.

Nonsense! We forget that life doesn't give a damn about the greatest good of the greatest number! What it gives a damn about is that all should be in bliss!

BROWN: Joe, do you think you have to give up your cognition, your thinking, in order to achieve what you're calling bliss?

CAMPBELL: No, but you've got to change it. This is the point that comes out all along the line in *Faust.* Goethe says,

Mephistopheles cannot control what Faust has done. All he can do is supply the means of Faust's achieving. But he cannot dictate what's to be achieved.

When the Mental Sheath becomes the dictator, that's a diabolical life. That's life governed by concepts instead of the dynamic of life.

DREESSEN: That's when you create your own disaster so that you can then have a rebirth of the bliss.

CAMPBELL: And you associate yourself, not with the thing that cracked up, but with the dynamic that transcends all of this.

BROWN: But you don't have to seek out disaster—

DREESSEN: Oh, no. It's there already [laughter].

CAMPBELL: Yes. Well, I think that those five sheaths are an enormously helpful thing. This is in the Vedanta tradition of India. If you think of the dialogue between the *monamayakosha,* the Mental Sheath, which is linking you to the body, and the Food Sheath, and the *rajasguna,* which is an expression of the real energy dynamic, you really see the sense of the shift of accent that mythology asks.

I've only recently seen it happen. Friends of mine, actually relatives of mine, suffered a very sudden shock with a death in the family that happened within hours. I mean, the person was in perfect health and then the aorta bursts and he's dead in a couple of hours.

You would have thought that the wife and sister of this man would have been shattered. No. They had already had a good base and they rode that thing.

They are people who have been thinking of these things for a long, long time in their lives and have suffered before and know how to place the center. And when you know how to place your center, you can take anything. You really can.

BROWN: They weren't locked into a psychological model that says you have to have a loving mother, a loving father, and the right school, and the appropriate profession in order to be free.

CAMPBELL: It doesn't do any harm, though.

ARRIEN: How would these five sheaths apply to relationships?

CAMPBELL: There are relationships that are based simply on the mental relationships. But the deep relationships—and there are two kinds—are the family relationship, the people with whom you are really of one body and are very deeply related. It's a relationship on the Wisdom Sheath side.

The other is the relationship that comes from a recognition of the common life, common goals, a kind of falling in love relationship, that is Wisdom Sheath stuff.

ARRIEN: Wisdom Sheath stuff?

CAMPBELL: You recognize mysterious spot relationships and the depth of being together is plenty. The only thing you've got to be taught if you're working on some project is just being together. That's Wisdom Sheath.

ARRIEN: And there's bliss?

CAMPBELL: Don't you feel it?

ARRIEN: Yes, or I wouldn't have asked!

COCKRELL: Can you expand on just *how* to follow your bliss—

CAMPBELL: I think there's no other way to live. There's a line at the end of Sinclair Lewis's *Babbit* where Mr. Babbitt says, "I never did a thing I wanted to in my life." He's a *dry stick.*

I actually heard a man use the expression in Bronxville one night before I was married. I was living there where I was teaching. And there was this one Greek restaurant where we used to like to go. Thursday night was the maid's night off so the restaurant would be full of families. And one night at the table next to me was a little family of a father, a mother, and a scrawny little twelve or thirteen-year-old boy.

And the father says to the boy—I heard this!—the father says to the boy, "Drink your tomato juice." The kid says, "I don't want to." And the father, in a louder voice, says, "Drink your tomato juice!" And then the mother says, "Don't make him do what he doesn't want to do!"

Then the father says, "*He* can't go through life doing what he wants to do. He'll be dead!" He said, "Look at *me*; I never did a thing I wanted to in all my life—"

I couldn't believe it! There it was right out of the book.

Now, I taught for one year in a boy's prep school, the prep school I'd gone to myself, and there was the moment for those boys when things were dawning on them. And then the question comes up, "Is there money in it?"

So all these people talk to me and I'd say, "Listen, do what *you* want to do, and don't worry about the money."

I'm enjoying life, so that's how I put my practice into teaching. And the little thing I have suggested for people who are trying to find their way is to follow your bliss. I've followed my bliss. And it's been a good way. But as for writing an autobiography, I feel so sad and nostalgic every time I look back at any period in my life, I can't bear to do it.

Joseph Campbell: The Theater of the Open Eye, New York, 1983

And what then is finally the best austerity, what is the best discipline? The best discipline is to enjoy your friends. Enjoy your meals. Realize what play is. Participate in the play, in the play of life. This is known as maha-suka, *the Great Delight.*

Joseph Campbell

And I have a firm belief in this now, not only in terms of my own experience, but in knowing about the experiences of other people. When you follow your bliss, and by bliss I mean the *deep sense of being in it,* and doing what the *push* is out of your own existence—it may not be fun, but it's your bliss and there's bliss behind pain too.

You follow that and doors will open where there were no doors before, where you would not have thought there were going to be doors, and where there wouldn't be a door for anybody else.

There's something about the integrity of a life. And the world moves in and helps. It really does.

And so I think the best thing I can say is follow your bliss. If your bliss is just your fun and your excitement, you're on the wrong track. I mean, you need instruction. Know where your bliss is. And that involves coming down to a deep place in yourself.

RICHARD BEBAN: It occurs to me, as we sit here tonight, just how truly remarkable it is that seven or eight of the top ten grossing films of all time, according to *Variety,* are in some way based on material that you have presented to their creators through your books. Films by George Lucas, George Miller, Steven Spielberg, that entire axis of people, have been deeply influenced by your work.

I heard a wonderful story, though, that you hadn't actually *gone* to a movie in over thirty years and then one rainy night in New York a few years back, you said to Jean, "Hey, let's go out and go to a movie."

CAMPBELL: Well, Jean looked kind of depressed that evening and I thought, God, what can we do to sort of help? So I said, "Jean, let's go to the movies." She said, "The movies? You haven't said a thing like that for years!" "Well," I said, "let's go."

So we walked out and the first movie we saw was this one of *2001*. We walked in and the first thing I see is chapter one from my book *Primitive Mythology,* with all the Australopithecines jumping around. But one of them was interested in something else

Joseph Campbell and panel at the Director's Guild, Los Angeles, for the West Coast premiere of The Hero's Journey. *At his right is John Densmore, to his left are moderator Richard Beban, Stuart Brown, and Phil Cousineau, 1987.*

besides sandwiches—he had a sense of awe and mystery. That's the whole theme, the sense of the awe and mystery of life. That means more to the development of the human spirit than economics. You have the division there of what I think of as the two orders of mankind: the one who is still the Australopithecine and is interested in economics primarily, and the one who is willing to follow the adventure. And so the adventure carries him around the moon and then out into the sky. And there it is still, that marvelous megalith he leaves behind, vibrating. I thought that was wonderful.

The other thing that they did that came out of chapter one was the image of the thigh bone of a gazelle that is used to hit someone. This idea came from a man named Raymond Dart, a South African anthropologist, who was dealing with the skulls of these sort of proto-human hominids. He found that some of the skulls had been dented by something shaped like a double knob. Then he found that the dent fit the thigh bone of a gazelle. He realized there were two kinds of creatures in the world. Those that were using weapons and those that weren't. Those that were using weapons to kill were meat-eaters; those that were getting killed were the vegetarians. That taught me a *big* lesson [laughter].

It's out of that higher consciousness, you might say, that the manipulation of material into tools comes. Now animals do use tools but they don't use tools with an intention to use them later. They use them right now. They pick up a stone and throw it at somebody. But to fashion a tool that will then fashion other tools, and all of this kind of thing, this is another kind of consciousness. This is the beginning of man, and the beginning of culture.

To see that bone in the movie hurled into the sky and turn into that great machine, that was a wonderful moment, this is a kind of *genial imaging* of enormous ideas, struck me in that film. I think there was a lot of it there.

Well then, it was another ten years when George Lucas got in touch with me and invited Jean and me to see *Star Wars*. I hadn't seen another movie since the *2001*. I caught up in one day on the whole movie industry. George invited us to that viewing theater in his place [Skywalker Ranch] there in San Rafael. In the morning I saw *Star Wars,* then talked about it with George, and in the afternoon I saw *The Empire Strikes Back,* and then in the evening I saw *The Return of the Jedi.* So it was a big day [laughter].

The next morning he showed Jean and me the two films that he had done before that. The most delicious thing is that *American Graffiti.*

BEBAN: Isn't that a wonderful movie?

CAMPBELL: After spending thirty-eight years teaching those kids, well, this was the whole generation! It was just wonderful. It started off exactly right. The young chap [Charles Martin Smith] gets off his motorcycle and knocks something over. He can't quite handle where he is! It was beautiful.

And then George showed the film before that he had done. And, my God, I was surprised. Years and years ago, Maya Deren and I and some other people formed a thing we called the Creative Film Foundation for little films that were made with hand-held cameras. Every year we gave an award for the best film of that particular year. We got all these films, films, films from all these young people. And the normal film was the one that George showed me that was the first film he'd done, of the misunderstood person with everything in him wandering through a city that doesn't know what a wonderful person he is. We had those by the dozen every year! It was a very thrilling thing to see that this man had started out where they all start, you might say, and then in two enormous leaps he had made these grand strides. I think this is a tremendous career. This is a young man with a mind that is magnificent. And I'm so proud that something I did helped him define his own truth.

Then the next great, proud moment was when Mickey Hart and Bob Weir [of the Grateful Dead] come along and tell me

I've helped them. Well, I never—the rock music never appealed to me at all. It was largely monotonous, it seemed to me [laughter]. Then they invited Jean and me to an event in Oakland [California] that just became a dance revelation. I got something there that made me note that this is magic. And it's magic for the future.

BEBAN: How so?

CAMPBELL: They hit a level of humanity that makes everybody at one with each other. It doesn't matter about this race thing, this age thing, I mean, everything else dropped out. The wonderful thing was, compared to the Hitler rallies that you see in the film [*The Hero's Journey*] that were used to a political purpose, here it was just the experience of the identity of everybody with everybody else.

I was carried away in a rapture. And so I am a Deadhead now [laughter].

Then a wonderful thing happened when Lynne Kaufman, who conducts the UC Berkeley Extension program, had the wonderful idea of a wonderful day of having Joe Campbell and John Weir Perry, a psychiatrist, and the Grateful Dead. I was to give a

Joseph Campbell shares the stage with Jerry Garcia and Mickey Hart of the Grateful Dead during a seminar entitled "From Ritual to Rapture." Palace of Fine Arts, San Francisco, 1986.

lecture on "Ritual and Rapture from Dionysus to the Grateful Dead." And I did.

John Perry gave a lecture on the imagery of schizophrenia and how in following it out you could have a spontaneous remission. He had an institute in San Francisco where he was taking people in trouble and letting them follow the mythological journey of their inward life, not abort the psychosis but carry it through and then let it come out. So that all fit.

Then Mickey Hart did a piece of music called the "African Queen meets the Holy Ghost." He told me he had about $500,000 worth of instruments on the stage. And, boy, that was just terrific. I don't want to try and describe it. But it was marvelous. He got a standing ovation for it. Then I sit on the stage like this with Jerry Garcia and Mickey Hart and it was one of the proudest moments of my life, the next proudest to this one.

BEBAN: Actually, that was my last day in San Francisco before I moved down here to Los Angeles. It was a once in a lifetime opportunity to see that. I believed that you should have taken the Jerry and Joe show on tour.

CAMPBELL: Well, you know, there's nothing like the moment. Repeating it again you don't get the same thing. It was a magic thing. And that's the way with the myth also, to catch that magical moment. Sometimes it's a moment, sometimes it's an impulse. So grab it and go.

BEBAN: You were talking earlier about the photograph in the film of you breaking the tape in [the Penn Relays in 1925] and talking about how that weekend you could do no wrong. You were in touch with something inside of yourself that was so transcendent that you could break tapes, or you could have done whatever it was you had been wanting to do all your life.

CAMPBELL: I wish I could have known in those years when I was in track what I know now about the psychological and spiritual aspect of athletics. I mean, this is a meditation system. The spiritual as well as physical control that a first-rate athlete represents is an enormous human achievement, really. There can come a moment—and I had one weekend in my career, it was a short career, it was three years—when I hit it. I was in perfect form. It was a big event, the Penn Relays. That picture was from that race, it was a gorgeous race. I ran my half-mile (I was running anchor on the relay) within one-fifth of a second of what was then the world record.

When I got home my father had all the newspapers there with streamer headlines: JOE CAMPBELL. And he said, "*What were you doing?*"

Well, it never happened again.

There are moments in the spiritual life that are like that when one is in perfect form and the mind is working. If you're fortunate enough to be trying to write a book at that time, it goes.

BEBAN: It seems to me that you've had more of those peak experiences, at least intellectually and spiritually, than most of the rest of us. I'm also jealous of the fact that during the Depression you took advantage of the fact and said, "Well, I'll go read for five years."

CAMPBELL: I didn't know I was going to take five years. I was five years without a job. No one knew how long that Depression was going to last. But people were wonderful to each other in those days.

For example, there I was in the woods. And it was at that time that I had just discovered, in Europe, James Joyce, Carl Jung, Thomas Mann, Freud, and the world of the arts, and I had also started my study of Sanskrit. It was off there—like that.

So I came back and went up to Columbia and found out that I didn't want to go back into the little bottle of the PhD thesis I was working on. I said to them, "There's a big thing opening up here" and they said, "No, no, no."

Well, my father was broke, and I was broke, and everybody was broke. I went up to the woods and just was reading, reading, reading. But when you're reading you have to buy the book. But there was an importing company in New York at the time, Steckett-Haffner, and I would write down to them for these expensive books by Leo Frobenius and Carl Jung and so forth and so on, and they would send them up to me. They didn't ask me to pay until years later when I got a job and I could pay the bill. That's the way that people behaved in those days.

You know, when real trouble comes your humanity is awakened. The fundamental human experience is that of compassion.

BEBAN: I was going to ask you that because in a world where, as you say, life eats life, where does compassion come from?

CAMPBELL: Human beings. The human heart. No other animal has it. Animals can have that feeling for their own little ones and animals can also have it for children. A dog will let a little child beat it around but it's the fundamental human experience. And it's the experience that politics won't let you have. Politics is based on fight, but real serious jungle fighting. This is why sports is so entirely different. The fellowship athletes have with each other is fundamental to the fight. It's there first. Whereas in the political arena you don't have that at all. I've never in my life met an order of young men to match those young men in the athletic arena. They were real human beings.

BEBAN: Yet people look at it from the outside as almost a circus, the way sports have become politicized.

CAMPBELL: Oh, well, that's another thing. Viewing a sport is one thing, being in it is another, they're not the same experience. You know, sitting down and looking at people beating each other up you participate as one who couldn't do it yourself but would also like to be beating the guy up. This is another order of experience.

BEBAN: But people sometimes look at sports as a metaphor for their own political tradition. Look at the tremendous soccer riots the world over. People look at competition in a political sense, you know, *my team*—

CAMPBELL: But there's more in it than that. The real fascinating thing in it is to see *competence in action*. Sport is really an elite experience. You can't have a game where everybody wins. But there's an awful lot of that kind of thinking in our sociological thinking now where nobody should be beating anybody else and let's fix it so he can't. Then you spend the rest of your life looking at a movie to see whether you can see a real elite performance. That's where life really is—in the upper brackets, not the lower ones.

AUDIENCE QUESTION: I just wanted to say thank for your lucid comments on Sam Keen's documentary "The Enemy with a Thousand Faces" [*Faces of the Enemy*] on PBS.

CAMPBELL: Oh yes. I would just like to say that I think that's an important book. It shows what ballyhoo has influenced the history of the twentieth century. I've lived through the whole century and it's been a mess [laughter]. It's been largely based on denigrating somebody over there and saying we've got to go in and knock them out. The main awakening of the human spirit is in compassion and the main function of propaganda is to suppress compassion, knock it out. Well, it's in public journalism all the time now, too. A cartoonist is someone who is showing a person as being not quite human, making him look like an insect or a bug.

This is an important point about propaganda that Sam Keen is making, a very important point.

BEBAN: What do you see as the way out?

CAMPBELL: I see the way out as tourism [laughter]. Go somewhere and meet somebody else. Perhaps even learn another language.

AUDIENCE QUESTION: What about the world myth? Are you familiar with *Gaia*, the James Lovelock book about the Gaia hypothesis?

CAMPBELL: Oh yes, the earth, the earth as a living entity. That's a basic mythological idea and it's one that is completely wiped out already in the book of Genesis where you hear, "Thou art made of dust and into dust you shall return." The earth is not dust. The earth is our mother. And here you have a deity who is trying to take over the job. And he does it by denigrating the other one.

Well, that's the way it works.

AUDIENCE QUESTION: Can someone please explain where the human capacity and feeling toward music came from when you consider that music has no real survival function?

CAMPBELL: It has an *awakening* function. Life is rhythm. Art is an organization of rhythms. Music is a fundamental art that touches our will system. In Schopenhauer's *The World as Will and Idea* he speaks of music as the sound that awakens the will. The rhythm of the music awakens certain life rhythms, ways of living and experiencing life. So it's an awakener of life. That's why.

For people who are really alive to have life awakened is more important than to get a sandwich. I mean, this is the problem of that Australopithecine thing again. And music is this one of the magic of that vibrating megalith while the rest of the apes are fighting for sandwiches. Those are the fighters, the ones without love for the other—*I want the sandwich!*

BEBAN: Edward T. Hall, the anthropologist, in his book *The Pulse of Life*, says that there is a myth about music, which is that the music is external. That what music really does is call out the rhythms that are within us, which are internal.

CAMPBELL: Oh, that's it. As Cézanne says, "Art is a harmony parallel to nature." The other thing about nature is that your nature and nature's nature are the same nature.

Recently I've come to realize the difference between two

basically contrary mythological orders. There is the order that is most concerned with linking you to a certain society and pointing out that this is different from another society. One of the strongest books on that category is the Bible. You're making a distinction between the chosen and other people and this gives them special privileges to behave in a nasty way to other people, and so forth and so on.

Then there's another kind of a religious system which has to do with the awakening of your nature and that's the Dionyisian one and that's the one that your art [turns to Densmore] is operating on. This is awakening the common humanity and it's a quite different rhythm system from that of marching to the bugle of "Onward Christian Soldiers." These two mythologies are in contrast all around.

And in the funny little talk I gave on "Ritual and Rapture" (by the way, Lynne Kaufman said this is the first time the word "rapture" has appeared in an academic catalog), that's what wakes the humanity. So I said, "I think that the Grateful Dead are the best answer today to the atom bomb." Because the atom bomb is separating us and this music is calling up the common humanity.

COUSINEAU: Joe, I remember standing next to you on stage in front of that blaring soundboard at the Grateful Dead concert in Oakland, and you elbowing me and saying, "Phil, this is one incredible Dionysian ritual! But do you know what the difference is? There are as many people here tonight standing up in a Dionysian rapture as there were living in ancient Athens! It's as if the rites of ancient Athens were compressed into one concert in one evening!"

CAMPBELL: Well, when Bob Weir goes out on the front of the stage and what—eight thousand people? That's sixteen thousand arms up in the air that go up like this! I just thought, Oh, boy, this is it [laughter].

AUDIENCE QUESTION: If the journey of the hero is the search for the self, then what is the ego and what is the self? And what is the relationship between the two?

CAMPBELL: The ego is you as you think of yourself. You in relation to all the commitments of your life, as you understand them. The self is the whole range of possibilities that you've never even thought of. And you're stuck with your past when you're stuck with the ego. Because if all you know about yourself is what you found out about yourself; well, that already happened. The self is a whole field of potentialities to come through.

AUDIENCE QUESTION: *The Tibetan Book of the Dead* talks about giving up the ego to transcend oneself into a larger whole. Maybe you have a comment about the theory or the evolution of man coming into a global community, the evolution of man's next step in the ego becoming the global consciousness rather than self-consciousness?

CAMPBELL: That's what I call "ego imperialism." Trying to impose your idea on the universe. That's what's got to go. The whole sense of the oriental reincarnation is that the ego has to be thrown off and these potentialities come through with ever more illuminated embodiments. Your ego is your embodiment and your self is your potentiality and that's what you listen to when you listen for the voice of inspiration and the voice of "What am I here for? What can I possibly make of myself?"

You're already made up to a certain extent and to try to hang on to that is egoism. Egoism is tightening. And so *The Tibetan Book of the Dead* keeps talking about *ahankara,* making the noise "I" as the thing that holds you back.

Now there's a certain danger in that. Freud's definition of ego is excellent. It is what he calls the "reality function." It is the function that puts you in touch with your personal relationship to time and space, here and now as you know it. That's the ego. Your judgment of things, also your evaluation of the moment. This is all ego stuff. The problem is not to eliminate ego, it's to turn ego and the judgment system of the moment into the servant of the self, not the dictator, but the vehicle for it to realize itself. It's a very nice balance, a very delicate one. And an awful lot of so-called "spiritual people" are very much against the ego and they turn themselves into—

Well, one of the problems about being psychoanalyzed is, as Nietzsche said, "Be careful lest in casting out your devils that you cast out the best thing that's in you." So many people who are really in deep analysis look as though and act as though they have been filleted. There's no bone there, there's no stuff! How to get rid of ego as dictator and turn it into messenger and servant and scout, to be in your service, is the trick.

AUDIENCE QUESTION: What myths do you feel dominate the American workplace? And what myths do you think should be instituted to make the American workplace a better place in which to work?

CAMPBELL: The American workplace is based upon the myth of money. Money is the bottom line today. No value can supersede the value of money. If you want to explain anything that you're doing, turning out third-rate material or anything else, it's cost. You can't turn out what you'd like to turn out because it would cost you too much. The hero is the one who will do it even sacrificing the money. The value that you stand for is your life. And if money is the final term, that's your mythology, and I'm afraid that's what's working.

BEBAN: So the myth that would replace that is the myth of the ability of the individual?

CAMPBELL: No. What I think about in the world today comes out in the film [*The Hero's Journey*] and that has to do with the question, To what society do you belong? Do you belong to this little in-group? Do you belong to the United States? Or do you belong to the planet, to mankind? Economically it's one planet now. There's no doubt about it.

I think one of the marvelous moments came a couple weeks ago when [Senator Richard A.] Gephardt said if the Japanese are outselling our automobiles because they make good automobiles that people want, then we must erect a punishment for them. And immediately the bond market dropped because the Japanese money is supporting the American market. Here you realize that we're not competitors, we're partners in a common action—namely the action of having a planetary society. And I think the Japanese are a little better than we are at realizing that partnership idea. That's the way it is in their management. For instance, even the unions in Japan cooperate so that they're not taking everything out of the institute that they're supposed to be controlling but helping it to survive. So they are asking, "What is an equitable distribution of money?" Not "We want this, this, this."

This pulling apart has to yield to the compassion principle. Otherwise you're in a jungle.

BEBAN: I think the key word is equitability with the multinationals that you're talking about and the idea that we're becoming one economic system. But still only 2 percent of the people control that wealth, no matter which country you're looking at.

CAMPBELL: No, I don't think that has anything to do with it.

BEBAN: No?

CAMPBELL: No [laughter]. In an equitable distribution system you never level people up, you always level down. And civilization comes from what's on top. I shouldn't say this, but—

BEBAN: I guess I'm trying to get back to the idea of compassion. Where does that come from? When people are, in fact, suffering because of a lack of goods—

CAMPBELL: Oh, well, that's something else. No, economic decency is not exploiting people. But our economic situation now is that there should not be anybody hungry in the world. That's really a fact. It's there for them to have it. The problem of distributing it is an enormous problem, by the way. And it's one thing to be equitable and give everything away; it's another thing to be equitable and give away yourself. Then you can't really help anybody, can you? That's a little bit like the ego-self problem. In actual economic situations this is complicated by the specifics of the situation, and I can't talk about that.

The basic thing is to think of society in its actuality, as a world society, which is what it is. When you look at the planet from the moon you don't see these divisions of nations; they're not there. That's what artificial. And it's the artificiality of this divisiveness that's the whole sense of Sam Keen's book and film, *Faces of the Enemy*. You turn your partner into an enemy and you have a war.

BEBAN: Is that the dominant mythological image now, the idea that we can see the earth from the moon? We have these photographs of our beautiful globe hovering there in outer space—

CAMPBELL: Yes, but it's not working except in pictures. A mythology doesn't come from the head; a mythology comes from the heart.

BEBAN But there's something so beautiful about finally seeing it—

CAMPBELL: Yeah, but how do you *feel* about people? Not how do you *think* about people. But what is the feeling system? A mythology comes from the feeling and an experience not from thinking. The difference between an ideology and a mythology is the difference between the ego and the self. Ideology comes from the thinking system and mythology comes from the *being*.

BEBAN: I think we have time for one more question.

JOHN DENSMORE: I'm going to try and put you on the spot.

CAMPBELL: I knew that moment would come.

DENSMORE: The essence of the world is sorrow and the trick is "joyful participation in the sorrows of the world." Say yes to it and watch it blow up. The world is okay, all rests in God.

Right?

CAMPBELL: That's a very nice lecture. I go with it all the way.

DENSMORE: Right. So for me, that gives me peace. But I feel like if I completely embrace that statement—well, I feel like I shouldn't completely embrace that statement until the moment before I die. Otherwise I think there's a danger of complacency. You know, I want to go out and fight against Fascists like Hitler or the nuclear thing. And I wonder whether this undermines me.

CAMPBELL: This is the problem that's come up two or three times tonight with the self and the ego. At the deep base, at the eternal center, this is the way it is. And how can my *moral* ideas and so forth be brought in accord with it? At the same time we see we have all the money over there, and we have poor people here. I can work for the human values as being not the essential ones but the potential ones.

At heart, I would say, no matter what happens, everything is okay. Suppose the world blows up—so what? You know, just absolutely, so what? But in terms of human values that's a real calamity! So in my human nature I'm going to do what I can to keep it from blowing up. My books have been working in that direction.

On the other hand if it did blow up, all right. Then there wouldn't be anybody here anymore and who'd be sorry?

BEBAN: And who would buy the books!

CAMPBELL: Yes—and who would buy the books! Now there's a wonderful saying in the Buddhist world: "Life is joyful participation in the sorrows of the world." All life is sorrowful. You are not going to change that. It's all right for everyone else to be sorrowful, but what about you being sorrowful? Well, participate. For me that is the sense of the Crucifixion. There's a beautiful passage in Paul's epistle to the Philippians: "For the Christ did not think the Godhood to be hung onto, but let go of, and he came into the world to participate in its sorrows, even to death on the Cross."

That is the act of joyful participation in the sorrows of the world. Do you see what I mean? You get a point of view, you get a—what can we call it—a nonegoistic, nonjudgmental point of view. And so go into the play and play a part. And at the same time know that this is a shadow reflex.

I was reading in one of the Sanskrit texts recently because in your old age, my dear friends, in your free time, you go back to what fed you most in your youth and childhood. So I found myself working again on the *Bhagavad Gita* and the *puranas* and brushing up on my Sanskrit. And there was something that came out of this that I had read before and it had never struck me this way.

The eternal cannot change. It's not touched by time. As soon as you have a historical act, a movement, you're in time. The world of time is a reflex of the energy of what is eternal. But the eternal is not touched by what is here. So the whole doctrine of sin is a false doctrine. It has to do with time. Your eternal character is not touched.

You are redeemed.

⧼ Epilogue ⧽

The Tiger and the Goat

CAMPBELL: The story I'd like to give is that of a tigress who was pregnant, and starving hungry. She came upon a little flock of goats. And in pouncing upon them, with the energy that she expended, she brought on the birth of her little one and her own death. So she died giving birth to a little tiger. The goats, meanwhile, had scattered, and they finally came back to their little grazing place, and they found this just-born little tiger and its dead mother. They had very strong parental instincts, and they adopted the little tiger, who grew up thinking he was a goat. He learned to bleat, he learned to eat grass, but the grass was very bad for his digestive system. He couldn't handle the cellulose. By the time he was an adolescent he was a pretty miserable specimen of his species.

At that time a male tiger pounced on the little flock, and they again scattered. But this little fellow was a tiger, he wasn't a goat. So there he was, standing. The big fellow looked at him. And he said, "What, *you* living here with these goats?"

The little tiger goes *Maaaaaa* and begins nibbling grass in a kind of embarrassed way. The big fellow is mortified, like a father coming home and finding his son with long hair; something like that. So he swats him back and forth a couple of times because the little fellow could only bleat and nibble grass. Then he takes him by the neck and carries him to a pond. There was no wind blowing; it was perfectly still.

Now the Hindus say of yoga that yoga is the art of making the mind stand still. The intentional stopping of the spontaneous activity of the mind itself. It's as though a pond was to be made to stand still. When the wind is blowing, the waters are rippling and all these little broken reflections come and go, come and go, come and go, and that's the way we are in our lives. We identify ourselves with one of these coming and going reflections, and we think— Oh dear, here I come, there I go. If you make the pond stand still, then the image stands still and you see your eternal presence, and identifying with that, you're relatively indifferent to the world.

So this little tiger is now being introduced to the principles of yoga. And the big fellow says, "Now look into that pond." And the little one puts his face over it. And for the first time in his little life he sees his actual face. The big tiger puts his face over there, and he says, "You see? You've got the face of a tiger, you're like me. *Be like me!*" (Now that's guru stuff: I'll give you my picture to wear and you'll know who you are.)

Anyhow, the little tiger's beginning to sort of get the message. The big fellow's next discipline is to pick him up and take him to his den, where there are the remains of a recently slaughtered gazelle. The big fellow takes a chunk of this bloody stuff, and he says to the little one, "Open your face."

The little one backs off. He says, "I'm a vegetarian."

"Well," says the big one, "none of that nonsense." And he shoves it down his throat. And the little one gags on it, as the text says, "As all do on true doctrine."

So, gagging on the true doctrine, it's nevertheless getting into his system since it is his proper food, and it activates his proper nervous system. Spontaneously moved by his proper food, he gives a little tiger roar, sort of Tiger Roar 101. Then the big guy says, "There we are. Now we've got it. Now we'll eat tiger food."

There's a moral here, of course. It is that we're all really tigers living here as goats. The function of sociology and most of our religious education is to teach us to be goats. But the function of the proper interpretation of mythological symbols and meditation discipline is to introduce you to your tiger face. Then comes the problem. You've found your tiger face but you're still living here with these goats. How are you going to do that?

What you will have learned is through all the forms of the world, the one radiance of eternity shows itself. You can regard the appearance of the miracle of life in all these forms. But don't let them know that you are a tiger!

When Hallaj or Jesus let the orthodox community know that they were tigers, they were crucified. And so the Sufis learned the lesson at that time with the death of Hallaj, around 900 A.D. And it is: You wear the outer garment of the law; you behave like everyone else. And you wear the inner garment of the mystic way. Now that's the great secret of life.

So with that I commit you all to be tigers in the world. But don't let anybody know it!

Books by Joseph Campbell

Where the Two Came to Their Father: A Navaho War Ceremonial
  (with Maud Oakes and Jeff King)
A Skeleton Key to Finnegans Wake
  (with Henry Morton Robinson)
The Hero with a Thousand Faces
The Masks of God: Primitive Mythology
The Masks of God: Oriental Mythology
The Masks of God: Occidental Mythology
The Masks of God: Creative Mythology
The Flight of the Wild Gander: Explorations in the Mythological Dimension
The Mythic Image
Myths to Live By
Tarot Revelations (with Richard Roberts)
Historical Atlas of World Mythology
  I. *The Way of the Animal Powers*
  II. *The Way of the Seeded Earth*
The Inner Reaches of Outer Space
The Power of Myth
  (with Bill Moyers)

BOOKS EDITED BY JOSEPH CAMPBELL

The Portable Arabian Nights

The Portable Jung

Myths, Dreams, and Religion

My Life and Lives: The Story of a Tibetan Incarnation
(with Rato Khyongla Nawang Losang)

Papers from the Eranos Yearbooks
(6 volumes)

BOOKS EDITED AND COMPLETED
FROM THE POSTHUMA OF HEINRICH ZIMMER

Myths and Symbols in Indian Art and Civilization

The King and the Corpse

Philosophies of India

The Art of Indian Asia
(2 volumes)

Bibliography

Alighieri, Dante. *The Convivio*. Trans. Philip H. Wicksteed. London: J. M. Dent and Sons, 1903.

———— *The Divine Comedy*. 6 vols. Trans. Charles S. Singleton. Bollingen Series LXXX. Princeton: Princeton University Press, 1975.

———— *La Vita Nuova*. Trans. Charles Eliot Norton. Boston and New York: Houghton Mifflin Company, 1867.

Arnold, Sir Edwin. *The Light of Asia*. London & Madras: The Theosophical Publishing House, 1980.

Arrien, Angeles. *The Tarot Handbook: Practical Applications of Ancient Visual Symbols*. Sonoma, CA: Arcus Press, 1987.

Bastian, Adolf. *Das Bestandige in den Menschenrassen und die Spielweite ihrer Veranderlichkeit*. Berlin: Dietrich Reimer, 1868.

Bédier, Joseph. *Le Roman de Tristan*. Trans. Hilaire Belloc. Compl. Paul Rosenfeld. Paris: Societé des Anciens Textes Français, 1902.

Blake, William. *Poetry and Prose of William Blake*. New York: Random House, 1927.

Bly, Robert. *Selected Poetry*. New York: Perennial Library, 1986.

Brown, Joseph Epes. *The Sacred Pipe: Black Elk's Account of the Seven Rites of the Oglala Sioux*. Norman: University of Oklahoma Press, 1963.

Campbell, Joseph, and Richard Roberts. *Tarot Revelations*. San Anselmo: Vernal Equinox Press, 1979.

Coomaraswamy, Ananda K. *Hinduism and Buddhism*. New York: Philosophical Library, n.d.

——— *The Transformation of Nature in Art.* Cambridge: Harvard University Press, 1934.

Daumal, René. *Mount Analogue.* Trans. Roger Shattuck. Baltimore: Penguin, 1974.

Dürkheim, Karlfried Graf. *Zen and Us.* Trans. Vincent Nash. New York: Dutton, 1987.

Eliade, Mircea. *Shamanism: Archaic Techniques of Ecstasy.* Trans. Willard R. Trask. Bollingen Series LXXVI. Princeton: Princeton University Press, 1964.

Eliot, T. S. *The Waste Land.* New York: Harcourt, Brace & World, 1922.

Eschenbach, Wolfram von. *Parzival.* New York: Random House, Vintage Books, 1961.

Evans-Wentz, W. Y. *The Tibetan Book of the Dead.* New York: Oxford University Press, 1960.

Ficino, Marselio. *The Book of Life.* Trans. Charles Boer. Dallas: Spring Publications, 1980.

Frankl, Dr. Viktor E. *Man's Search for Meaning: An Introduction to Logotherapy.* New York: Washington Square Press, 1963.

Frazer, Sir James George. *The Golden Bough.* (abridged). Ed. Theodor H. Gaster. New York: Mentor Books, 1964.

Freud, Sigmund. *Collected Papers.* New York: Basic Books, 1959.

Frobenius, Leo. *Voice of Africa.* 2 vols. Reprint of 1913 ed. Salem: Ayer Press, 1969.

Goethe, Wolfgang. *Faust.* Boston and New York: Houghton Mifflin Company, 1870.

The Gospel According to Thomas. Trans. A. Guillaumont, et. al. Leiden: E. J. Brill; New York: Harper & Row Publishers, 1959.

Grof, Stanislav. *East and West: Ancient Wisdom and Modern Science.* Mill Valley, CA: Robert Briggs, 1985.

——— *LSD Psychotherapy.* San Bernardino, CA: Borgo Press, 1986.

Grinnell, George Bird. *Blackfoot Lodge Tales.* New York: Charles Scribner's Sons, 1916.

Hall, Edward T. *The Dance of Life: The Other Dimension of Time.* New York: Doubleday, 1984.

Highwater, Jamake. *The Primal Mind: Vision and Reality in Indian America.* New York and Scarborough, Ontario: Meridian, 1981.

Hill, Gareth., ed. *The Shaman from Elko: Papers in Honor of Joseph Henderson's 75th Birthday.* San Francisco: C. G. Jung Institute, 1978.

Jeffers, Robinson. *Selected Poems.* New York: Random House, 1953.

Jianou, Ionel and Michel Dufet. *Bourdelle.* Paris: Arted Editions d'Art, 1971.

Joyce, James. *Finnegans Wake.* New York: Viking Press, 1939.

———— *A Portrait of the Artist as a Young Man*. New York: The Viking Press, 1964.

———— *Ulysses*. New York: Random House, The Modern Library, 1934.

Jung, C. G. *Symbols of Transformation*. New York: Pantheon Books, 1956.
———— *Memories, Dreams and Reflections*. Recorded and ed. Aniela Jaffe. Trans. Richard and Clara Winston. New York: Pantheon Books, 1963.

Kant, Immanuel. *The Critique of Pure Reason*. Trans. and ed. Norman K. Smith. New York: St. Martin's Press, 1987.
———— *Prologemena to Any Future Metaphysics*. Trans. Paul Carus. Peru, IL: Open Court Press, 1985.

Keen, Sam. *The Faces of the Enemy*. San Francisco: Harper & Row Publishers, 1986.

Keleman, Stanley. *Somatic Reality*. Berkeley: Center Press, 1979.

Kühn, Herbert. *The Rock Pictures of Europe*. New York: October Press.

Lewis, Sinclair. *Babbit*. New York: Harcourt, Brace and Jovanovich, 1949.

Malory, Sir Thomas. *Le Morte d'Arthur*. 2 vols. Ed. Janet Cowen. London: Penguin, 1970.

Mann, Thomas. *Buddenbrooks*. New York: Random House, 1984.
———— *Magic Mountain*. New York: Random House, 1969.

Merejkowski, Dmitri. *The Romance of Leonardo da Vince*. Trans. Bernard Guilbert Guerney. New York: The Modern Library, 1928.

Murphy, Michael, and Rhea A. White. *The Psychic Side of Sports*. Reading: Addison-Wesley Publishing, 1978.

Neihardt, John. *Black Elk Speaks*. Lincoln: University of Nebraska Press, 1968.

Nietzsche, Friedrich. *Thus Spake Zarathustra*. London: Penguin, 1961.
———— *The Birth of Tragedy*. New York: Vintage Books, 1967.

Nilsson, Martin P. *A History of Greek Religion*. Trans. F. J. Feilden. Westport: Greenwood Press, 1949.

Ortega y Gasset, José. *Meditations on Quixote*. Trans. Evelyn Rugg and Diego Marin. New York: W. W. & Company, 1961.

Ovid. *Metamorphoses*. Trans. Frank Justus Miller. The Loeb Classical Library. Cambridge: Harvard University Press, 1916.

Pagels, Elaine. *The Gnostic Gospels*. New York: Vintage Books, 1981.

Pound, Ezra. *Selected Poems: 1908–1959*. London: Faber & Faber, 1975.

Proust, Marcel. *Rembrances of Things Past*. Trans. C. K. Scott Moncrieff and Terence Kilmartin. New York: Random House, 1981.

Ramakrishna, Sri. *The Gospels of Sri Ramakrishna*. Trans. Swami Nikhilananda. New York: Ramakrishna-Vivekananda Center, 1942.

Rougemont, Denis de. *Love in the Western World*. Trans. Montgomery Belgion. Princeton: Princeton University Press, 1983.

Schopenhauer, Arnold. *The World as Will and Representation*. 2 vols. Trans. E. F. Payne. New York: Dover, 1966.

Schroedinger, Edwin. *My View of the World*. Trans. Cecily Hastings. Cambridge: Cambridge University Press, 1964.

Spengler, Oswald. *The Decline of the West*. Trans. Charles Francis Atkinson. New York: Alfred A. Knopf, 1926.

Strassburg, Gottfried Von. *Tristan*. Trans A. T. Hatto. Baltimore: Penguin Books, 1960.

Suzuki, Daisetz. *Zen and Japanese Culture*. Bollingen Series LXIV. Princeton: Princeton University Press, 1959.

Troyes, Chretien de. *La Queste del Sainte Graal*. Ed. Albert Pauphilet. Paris: Champion, 1949.

Tzu, Lao. *Tao Te Ching*. Trans. Arthur Waley. New York: The Macmillan Co., 1954.

Underhill, Evelyn. *Mysticism*. Cleveland and New York: Meridian, 1970.

Watts, Alan. *In My Own Way*. New York: Vintage Books, 1972.

Yeats, W. B. *A Vision*. New York: Macmillan Company; First Collier Books Edition, 1966.

———— *Irish Folk Tales*. New York: The Modern Library, n.d.

———— *The Collected Poems of W. B. Yeats*. London: Macmillan, 1966.

Contributors

BETTE ANDRESEN is a photographer and therapist from Northern California.

ANGELES ARRIEN is a Basque mystic, anthropologist, and teacher. She is the author of *The Tarot: Practical Applications of Ancient Visual Symbols.*

RICHARD BEBAN is a Los Angeles-based screenwriter and journalist. His radio interviews have been broadcast worldwide.

ROBERT BLY is a poet, minstrel, and translator. His many books include *The Light Around the Body,* which won the National Book Award, *News of the Universe,* and numerous translations.

ROBERT COCKRELL is a physician and filmmaker from Los Angeles. He was associate executive producer of *The Hero's Journey.*

JOHN DENSMORE is a musician and actor. He was the drummer for the Doors and is the author of the upcoming autobiography *Riders on the Storm.*

EDWARD DREESSEN is an Aikido master who currently lives in Northern California.

LAWRENCE FAVROT is director of the preventive medical program of Sharp Memorial Hospital in San Diego, California, and assistant chief of cardiology. He is a Fellow of the American College of Cardiology.

STANISLAV GROF was formerly chief of psychiatric research at the Maryland Psychiatric Research Center and assistant professor of psychiatry at Johns Hopkins University School of Medicine. He is currently Scholar-in-Residence at Esalen Institute. He is author of *Beyond Death* and *Beyond the Brain,* among many other volumes.

ROGER GUILLEMEN is a Nobel Prize Laureate for his research in brain chemistry.

JOAN HALIFAX is an anthropologist, lecturer, and author of *Shaman: Wounded Healer* and *Shamanic Voices: A Survey of Visionary Narratives.*

JAMAKE HIGHWATER is a writer and lecturer on the arts and American Indian culture. His many books include *The Primal Mind: Vision and Reality in Indian America* and *Anpao: An American Indian Odyssey.*

DAVID KENNARD is a documentary filmmaker from London, England. His credits include work on the television productions of "Connections" and "China." He was location director for the Esalen filming on *The Hero's Journey.*

RICHARD TARNAS is a writer, astrologer, and teacher, who lives in Big Sur, California.

ROZANNE ZUCCHET was administrative assistant to the producer on *The Hero's Journey.* Currently she is vice president of a public relations firm in San Diego, California.

Credits

Index

*Page numbers in italics refer to illustrations; page numbers in boldface refer to sidebars.

Yeats, William Butler, 39, 100
Yoga, 10; Kundalini, 24, 138

Zen, 41, 152
Zimmer, Heinrich, 41, 48, 60,
 79, 114, 121–24, *122,* **126,**
 145; American lectures of, on

Indian art and mythology
 (*The Art of Indian Asia,*
 Campbell, ed.), 115, 126; as
 J. C.'s mentor, 126, **126**
Zoroaster, 10, 173
Zucchet, Rozanne, 92, *92,* 93